TAROT MAGIC FOR THE REALITY HACKER

TAROT MAGIC FOR THE REALITY HACKER
Divination in the Modern World

Ari Freeman

AEON

First published in 2025 by
Aeon Books

Copyright © 2025 by Ari Freeman

The right of Ari Freeman to be identified as the author of this work has been asserted in accordance with §§ 77 and 78 of the Copyright Design and Patents Act 1988.

All rights reserved. No part of this publication may be reproduced, stored in a retrieval system, or transmitted, in any form or by any means, electronic, mechanical, photocopying, recording, or otherwise, without the prior written permission of the publisher.

British Library Cataloguing in Publication Data

A C.I.P. for this book is available from the British Library

ISBN-13: 978-1-80152-196-3

Typeset by Medlar Publishing Solutions Pvt Ltd, India

www.aeonbooks.co.uk

Thanks

*Ciaran MacConneach for all his efforts and friendship
during the writing of this book*

Marcus Mattern for his magical advice

Lionel Snell for his clarifications

TABLE OF CONTENTS

INTRODUCTION	xi
Tarot's inner structure	xii
Neo-Pythagorean numerology	xii
Card meanings at a glance	xiv
The Suits	xv
The Major Arcana	xvi
The Court Cards	xix
The Minor Arcana	xxiv
LEVEL 4	
Really advanced Tarot reading	1
Tarot astrology	2
Aristotle's cosmology	4
Heavenly spheres	5
The meaning of the seven classical planets	7
The outer planets	14
The meanings of the outer planets	15
Essential dignity	17
Other astrological concepts	18

The twelve signs of the zodiac	19
The houses	27
Southern hemisphere astrology	30
Decans	30
Tarot Kabbalah	34
What is Kabbalah?	34
A history of Kabbalah	35
The core principles of Kabbalah	42
Key figures of Christian Kabbalah and the Western magical tradition	44
Kabbalah explained	55
The Three Veils	55
The Four Worlds	56
Etz Hayim, the Tree of Life	58
The Three Pillars	59
The Sefirot	60
A fractal system	66
The Hebrew alphabet	68
Letters as numbers	70
The thirty-two paths of the sefirot	71
Angels in Tarot	74
Chayot and the Merkabah	75
Cherubim/Kerabim	76
Gabriel	76
Holy Guardian Angel	77
Michael	78
Raguel	79
Raphael	79
Uriel	79
The Shem HaMephorash	79
Kabbalistic Secrets	80
Kabbalistic Angels	80
What is the Shem HaMephorash?	83
How did it get attributed to Tarot?	86
Biblical verse	87
The Zodiac and the Names	92
Get better imaginary friends	103
Angel-summoning methods	104

High information decks	124
High information spreads	127
MacGregor Mathers' method of divination by the Tarot	128
Multiple decks	148

LEVEL 5

Bending the fabric of the universe with Tarot	157
Tarot spells	157
Manifesting an intention	159
Engaging cards in conversation	163
Irreverent tarot experiments	164
Reduced decks	165
Reading with only the major arcana:	
The jodorowsky method	166
Reading with playing cards	172
Playing card example reading	172
Choosing cards rather than shuffling	174
Low information decks	175
Oblique Strategies	175
My minimalist deck	177
Tarot reading without cards	181
Using Artificial Intelligence for divination	183
Interpretation into cards	183
Divination by radio surfing	186

CONCLUSION

	189
The twenty-first century occult revival	189
Tarot as a magical framework	190
Where will Tarot head in the future?	191
Slaughtering the sacred cow	191

APPENDICES

	193
Mythology	193
Greco-Roman gods	193
Egyptian gods	224
Norse gods	246
Gods from other cultures	255
Tables of correspondences	260

REFERENCES 285
    Bibliography 285
    Web pages 286

INDEX 287

INTRODUCTION

This book can be considered the second part of a gradated course in Tarot. Unless you are already an expert Tarot reader, it is assumed that you have read the first book, *Tarot for Sceptics: The Practical Usage of Divination for Psychic Results*. For those who are already doing Tarot readings however, it works as a stand-alone volume. Likewise, it is suitable if you are a Tarot reader who is ready to get further into the occult, or an experienced occultist who wants to incorporate some Tarot into your system and gain some magical theory to boot.

In this volume there are many unique approaches:

This book serves as a deeper dive and an expansion pack. First, we will go in depth into the inner structures of Tarot that produced the card meanings. This is vital information for anyone who wants to engage with Tarot at the deepest level, the type of information that will allow one to create one's own deck. Later, we will explore the occult connections, occult history, and legends about Tarot. Included are methodical explanations of Tarot's connections to Kabbalah, astrology, angels, mythology, spells and magical operations; if you wanted to, this would allow you to bluff your way into secret occult orders, or could be used as part of a core curriculum for a coven of witches, hermetic magi, chaos magicians, or otherwise to raise your magic street cred to head-swelling proportions. If you are planning on using Tarot as part of a wider system of magic, this is the perfect guide.

After that, we will don the sceptic's hat again. I am going to show you how to be a 'Tarot hacker', in order to get to the bottom of what is really going on with divination. In this part of the book, I dissect the structure, the symbols, and the rules, all in the spirit of understanding what a good reading is, what might really be going on with 'psychic phenomena', and how this is affected by increasing or reducing the information in a deck (or even dispensing with the deck altogether!). These approaches are unique to this book.

I hope that these teachings will guide the reader to a new twenty-first century approach to cartomancy, informed by—but not shackled to—the past.

Tarot's inner structure

At its core, Tarot symbolism was built primarily from these sources:

- Neo-Pythagorean numerology, in particular the numbers one to ten, and their qualities.
- Astrology, especially the seven classical planets, the twelve signs of the zodiac, and the thirty-six decans.
- Kabbalah, especially the Tree of Life, עֵץ חַיִּים (etz chaim), its ten sefirot (numerations, or 'spheres') an the twenty-two paths connecting them, each representing a type of consciousness.

Neo-Pythagorean numerology

Zero: The state of pre-existence, and pure potentiality. Connected to the sefirah Keter and the Fool card.

The first four numbers are the core concepts that were thought by Pythagoreans to be able to generate all other numbers, and by extension all information: the universe.

Pythagoras was also the father of music theory and thought that his musical ideas were the same rules by which the cosmos was ordered.

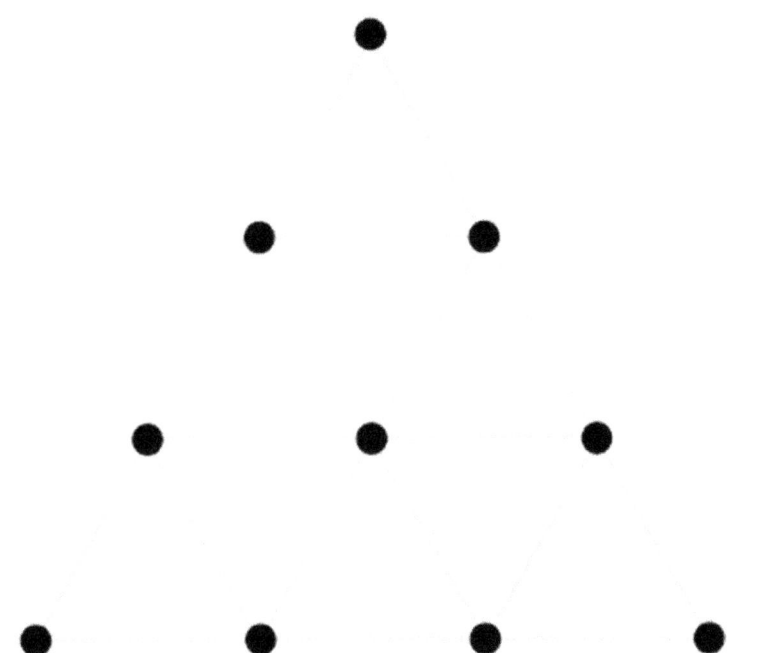

Figure 1. The Tetractys of Pythagoras, showing how the number ten can be generated from the first four numbers.

One: The concept of unification. Here we have 'position' and 'selfhood'. This is zero dimensions of space. One is of course the number of commencement, and in Tarot of inspirations.

Two: The first relationship. Now one can be measured in relation to another. Here is also the first decision, and the first true comprehension. One thing related to another. We can also draw a line, which implies travel, change, and time. This is one dimension of space. In Tarot, two is a number of response. The splitting into what is and what isn't, the Logos.

Three: With a third dimension we have the idea of surface. Now an enclosure can be drawn, implying territory. The relationships are now threefold; point one may say, 'I prefer point three to point two.' This is the first analysis. One may choose one path at the expense of another. A tension. Three is the number of communication in small groups. The union of opposites.

Four: We now have a third spatial dimension and we can build solid shapes such as four-pointed pyramids. This is a stability. Most animals stand on four legs. As it is stable, it can also present a hurdle which is hard to overcome. The four elements of which all other things are made.

Five: This can be motion, change or time. Our objects can now move, or be 'excited'. This is a tension. It is the overcoming of the stability of four, for better or worse.

Six: The number of the self and of man. Here time can be divided into past, present, and future in relation to our object. So now we have narrative.

Seven: To the ancients the number seven symbolised 'many' or 'several'. It can also imply a complete set: the seven virtues, the seven deadly sins, the seven classical planets, the seven colours of the rainbow, the seven different notes in the major scale, the seven seas.

Eight: This is the action part of our narrative. The climax. It is ambition put to work.

Nine: Nine is like the last page of a book. The resolution of a storyline and the final part of a cycle. With it comes rationalism. The loose ends of the story are tied.

Ten: The number of transcendence to a new cycle. Ten is a higher order of the number one, and thus as the old narrative comes to an end, so a new narrative may be started again from one.

Card meanings at a glance

In my first Tarot book, *Tarot for Sceptics*, each card is explained in depth. Here we will start with a recap.

The Suits

	Element	Qualities	Letter	Gender	Temperament	Roles	Meanings
Wands	Fire	Hot and dry	Yod ׳	Masculine/Active	Choleric. Dominating, competitive, striving, intuitive, assertive	Artists Musicians Magicians Adventurers	Willpower. Creativity, assertiveness, leadership
Cups	Water	Cold and wet	Heh ה	Feminine/Receptive	Phlegmatic. Curious, experiencing, accommodating, reacting, supportive, emotional	Singers Poets Healers Counsellors Carers Romantics	Emotions. Relationships, romance
Swords	Air	Hot and wet	Vav ו	Masculine/Active	Sanguine. Talkative, impressionable, expressive, social, conceptual	Inventors Designers Engineers Sportspeople Military Gamers Teachers	Intellect. Competition, education, debate
Pentacles	Earth	Cold and dry	Heh ה (Final)	Feminine/Receptive	Melancholic. Gentle, irritable, relating, critical, soulful, sensual, tactile	Tradespeople Manufacturers Miners Fashion Industry Merchants Builders	Manifestation. Time, energy, money, body

The Major Arcana

Card	Letter	Path	Planet or sign	Meanings
0 Fool	Alef א Ox	11 Keter to Chokhmah	Primum Mobile	One who knows nothing. Breaking out into a new order. Something from nothing.
I Magician	Bet ב House	12 Keter to Binah	Mercury	A master of their craft. Having one's life in order.
II Priestess	Gimel ג Camel	13 Keter to Tiferet	Moon	Knowledge from direct experience. Intuition.
III Empress	Dalet ד Door	14 Chokhmah to Binah	Venus	Motherhood. Mother earth. Fertility. Anima.
IV Emperor	Heh ה Window	15 Chokhmah to Tiferet	Aries	Rulership. Empires. Governance. Stability.
V Hierophant	Vav ו Nail/Hook	16 Chokhmah to Chesed	Taurus	Initiations. Religion. Education. Psychopomp. Institutions.
VI Lovers	Zayin ז Sword	17 Binah to Tiferet	Gemini	Romance. Union of opposites. Trust. A leap of faith. Synthesis.
VII Chariot	Chet ח Boundary/Fence	18 Binah to Gevurah	Cancer	Leadership. Unifying forces. Ambition. Taking on challenges with confidence.
VIII Strength (Justice in Marseilles and Thoth)	Tet ט Serpent	19 Chesed to Gevurah	Leo	Charming others. Inner strength. Overcoming difficulties. Healing.

IX Hermit	Yod י Hand	20 Chesed to Tiferet	Virgo	Solitude seeking wisdom. Individuation. Study and practice. A teacher.
X Wheel of Fortune	Kaf כ cupped hand/ Spoon/ Submission	21 Chesed to Netzach	Jupiter	Taking a chance. Fortune whether good or bad. Fate. Transcendental cycles of time.
XI Justice (Strength in Marseilles and Thoth)	Lamed ל Ox Goad/Yoke	22 Gevurah to Tiferet	Libra	Diplomacy. Balance. Compromise. Objectivity. Forgiveness. Vindication.
XII Hanged Man	Mem מ Water	23 Gevurah to Hod	Neptune	Self-martyrdom. Rebellion. Self-sacrifice. Apostates. Searching for inner wisdom. Facing one's shadow.
XIII Death	Nun נ Fish	24 Tiferet to Netzach	Scorpio	Grief. Death. Necessary change. End of a cycle of time. Autumn.
XIV Temperance	Samekh ס Support/Pillar	25 Tiferet to Yesod	Sagittarius	Rebalance. Abstinence. The straight and narrow. Higher purpose.
XV The Devil	Ayin ע Eye	26 Tiferet to Hod	Capricorn	Corruption. Hedonism. Addiction. Self-destruction. Cynicism and negativity. Necessary evils.
XVI Tower	Peh פ Mouth	27 Netzach to Hod	Mars	Catastrophe. Loss of faith. Evil uncovered. A purge of a failed system.

(*Continued*)

(Continued)

Card	Letter	Path	Planet or sign	Meanings
XVII Star	Tzaddi צ Fishhook	28 Netzach to Yesod	Aquarius	Faith in an ideal. Lofty goals. Inspiration.
XVIII Moon	Qof ק Back of the head	29 Netzach to Malkut	Pisces	An ordeal. Occult knowledge. A journey of self-discovery. Working to unify oneself. Liminal states.
XIX Sun	Resh ר Head	30 Hod to Yesod	Sun	A day in the sun. Joy. Rose-coloured spectacles. Innocence.
XX Judgement	Shin ש Tooth	31 Hod to Malkut	Pluto	Unveiling. The past coming back to haunt. A day of reckoning. Court proceedings. Facing trauma.
XXI World	Tav ת Cross/Mark	32 Yesod to Malkut	Saturn	Expansion of one's worldview. Travel. The bigger picture. World news. Macrocosm.

The Court Cards

	Letter	Element	Roles
Kings	Yod ׳	Fire	Grandfathers. Fathers. Older husbands. Elders. Teachers. Male bosses. Patriarchs. Masters in their field.
Queens	Heh ה	Water	Grandmothers. Mothers. Older wives. Elders. Teachers. Female bosses. Masters in their field. Matriarchs.
Knights	Vav ו	Air	Colleagues. Peers. Skilful workers and practitioners. Doers.
Pages	Heh ה (final)	Earth	Newbies, apprentices, youth, children.

Card	Zodiacal sign or quadrant	Ruling planets	Elements	Meaning	Roles
King of Wands	21° Scorpio to 20° Sagittarius	Mars (Pluto) and Jupiter	**Fire of Fire** Electricity, lightning bolts, explosions, ignitions.	Pure intention, or one intention causes another.	An ambitious and charismatic leader. A 'cult leader'. They work on instincts and self-belief more than logic.
King of Cups	21° Aquarius to 20° Pisces	Saturn (Uranus) and Jupiter (Neptune)	**Fire of Water** Fast flows of water, foods, tidal waves.	Intention causes emotion.	A godfather. They put family bonds above all other morals. Alternatively, a romantic, who is a master at conveying emotion.
King of Swords	21° Taurus to 20° Gemini	Venus and Mercury	**Fire of Air** High winds, storms, hurricanes and cyclones.	Intention drives intellect.	An authoritative judge, scientist, general, philosopher, or leading thinker in their field. They are an idealist with fixed rational beliefs.
King of Pentacles	21° Leo to 20° Virgo	The Sun and Mercury	**Fire of Earth** Earthquakes, landslides, rockfalls.	Intention causes motion or manifestation.	A hard-working boss, or master craftsperson. Alternatively, someone who has made their fortune working the earth: farming, mining, etc. They are materialistic.
Queen of Wands	21° Pisces to 20° Aries	Jupiter (Neptune) and Mars	**Water of Fire** Combustible liquids.	Emotion causes intention.	A woman who has found power in a role traditionally prescribed to men, or in a role that rules over men. A female elder with authority in her community. (Alternatively, a male 'Queen'.)

Queen of Cups	21° Gemini to 20° Cancer	Mercury and the Moon	**Water of Water** Waves, volumes of liquids.	Pure emotionality or one emotion driving another.	A mystical woman who is powerfully emotionally expressive. Often an artist or poet who creates beautiful things that move people. Alternatively, a skilled female fortune teller.
Queen of Swords	21° Virgo to 20° Libra	Mercury and Venus	**Water of Air** Mist and rain.	Emotion drives intellect.	A female academic, politician, thinker, champion sportsperson, or military leader.
Queen of Pentacles	21° Sagittarius to 20° Capricorn	Jupiter and Saturn	**Water of Earth** Rivers, swamps, springs.	Emotion manifested or acted out.	A woman of means. Materialistic, conservative and private. She is usually found in roles serving the community.
Knight of Wands	21° Cancer to 20° Leo	The Moon and the Sun	**Air of Fire** Volatile chemicals and combustible gases, shockwaves.	Intellect drives intention.	A 'prima donna' personality. Full of charisma and drama, they are a person with rare talent. They can appear to be narcissistic to those that cross them.
Knight of Cups	21° Libra to 20° Scorpio	Venus and Mars (Pluto)	**Air of Water** Steam and vapour.	Intellect, symbols or concepts drive emotions.	An escapist talent, prone to experimentation. Rebellious and melancholic.

(*Continued*)

(Continued)

Card	Zodiacal sign or quadrant	Ruling planets	Elements	Meaning	Roles
Knight of Swords	21° Capricorn to 20° Aquarius	Saturn and Saturn (Uranus)	**Air of Air** Unseen forces such as gravity. Physical fields such as electromagnetism.	Pure intellect. Pure spirit.	A 'daredevil' personality. Brash, intense and brave. They have big goals and take no prisoners. They are better at debate than at preaching the truth. They often achieve the improbable as they never hold back.
Knight of Pentacles	21° Leo to 20° Aquarius	The Sun and Saturn (Uranus)	**Air of Earth** Dust storms, flying objects.	Concepts manifested.	A slow, cautious and responsible person. They are hard-working and skilled, producing fine things. Ever the pragmatist, they emphasise the phrase 'seeing is believing'. As friends they are highly dependable.
Page of Wands	Cancer, Leo and Virgo. (The months transitioning from summer to autumn in the northern hemisphere.)		**Earth of Fire** Solid fuels, contained fires.	The manifest drives intent.	An enthusiastic and wilful youth. Highly individualistic and impulsive.

INTRODUCTION xxiii

Page of Cups	Libra, Scorpio and Sagittarius. (The months transitioning from autumn to winter the northern hemisphere.)	Earth of Water Ice, snow.	The manifest drives emotion.	A young romantic dreamer. They are kind but not confident. They are usually on a voyage of self-discovery, or lost in their relationships. They have trouble settling down.
Page of Swords	Capricorn, Aquarius and Pisces. (The months transitioning from winter to spring in the Northern Hemisphere.)	Earth of Air Writing, recordings, discoveries from observing matter.	The manifest drives conceptualisation.	A 'gate-keeper' who would like to be considered an expert, but who has not yet put in the hard work. They profess strong beliefs but have not thought them through. Book-worm kids.
Page of Pentacles	Aries, Taurus, Gemini. (The months transition from spring to summer in the northern hemisphere.)	Earth of Earth Crystallisation, hard substances.	Matter working on matter.	A hard-working apprentice in an entry-level role. They seek material gain but have yet to achieve it.

The Minor Arcana

Card	Sefirah	Zodiacal decan	Act	Meaning
Ace of Wands	Fire in Keter	(None, or the three fire signs: Aries, Leo and Sagittarius)	Act I beginning	A new inspiration. A drive to express oneself.
Ace of Cups	Water in Keter	(None, or the three water signs: Cancer, Scorpio and Pisces)	Act I beginning	A spark of a new relationship. A crush.
Ace of Swords	Air in Keter	(None, or the three air signs: Libra, Aquarius, Gemini)	Act I beginning	A decision first rationalised. The beginning of a competition or debate.
Ace of Pentacles	Earth in Keter	(None, or the three earth signs: Capricorn, Taurus, Virgo)	Act I beginning	A new opportunity to act in the world. A new job opportunity. A new investment, or the desire to acquire a new object.
Two of Wands	Fire in Chokhmah	Mars in Aries (Domicile)	Act I first tension	A decision between life goals. One must be sacrificed in order that the other can be pursued.
Two of Cups	Water in Chokhmah	Venus in Cancer	Act I first tension	A new relationship is reciprocated for the first time. A new partnership. Good news for love.
Two of Swords	Air in Chokhmah	Moon in Libra	Act I first tension	A weighing up of two rational decisions. A rational choice. A decision to engage in an argument, a debate, or a cause.
Two of Pentacles	Earth in Chokhmah	Jupiter in Capricorn (Fall)	Act I first tension	The balancing of resources: time, health, and money. Usually due to a change in circumstances.

INTRODUCTION xxv

Three of Wands	Fire in Binah	Sun in Aries (Exalted)	Act I first resolution	Commitment to an ambition, and putting other possibilities on hold, or abandoning them.
Three of Cups	Water in Binah	Mercury in Cancer	Act I first resolution	Success in connecting emotionally with others. Especially in small groups.
Three of Swords	Air in Binah	Saturn in Libra (Exalted)	Act I first resolution	A heartbreak, a betrayal, an upsetting argument.
Three of Pentacles	Earth in Binah	Mars in Capricorn (Exalted)	Act I first resolution	The first success in mastering a craft or in a new job position. Other people are impressed by one's work.
Four of Wands	Fire in Chesed	Venus in Aries (Detriment)	Act II stability (hurdle)	Good early results achieving one's ambitions. Stability is found. Further success will require a big push and the taking of a risk.
Four of Cups	Water in Chesed	Moon in Cancer (Domicile)	Act II stability (hurdle)	An uncomfortable emotional stability. The novelty has worn off in a relationship. One is dissatisfied and pessimistic despite things not yet being that bad.
Four of Swords	Air in Chesed	Jupiter in Libra	Act II stability (hurdle)	A respite after a struggle of will. Or pulling out of a fight, an act of mercy. The saving of one's strength.
Four of Pentacles	Earth in Chesed	Sun in Capricorn	Act II stability (hurdle)	Saving for a rainy day. A miser. Some resources need to be spent to move forward, but one is reluctant to move.
Five of Wands	Fire in Gevurah	Saturn in Leo (Detriment)	Act II conflict	A competition amongst equals. 'Every man for himself.' The winners will be initiated into the hierarchy. Often comes up for job applications, for exams, or for workers trying to get promoted.

(Continued)

(Continued)

Card	Sefirah	Zodiacal decan	Act	Meaning
Five of Cups	Water in Gevurah	Mars in Scorpio (Domicile)	Act II conflict	'Crying over spilt milk.' One has suffered an emotional loss, but also there is a failure to regard what one still has.
Five of Swords	Air in Gevurah	Venus in Aquarius	Act II conflict	Winning a competition by sneaky means. A debate for 'points' rather than for truth. The querent may be the sneak or they may be the victim of the sneak depending on the card's position in relation to other cards.
Five of Pentacles	Earth in Gevurah	Mercury in Taurus	Act II conflict	Trying to maintain one's dignity through a difficult time. One is reluctant to receive charity. Sticking by one's partner through a difficult time. The difficulty is usually bad health or a loss of finances.
Six of Wands	Fire in Tiferet	Jupiter in Leo	Act II resolution	A celebration after a success. One battle has been one. The halfway point. 'Victory.'
Six of Cups	Water in Tiferet	Sun in Scorpio	Act II resolution	Nostalgia. Reunion. A return to the past.
Six of Swords	Air in Tiferet	Mercury in Aquarius	Act II resolution/ realisation	Taking one's troubles with one. Unsuccessfully trying to run away from emotions. The halfway point in healing from mental trauma. Though painful, a breakthrough is made. Work is still to be done.
Six of Pentacles	Earth Tiferet	Moon in Taurus (Exalted)	Act II resolution	Newfound resources. Abundance. A charitable mindset after a financial gain. Though a good sign, some money needs to be put away for a rainy day.

Seven of Wands	Fire in Netzach	Mars in Leo	Act III tension	The hard fight to get what one wants. Defending what one has. A struggle of wills. The 'suffering artist'. 'Kicking against the pricks' (Acts 9:5).
Seven of Cups	Water in Netzach	Venus in Scorpio	Act III tension	Temptation, debauchery, the curse of choice. Living in a temporary luxury. The high before the comedown.
Seven of Swords	Air in Netzach	Moon in Aquarius	Act III tension	A theft. A loophole. Taking someone's ideas. The loss of things unguarded.
Seven of Pentacles	Earth in Netzach	Saturn in Taurus	Act III tension	Waiting for an investment to deliver a return. Impatience. A slowing of progress after the hard work has been done. Success or failure is around the corner.
Eight of Wands	Fire in Hod	Mercury in Sagittarius (Detriment)	Act III action	A speedy delivery. A breakthrough in communication. A time of rapid change in relation to one's ambitions.
Eight of Cups	Water in Hod	Saturn in Pisces (Domicile)	Act III action	Abandoning ship. Walking away from one's problems. Leaving a long relationship.
Eight of Swords	Air in Hod	Jupiter in Gemini (Detriment)	Act III action/ ordeal	A self-inflicted ordeal. Making things hard for oneself.
Eight of Pentacles	Earth in Hod	Sun in Virgo	Act III action	The final stretch of hard work in a project. A productive time. Pride in one's work.
Nine of Wands	Fire in Yesod	Moon in Sagittarius	Act III resolution	Surviving a struggle. Exhaustion after a narrow success against great odds. Bravery.

(*Continued*)

(Continued)

Card	Sefirah	Zodiacal decan	Act	Meaning
Nine of Cups	Water in Yesod	Jupiter in Pisces (Domicile)	Act III resolution	Playing host. A party. A feeling of satisfaction in one's relationships. Providing joy for others.
Nine of Swords	Air in Yesod	Mars in Gemini	Act III resolution/ tragedy	Anguish, anxiety, or grief. One's inner problems outweigh the reality of the situation. Grounding is needed.
Nine of Pentacles	Earth in Yesod	Venus in Virgo (Fall)	Act III resolution/ happy ending	Abundance and material gain. Feeling wealthy. Financial security. Feeling in control of one's environment.
Ten of Wands	Fire in Malkut	Saturn in Sagittarius	Overture (burden)	The burden of success. Biting off more than one can chew. Overwhelmed by responsibility.
Ten of Cups	Water in Malkut	Mars in Pisces	Overture (happiness)	Emotional fulfilment in relationships and family.
Ten of Swords	Air in Malkut	Sun in Gemini	Overture (defeat)	Defeat. Loss of face. Despair. Rock bottom. Reluctant admission of fault. The only path forward is upward.
Ten of Pentacles	Earth in Malkut	Mercury in Virgo	Overture (fulfilment)	The fulfilment of fate. A meeting of generations. Satisfaction in achieving one's life goals.

LEVEL 4

Really advanced Tarot reading

Level 1 (Tarot Reading), Level 2 (Advanced Tarot Reading) and Level 3 (Understanding Tarot), were covered in the first book *Tarot for Sceptics*. If you are continuing on, you might want to have that volume to refer back to. If you are reading this book to expand on the Tarot reading you have learned elsewhere, feel free to plow on ahead.

At this point the Tarot becomes a scaffold for a diverse range of esoteric, syncretic ideas. Since the nineteenth century, Western occultists have tried to slap as much clothing onto the core skeleton of Tarot as possible, with Tarot de Marseilles being the original 'simple' form from which all the other decks and techniques are derived.

None of this extra information is necessary to get practical fortune-telling results. However, if one thinks of the core Tarot as a kind of telephone network for the transmission of concepts, this extra stuff (deep esoteric wisdom) is like an attempt to hack that network for ever wider forms of communication and to integrate it with ideas. This is akin to building an internet on the original network. The extra expansions are astrology, spirit contact in the form of archetypes, angels and gods, the Hebrew alphabet (used as a core 'magical language' from which to manipulate the universe), the Kabbalistic Tree of Life (itself an entire map of creation from the world of concepts), and perhaps the most 'out there' expansion, the Shem HaMephorash, a set of constructed angels or angel contacts, derived from the original Hebrew of Exodus 14:19–21 of the Old Testament.

It is entirely optional whether you incorporate this extra stuff into your readings, and it is entirely possible to have a lifelong professional career as a Tarot reader without any of it. My reason then for including it is to show by example how a magical system can be created from parts, in order that, in Level 5, I can show how you may construct your own system! To my knowledge, nobody has previously attempted to impart this approach to Tarot in this way. As such, some of you—especially the 'show me the results' magicians—may read Level 5 before Level 4. Well, I can't stop you, can I?

If however, one-upmanship is your game, and you wish to have one over all those inferior magicians who skipped this section, the full utilisation of this esoterica will certainly empower your ego and turn you into the magical equivalent of a bebop jazz musician, capable of impressing all with your vast theory, improvisational prowess and ability to get weirder results than all the other 'Tarot warlocks'. I mean even owning this book and flashing the pages of this section at your friends will boggle them in the best way, a 'charm spell' in and of itself.

Finally, this section is a great introduction to some occult ideas that might become your new thing!

Have fun, and may your results be reality-redefining.

Tarot astrology

Astrology is one of the core systems that informed the meanings of the cards for both the Rider Waite Smith deck and Crowley's Thoth deck (as well as the Golden Dawn deck, and the teachings which were the basis for all these decks).

In the modern world, astrology holds its place in a small corner in the fringe of culture, where the occult, magic, and 'new age' hang out. Because of this, it is usually forgotten that astrology was once the dominant framework that was used to understand the physical world from Europe to Persia to India, with comparable systems used in China and numerous other cultures. The astrology most visible today is the

Hellenistic tradition dating back at least as far as 332 BCE, which in turn was based upon Egyptian and Babylonian forms which date back to 2100 BCE and 1800 BCE respectively.

Since the Enlightenment (from around 1715 CE), the physical theories in astrology have mostly been dropped, with most practitioners using a psychological explanatory model or else ideas about subtle 'energy' which can mean anything from emotional influences to some invisible physical force that currently eludes science. Of all divinatory systems, astrology has perhaps been most adversely affected by the evolution of scientific models of reality. Especially damaging was the move away from the model of the geocentric universe—which placed the Earth and humankind at the centre of a 'small' universe—to the heliocentric model[1] which eventually reduced us to a speck in an unfathomably large cosmos.

For this reason, learning astrology as a modern practitioner can be a very messy exercise, and there is no longer any clear consensus, even amongst astrologers, on why astrology should work. Having struggled with this myself, I've come to the conclusion that the easiest way into astrology is through the classical system which has its origins in the ancient Greek system, especially of Aristotle. Even though we no longer describe the solar system using a geocentric model of layered spheres, this at least gives us an understanding of the beliefs of the past. 'Modern astrology', by comparison, is a mish-mash of modern and defunct ideas jury-rigged together like a vehicle made out of bits of horse-drawn carts, cars and aeroplanes. It might, despite itself, get you from point A to point B, but learning how to drive the thing is complex and confusing. Astrology, done properly, like Tarot, fits into that odd category of things that should not work but appear to work anyway, even though most of the attempts to explain why it works look like nonsense...

Did I mention that it works?

One of my eventual goals is to try and fix some of the problems with magical systems that rely too heavily on old, defunct science, and to

---

[1] Credited to Nicolaus Copernicus (1473–1543) and his 1543 publication of *De revolutionibus orbium coelestium,* though earlier Heliocentric models had been proposed by Aristarchus of Samos in the third century BCE, and in the fifth century BCE by the Greek philosophers Philolaus and Hicetas.

bring magical explanations closer to contemporary consensus reality. What follows however will simply be a summary of astrology in the ways it is used with Tarot. As astrology is probably the most complex of all forms of divination, I am not offering a full explanation of it here, nor trying to solve all its problems, and a book that tried to do so could be tens of thousands of pages long! As far as Tarot reading is concerned, astrology is mostly used as an interface to the archetypes and symbols of Greco-Roman mythology, and it functions as such very well. I will start however by describing the universe of classical Western astrology, the universe as understood before complex telescopes, space probes and empiricism. The hope is that one day some other writer will come and reorganise astrology to better fit our current scientific model of the universe.[2]

Aristotle's cosmology

Aristotle (384–322 BCE) is perhaps more than any other ancient thinker, responsible for our modern worldview. He was the first to organise philosophy into formal logic, to categorise organisms by their common physical attributes, especially species, to add a fifth element 'aether' (spirit) to the four classical elements of fire, water, air and earth (the system presented by Empedocles, c. 494–434 BCE), which is still used in Western magic, and perhaps most importantly, he organised the study of nature by organising it into a chain of causes and effects.

From the twelfth century CE until the rediscovery and republishing of the works of Plato in Italy by Marsilio Ficino in 1484 CE (brought to him by Islamic scholars, and to them by the Byzantines), Aristotle was the dominant philosopher of the European Christian world.

Aristotle's book *On the Heavens*, written around 350 BCE, contained his astronomical ideas and was the influence for late medieval and Renaissance astrology.

---

[2] One nice thing about the old Western scientific models, even if they were physically wrong, is that they tried to align human spiritual and subjective conscious experiences with the physical model. Many scientists are back on this mission after centuries of materialism. For this reason, the geocentric cosmology still has some utility as a psychological model, and as Tarot readers and magicians, this is what we are interested in.

Schema huius præmissæ diuisionis Sphærarum.

Figure 2. Peter Apian's 1524 representation of the universe, heavily influenced by Aristotle's ideas.

Heavenly spheres

In Aristotle's cosmology, the Earth is the centre of the universe, which makes perfect sense in an age where no human had ever left the Earth. Around this are ten nested spheres, each one surrounding the last. These were laid out in order of the perceived speed of the bodies that moved in them. This has come to be known in astrology as 'the Chaldean order'.[3] Aristotle's cosmology was added to later by Ptolemy (100–170 CE) in his astronomical work *Tetrabiblos* ('Four books') and it is his system that has become dominant for Western astrologers. In order, the spheres are:

0. The Earth.
1. The sphere of Luna, through which the Moon travels around the Earth. The fastest observable body, correctly understood to be the closest to the Earth.
2. The sphere of Mercury.
3. The sphere of Venus.
4. The sphere of the Sun. It was not at this time understood that the apparent speed of the Sun is actually the speed of the Earth around it.
5. The sphere of Mars.
6. The sphere of Jupiter.
7. The sphere of Saturn. Correctly understood to be the slowest planet.
8. The firmament, which is the sphere of the 'fixed stars'. Largely understood to not move at all, we now know that the stars move very slowly in relation to the Earth.
9. The Crystallinum (Crystal sphere). Added in by astrologers later, this is the sphere of the zodiac, through which the twelve divisions of the sky—named after constellations that they once aligned with—have their effect on us.[4]
10. The Primum Mobile or 'prime mover', which was said to rotate every twenty-four hours, taking the other spheres with it, and accounting for the motion that we now understand to be the rotation of the Earth.

Outside of this was things yet uncreated, the realm of God.

---

[3] Chaldean is an old name for the Aramaic language, and for the race of semitic people who had a small nation from approximately the late tenth to mid-sixth centuries BC. After this period, they were absorbed by the neighbouring Babylonians.

[4] Due to the precession of the equinoxes, the constellations no longer align to the divisions of the sky which are named after them. In Western astrology, the divisions of the sky are what matters. The Indian system, which also descends largely from the Greek system, is sidereal. That is, the constellations are used instead of the 'tropical' divisions of the sky. For our purposes, the Western system is the correct one for Tarot.

Each of these spheres was considered to transmit a type of influence, in line with the symbolism or spiritual nature of the body and of the god that ruled that sphere. In this sense the planet Mars was the transmitter and link to the influence of the concepts and forces governed by the god Mars.

This can be hard to relate to for someone educated in our modern world and education system, but becomes easier if one understands that before the scientific age, there was no division between the world of concepts and the world of spirits. Instead, they were thought to either overlap, or else to be the same thing. Astrologically speaking, Mars the planet is therefore the conveyer of all 'Martian' and 'martial' concepts. An angry or combative mood in a human being then was not only thought of as behaving 'like Mars' but also as 'invoking' Mars, and the planet Mars was one of the transmitters of the qualities of Mars.

The meaning of the seven classical planets

The term 'planet' comes from ancient Greek πλανήτης (planétēs) originally meaning 'wanderer'.

Therefore planets in astrology are those objects that move around the sky in relation to our observation point on Earth. The 'stars' by comparison were considered 'fixed', moving as an entire sphere rather than as independent objects. For this reason, the Sun and Moon are 'planets' in astrology, while the Earth is not.

The seven classical planets, though Roman, draw from the gods of Greek myth, which were syncretised by the Romans with their own gods. This came from the period where the Roman Empire was expanding and modelling itself on the earlier Greek Empire of Alexander the Great. Though the Roman gods are thought to have once been different, they have been treated as equivalent to the Greek gods for so long that we are no longer able to discern a difference.

Each of these seven planets is paired with an opposite: Saturn/Jupiter, Mars/Venus and Sun/Moon. The exception is Mercury, who is a free agent and a trickster, never settling on a true nature. He acts as his own opposite, hence the term 'mercurial', meaning of changeable or volatile character. Mercury is also often said to be androgynous, which is useful for the symbolism of Tarot. I have included more detail on the gods in an appendix titled 'Mythology: Greco-Roman Gods'.

Saturn (Cronus)

The ruling Titan who is the father of Jupiter (Zeus) and the Olympians. Saturn represents the establishment, old traditions, slow-moving and monolithic societal structures, and old people, such as grandparents. Without old ways there is no society, but often these structures need to be subverted in order to achieve progress. Where Jupiter, who rebelled against his father, represents empires in expansion, Saturn is empires in stasis and decline. The positive side of this is the preservation of the past: museums, archaeology, tradition. The negative is bloated bureaucracy, dynasties that guard their power, depression and decline. Where Jupiter expands, Saturn retracts. He therefore represents times in our lives where we pull back. Saturn has staying power and an ability to concentrate. He is the correct influence for lifelong pursuits, routines, and discipline. My favourite astrologer, John David Ebert, also refers to him as 'the king in a bad mood'. Saturn is a pessimist: he readily spots the bad in things, he is ready for any trap that is waiting. He therefore also represents caution, safety, and treading the well-known path. The old-school. He is the building of walls and fences. Other associations include gravity and pressure, weight and rigidity. The weight of tradition.

Saturn corresponds to the following Tarot cards:

- Five of Wands—Saturn in Leo.
- Ten of Wands—Saturn in Sagittarius.
- Eight of Cups—Saturn in Pisces.
- Three of Swords—Saturn in Libra.
- Seven of Pentacles—Saturn in Taurus.
- Knight of Swords—21° Capricorn to 20° Aquarius. Both are ruled by Saturn in the classical system. (In modern astrology, Aquarius is ruled by Uranus.)
- Queen of Pentacles—21° Sagittarius to 20° Capricorn. Capricorn is ruled by Saturn.
- King of Cups—21° Aquarius to 20° Pisces. Aquarius is classically ruled by Saturn, but by Uranus in the modern system. Pisces is classically ruled by Jupiter, and by Neptune in modern astrology.
- XV The Devil—Capricorn, ruled by Saturn.
- XXI The World—Saturn.

Jupiter (Zeus)

In relation to Saturn's tradition, Jupiter is the avant-garde. He is the 'king in a good mood'. Jupiter is kingdoms expanding, economic growth, optimism, good fortune, good luck, and opportunity. He is the archetype for entrepreneurs. The power of youthful energy and its effect on the establishment. He is new institutions, positive leadership, and the charm of leaders. He represents reform, and progressive politics. As the will to power, he is triumph, exploration, and incorporating the world into one's own will. Finally, Jupiter is associated with good health and the will to explore and to conquer.

Jupiter corresponds to the following Tarot cards:

- 6 of Wands—Jupiter in Leo.
- 9 of Cups—Jupiter in Pisces.
- 4 of Swords—Jupiter in Libra.
- 8 of Swords—Jupiter in Gemini.
- King of Wands—21° Scorpio to 20° Sagittarius, ruled by Jupiter. (Scorpio is traditionally ruled by Mars, and in modern astrology by Pluto.)
- Queen of Wands—21° Pisces to 20° Aries. Pisces is classically ruled by Jupiter (by Neptune in modern astrology). Aries is ruled by Mars.
- Queen of Pentacles—21° Sagittarius to 20° Capricorn. Sagittarius is ruled by Jupiter. (Capricorn is ruled by Saturn.)
- X The Wheel of Fortune—Jupiter.
- XVIII The Moon—Pisces, classically ruled by Jupiter (in modern astrology by Neptune).
- XIV Temperance—Sagittarius, ruled by Jupiter.

Mars (Ares)

As the most energetic of all the gods, Mars is the ambition and the pure desire that motivates Jupiter's expansion. He is also the action on the ground in relation to Jupiter's leadership. Where Saturn is defence, Mars is aggression and attack. He is the hunter, the wooer, and the competitor. He represents movement, force, excitement, active sexuality and violence. He strives to win. He is battle and sports, arguments and debates, competitions and competitiveness. He is confident, but also reckless, when not balanced by other forces such as Saturn or Venus.

Venus is his opposite, and she represents the things and people he desires. Mars is associated with the Tower card. In Taoism, Mars aligns to the Yang. The will to competition.

Mars corresponds to the following Tarot cards:

- 2 of Wands—Mars in Aries.
- 7 of Wands—Mars in Leo.
- 5 of Cups—Mars in Scorpio.
- 10 of Cups—Mars in Pisces.
- 9 of Swords—Mars in Gemini.
- 3 of Pentacles—Mars in Capricorn.
- Knight of Cups—21° Libra to 20° Scorpio. Scorpio is classically ruled by Mars (by Pluto in modern Astrology.) Libra is ruled by Venus.
- Knight of Pentacles—21° Aries to 20° Taurus. Aries is ruled by Mars. (Taurus is ruled by Venus.)
- Queen of Wands—21° Pisces to 20° Aries. Aries is ruled by Mars. (Pisces is classically ruled by Jupiter, and by Neptune in modern astrology.)
- King of Wands—21° Scorpio to 20° Sagittarius. Scorpio is classically ruled by Mars (by Pluto in modern Astrology). Sagittarius is ruled by Jupiter.
- IV The Emperor—Aries, ruled by Mars.
- XIII Death—Scorpio, classically ruled by Mars (by Pluto in modern astrology).
- XVI The Tower—Mars.

Sun (Apollo)

The Sun is one's sense of self, especially the outer parts of one's personality and one's persona. It is that which you know about yourself, as well as the overt roles you play for others. It is knowledge and things out in the light for all to see. It is the visible outward surfaces of everyone and everything. It is the facts laid bare. It radiates and 'sheds light' on the things around it and therefore represents charm and self-esteem and celebrity. In the philosophy of Friedrich Nietzsche, the 'Apollonian' (a sun god) represents harmony, progress, clarity, logic, the principle of individuation, rationality, and ordered states of consciousness. Its opposite, the 'Dionysian', would be represented by the moon. The sun is the will to being and the animus, or 'male' half of the soul.

The Sun corresponds to the following Tarot cards:

- 3 of Wands—Sun in Aries.
- 6 of Cups—Sun in Scorpio.
- 10 of Swords—Sun in Gemini.
- 4 of Pentacles—Sun in Capricorn.
- 8 of Pentacles—Sun in Virgo.
- Knight of Wands—21° Cancer to 20° Leo. Leo is ruled by the Sun. (Cancer is ruled by the Moon.)
- King of Pentacles—21° Leo to 20° Virgo. Leo is ruled by the Sun. (Virgo is ruled by Mercury.)
- VIII Strength—Leo, ruled by the Sun.
- XIX—The Sun.

Venus (Aphrodite)

Where Mars is the desirer, Venus is that which is desired. Where Mars hunts with a spear or bow and arrow, Venus is the lure of the fisherman. She is aesthetics, art, beauty and attraction. She is receptive sexuality, the 'chooser' of lovers and the discernment and the judge of the worthy and unworthy. She represents refinement, beautiful music and art, romance, temptation and peace. She is heart over mind, and can intoxicate the unwise: for instance, Romeo and Juliet and the folie à deux.[5] She is the drive towards company, romance, love and binding. In Daoism, Venus aligns to the Yin. She is the will to bond.

Venus corresponds to the following Tarot cards:

- 4 of Wands—Venus in Aries.
- 2 of Cups—Venus in Cancer.
- 7 of Cups—Venus in Scorpio.
- 5 of Swords—Venus in Aquarius.
- 9 of Pentacles—Venus in Pentacles.
- III The Empress—Venus.

---

[5] The 'madness of two', a charming French term for a romantic pairing based on the shared delusions of the two partners.

- V The Hierophant—Taurus, ruled by Venus.
- XI Justice—Libra, ruled by Venus.
- Queen of Swords—21° Virgo to 20° Libra, ruled by Venus. (Virgo is ruled by Mercury.)
- Knight of Cups—21° Libra to 20° Scorpio. Libra is ruled by Venus. (Scorpio is ruled by Mars or Pluto.)
- Knight of Pentacles—21° Aries to 20° Taurus. Taurus is ruled by Venus. (Aries is ruled by Mars.)
- King of Swords—21° Taurus to 20° Gemini. Taurus is ruled by Venus. (Gemini is ruled by Mercury.)

Mercury (Hermes)

This planet governs communication, commerce, economics, information transfers, the internet, cybernetic systems, medicine, and conceptual breakthroughs. Mercury is information both overt and occulted, codes, books, propaganda, and the manipulation of perception. The inherent qualities of Mercury are metamorphosis and the ability to change, the ability to transcend boundaries and dichotomies, classes, worlds, languages, genders etc. Mercury is the world of concepts. While all the other planets are arranged in opposite pairs, Mercury, the shapeshifter, is its own opposite and is therefore androgynous. The will to know.

Mercury corresponds to the following Tarot cards:

- 8 of Wands—Mercury in Sagittarius.
- 3 of Cups—Mercury in Cancer.
- 6 of Swords—Mercury in Aquarius.
- 5 of Pentacles—Mercury in Taurus.
- 10 of Pentacles—Mercury in Virgo.
- Queen of Cups—21° Gemini to 20° Cancer. Gemini is ruled by Mercury. (Cancer is ruled by the Moon.)
- Queen of Swords—21° Virgo to 20° Libra. Virgo is ruled by Mercury. (Libra is ruled by Venus.)
- King of Swords—21° Taurus to 20° Gemini, ruled by Mercury. (Taurus is ruled by Venus.)
- King of Pentacles—21° Leo to 20° Virgo, ruled by Mercury. (Leo is ruled by the Sun.)

- The Magician—Mercury.
- The Hermit—Virgo, ruled by Mercury.
- The Lovers—Gemini, ruled by Mercury.

Moon/Luna

Represents short cycles of time, such as days, weeks and months. She is moods and emotions, especially those which are temporary. She is hormonal influences on the mind such as menstrual cycles, or the daily testosterone cycle in men. The Moon is hidden things come to light, liminality, and lunatics. She is tied to direct personal experience, especially that which cannot be easily explained. In Nietzsche's philosophy, the opposite of the 'Apollonian', which I attribute to the Sun, is the lunar, 'Dionysian', representing dissolution of boundaries, intoxication and other altered states of consciousness, dream, emotion, ecstasy and unity, the dissolution of the individual, the influence of the body, the intuition, and knowledge gained through purely subjective experiences. These attributes all fit the Moon. Even though there is a moon card in Tarot, the astrological Moon is somewhat confusingly associated with the High Priestess. The Moon card is associated instead with Pisces. The Moon is the liminal area between the known and the unknown, just as the night's moon is the light in the dark, which casts many shadows. Therefore, she is a symbol for the occult (the hidden) and most new ideas come from this place. She is the anima, the feminine part of the soul. She is the will to experience and to 'feel'.

The Moon corresponds to the following Tarot cards:

- 9 of Wands—Moon in Sagittarius.
- 4 of Cups—Moon in Cancer.
- 2 of Swords—Moon in Libra.
- 7 of Swords—Moon in Aquarius.
- 6 of Pentacles—Moon in Taurus.
- Queen of Cups—21° Gemini to 20° Cancer, ruled by the Moon. (Gemini is ruled by Mercury.)
- The High Priestess—The Moon.
- The Chariot—Cancer, ruled by the Moon.
- The Knight of Wands—21° Cancer to 20° Leo. Cancer is ruled by the Moon.

The outer planets

While most modern astrologers have incorporated the outer planets into their divination, they were discovered late, not being visible to the naked eye,[6] and are not part of classical astrology. Their inclusion as full planets is somewhat disruptive to the classical numerology of seven, and as they move slowly in comparison to the inner planets, their influence on people is generational rather than individual. Likewise, there is a certain beauty to the symmetry of the classical system of planets where each is in a male/female dichotomy, with Mercury as an androgyne. When practising astrology, I consider the outer planets as an 'expansion pack', and for this they work very well. For Tarot these problems are less of an issue as we are mostly working with the planets as archetypes. Many astrologers leave the outer planets out entirely and still get good readings.

The discovery of the outer planets

Neptune was widely thought to be a star until it was catalogued as a planet around 1846. There is much contention about exactly who 'discovered' it, though several astronomers contributed, including Johann Gottfried Galle, Heinrich Louis d'Arrest, John Couch Adams, Urbain Le Verrier, and James Challis. Galle, Le Verrier and Adams were eventually granted joint credit. Le Verrier named the planet Neptune in accordance with the theme of Roman gods and this name was eventually accepted.

Since then, Neptune has been incorporated into astrology. As the 'classical' planets have thousands of years of mythological association and the outer planets much less, they don't necessarily fit their Roman namesakes as clearly.

Uranus was also largely recorded as a star until its discovery as a planet by Sir William Herschel in 1781. Pierre Charles Le Monnier had also contributed to the discovery with his earlier observations between 1750 and 1769. Originally it was named 'Herschel' for its discoverer, or 'Georgium Sidus' after Herschel's patron, King George III. In 1782 Johann Elert Bode proposed the name 'Uranus' as a better fit for the theme of the Roman gods of the other planets, and this was eventually accepted

---

[6] Uranus is right on the edge of what is visible on the clearest of nights, with no light pollution.

and published in 1850 by His Majesty's Nautical Almanac Office, a primary publisher of astronomical data. Of all the planets, the name Uranus is perhaps the worst fit with the accepted astrological attributes, and some astrologers suggest that a better fit would be 'Prometheus'.

Pluto was officially discovered in 1930 by Clyde Tombaugh, though a 'Planet X' had been predicted since as far back as the 1840s. Upon the announcement of the discovery of Pluto, a competition was held by the staff of the Lowell Observatory to name the planet. The name 'Pluto' had received some 150 nominations, the first of which was from Venetia Burney (1918–2009), an eleven-year-old schoolgirl from Oxford, England, who was interested in classical mythology. Her suggested name was apt, as the planet inhabits the cold outer regions of the solar system, akin to 'Hades'. This symbolism, and the attributes later assigned by astrologers to this planet, fit the god of the underworld very well.

Since 2006, Pluto has been reclassified as a 'dwarf planet' to allow the inclusion of several other solar system objects.[7] A dwarf planet is any small body that still has enough gravitation to form a sphere or an ellipsoid. Smaller, more irregular objects are called 'minor planets'. These extra objects currently have no place in Tarot but are slowly being worked out by modern astrologers.

One curious minor planet that has a strong following in modern Astrology is 2060 Chiron, which is classified as both a minor planet and a comet by astronomers. It lives between Saturn and Uranus and is named for the Greek centaur who was a master healer. Perhaps there is scope to one day create a Tarot deck based on up-to-date astronomy.

The meanings of the outer planets

Uranus

Mythologically and astrologically, it is easier to think of this planet as having the properties of Prometheus, the Greek titan who brought fire and technology to man in rebellion against the Olympian hegemony.

---

[7] If you would like to make a name for yourself in history as an astrologer, see if you can decipher the meanings of all the dwarf planets: Pluto, Eris, Haumea, Makemake, Gonggong, Quaoar, Sedna, Ceres, and Orcus. By the time you are finished, undoubtably more will have been discovered. Such is the confusing state of modern astrology. Some astrologers also include smaller, 'minor planets' (also called centaurs), with Chiron having become very popular. There are more than 1,131,201 of these currently counted. I'm sorry to present you with this state of affairs.

Uranus is the signifier of cultural breakthroughs and zeitgeist events. It is associated with generational breaks from tradition. It represents utopian and dystopian thinking and group ideology. Some astrologers also associate Uranus with natural and societal events that shake people up, such as earthquakes, natural disasters, wars and national conflicts. Taking eighty-four years to move round the zodiac, it signifies time cycles roughly the length of a human life. When used with the Tarot, Uranus is usually associated with the Fool. It is the tension which forces evolution. The will to change. The Star card, which is assigned to Aquarius, has Uranus as its ruler in modern astrology (Saturn in classical astrology).

Neptune

Named for the god of the sea, this is interpreted rather metaphorically by astrologers. Here water is the dissolution of boundaries, the subconscious, and psychedelic or liminal conscious states. Neptune is thus the blurring of boundaries, and especially the effects of the 'weird' on groups of people: psychedelia, drugs, pop culture, dreams, delusions, fiction, poetry, imagination, groupthink, psychosis, personal spirituality, divination, and myth. Neptune takes 165 years to move through the zodiac, so it represents societal 'eras' more than individual experience. When used in Tarot, Neptune belongs to the Hanged Man card. It is transcendental experiences. The will to transcend the self.

Pluto

Generally considered the most negative planet by modern astrologers, Pluto signifies cultural upheavals, and cycles of death or destruction which precede rebirth. It is a planet of grand powers unleashed and great uncoverings. Pluto takes 248 years to move through the zodiac, and therefore represents whole traditions of human influence.

As Pluto is the ruler of Scorpio in modern astrology (ruled by Mars in classical astrology) it may be assigned to the Death card. Pluto can be associated with the Jungian shadow and the death drive.

Tarot readers also often assign it to the Judgement card, for which it is a good fit; things from the underworld brought to awareness.

Essential dignity

These are four categories applied to the zodiacal signs for each planet, that affect its ability to perform:

- **Domicile:** The sign that a planet is the ruler of. Here the planet has full freedom to act in its nature. It will also be most stable in this sign.
- **Detriment:** The sign opposite the sign of domicile. This will put the planet in the opposite season. Here the planet with be stifled or blocked from expressing itself. A negative stability.
- **Exaltation:** The sign where the planet is a 'welcome guest'. Here the planet is partially amplified, but not as expressive or as stable as it would be in its own domicile. One can think of this as a positive tension.
- **Fall:** The sign opposite the sign of exaltation. A negative tension.

All other planetary placements are considered neutral. As Mercury is a duplicitous planet, its Domicile is the same as its Exaltation and its Detriment is the same as its Fall.

The classical attributions are most useful for Tarot. In this system all the planets rule two signs, except for the Sun and Moon, which rule one sign each. This is because the Moon was understood to be a reflector of the Sun and the two bodies were thought to be in sympathy.

Classical Planets	*Domicile (Rulership)*	*Detriment*	*Exaltation*	*Fall*
Saturn	Capricorn & Aquarius	Cancer & Leo	Libra	Aries
Jupiter	Sagittarius & Pisces	Gemini & Virgo	Cancer	Capricorn
Mars	Aries & Scorpio	Taurus & Libra	Capricorn	Cancer
Sun	Leo	Aquarius	Aries	Libra
Venus	Taurus & Libra	Aries & Scorpio	Pisces	Virgo
Mercury	Gemini & Virgo	Sagittarius & Pisces	Virgo	Pisces
Moon	Cancer	Capricorn	Taurus	Scorpio

There is however a modern set of attributions below which include the outer planets and which have a few differences. I realise that these differences can be frustrating for some, and yet they abound in magical systems. Therefore my recommendation is to choose one or the other and stick to it. In this system only Venus and Mercury rule two signs.

Outer Planets	Domicile (Rulership)	Detriment	Exaltation	Fall
Saturn	Capricorn	Cancer	Libra	Aries
Jupiter	Sagittarius	Gemini	Cancer	Capricorn
Mars	Aries	Libra	Capricorn	Cancer
Sun	Leo	Uranus	Aries	Libra
Venus	Taurus & Libra	Aries	Sagittarius	Gemini
Mercury	Gemini & Virgo	Sagittarius	Virgo	Sagittarius
Moon	Cancer	Capricorn	Taurus	Scorpio
Uranus	Aquarius	Leo	Scorpio	Uranus
Neptune	Pisces	Virgo	Leo	Aquarius
Pluto	Scorpio	Taurus	Aquarius	Leo

Other astrological concepts

These attributes are used in combination to categorise and understand the signs of the zodiac. Each divides the twelve signs into a subgroup, which has an underlying numerology: Twos, Threes, and Fours.

Polarity

These divide the twelve signs into two groups of six.
Sometimes called 'gender', this is a dichotomy of:

- Active (Masculine).
- Passive (Feminine).

The active signs are the Fire and Air signs: Aries, Gemini, Leo, Libra, Sagittarius, and Aquarius. The passive signs are the Water and Earth signs: Taurus, Cancer, Virgo, Scorpio, Capricorn, and Pisces. (Astrologers sometimes refer to these as 'positive' and 'negative' signs, but I personally find that a bit misleading for new learners, as by this they simply mean 'active' and 'passive'.)

Qualities (Quadruplicity)

These divide the twelve signs into three groups of four.

- Cardinal. The beginning of a season.
- Fixed. The middle of a season.
- Mutable. The end of a season.

Cardinal signs are instigators, leaders, people with ambition who take charge. Fixed signs like to stay as they are. Mutable signs are shape-changers, always ready to try something new.

The Cardinal signs are Aries, Cancer, Libra and Capricorn. The Fixed signs are Taurus, Leo, Scorpio, and Aquarius. The Mutable signs are Gemini, Virgo, Sagittarius, and Pisces.

Element (Triplicity)

These divide the twelve signs into four groups of three.

By now you will be very familiar with the four elements: Fire, Water, Air, Earth.

The Fire signs are Aries, Leo and Sagittarius. The Water signs are Cancer, Scorpio, and Pisces. The Air signs are Gemini, Libra, and Aquarius. The Earth signs are Taurus, Virgo, and Capricorn.

The twelve signs of the zodiac

The signs of the zodiac are twelve equal divisions of the ecliptic, that is, the Sun's (apparent) path around the Earth. From Earth they can be understood as moving divisions of the sky. These are named for the constellations that they once aligned to, but due to the precession of the equinoxes, the Earth has moved away from these exact positions. In Western astrology the divisions of the ecliptic are what are important and the constellations are disregarded. Sidereal astrological systems such as Vedic astrology instead use the constellations in their current positions rather than the ecliptic but are not important to us here.

Each of the signs represents personality traits that can be found in individual people as well as archetypes that play out in the world through groups of people, corporations, fiction, nations, politics and any observations that can be assembled into a narrative. Though it has become popular for people to identify with their zodiacal Sun sign (the sign where the Sun was positioned when they were born), I have found that the full power of astrology as a divinatory system only comes into play when all the planets and signs are read in their combinations.[8]

Aries ♈

Date: 21 March–19 April
Polarity: Active
Quality: Cardinal
Element: Fire
Tarot card: The Emperor
Season: Beginning of spring
Ruling planet: Mars
Planet in detriment: Venus
Planet in exaltation: Sun
Planet in fall: Saturn

People born in Aries are determined, motivated, resourceful, adventurous, quick to act, brave, quick to bore, and passionate. They like to express their will to the outside world. They can be self-centred and single-minded. They are competitive and don't like to 'lose' arguments or games. They also tend to play 'to win' instead of playing to be 'right'. They enjoy status and hate being restricted or made to wait. They often appear energetic to other people.

Aries teaches the importance of the self to the previous sign, Pisces, and learns the importance of patience from the next sign, Taurus.

Taurus ♉

Date: 20 April–20 May
Polarity: Passive

---

[8] Though I will not be explaining how to read a full astrological chart here, as our purpose is Tarot reading, I am of the opinion that the minimum useful information to give an accurate astrological reading is one's Sun sign, one's ascendant and one's Moon sign. If you want a useful side quest, go find out these three core aspects of your natal chart and then read this section again.

Quality: Fixed
Element: Earth
Tarot card: The Hierophant
Season: Middle of spring
Ruling planet: Venus
Planet in detriment: Mars or Pluto
Planet in exaltation: Moon
Planet in fall: None or Uranus

People born in Taurus are homebodies. They like nice things, nice people, good food, art and a nice home. They are slow to anger or upset, but can burst in a quick rage like the proverbial bull if pushed beyond their boundaries. This usually happens if they perceive a broaching of their 'territory'. They are attracted to beautiful things and beautiful people, but less concerned over their own glamour. They have the stubbornness of the bull and can be hard to motivate.

Taurus teaches Aries patience and learns from Gemini the importance of flexibility.

Gemini ♊

Date: 21 May–21 June
Polarity: Active
Quality: Mutable
Element: Air
Tarot card: The Lovers
Season: End of spring
Ruling planet: Mercury
Planet in detriment: Jupiter
Planet in exaltation: Mercury
Planet in fall: None or Venus

These are people who are full of ideas and live in the world of concepts. Even when this sign is embodied in a single person, that individual is able to think like a committee, understanding multiple points of view. For this reason, they can be excellent teachers but are often demanding students. The primary attribute is adaptability and being a jack-of-all-trades. They often seem to be contradictory and complex to get to know, being 'mercurial' by nature. To the fixed signs they can seem impractical, but Geminis' problem-solving abilities usually find a way through. Geminis tend to annoy down-to-earth people.

Gemini teaches Taurus how to be more flexible and learns from Cancer that rational thought has limitations and emotions have their place.

Cancer ♋

Date: 22 June–22 July
Polarity: Passive
Quality: Cardinal
Element: Water
Tarot card: The Chariot
Season: Beginning of summer
Ruling planet: The Moon
Planet in detriment: Saturn
Planet in exaltation: Jupiter
Planet in fall: Mars

'Hard on the outside, soft on the inside', like the crab, people born in Cancer are private, family- and friend-oriented, loyal, seeking close relationships. They are highly protective of themselves and their loved ones. As cardinal Water, they are empathetic, sympathetic and intuitive. A good sign for a counsellor. In the negative, they can be clingy, moody or emotionally manipulative. They like to keep up appearances, almost as a mask to protect their privacy.

Cancer teaches Gemini the value of emotions and learns from Leo the power of self-expression.

Leo ♌

Date: 23 July–22 August
Polarity: Active
Quality: Fixed
Element: Fire
Tarot card: Strength
Season: Middle of summer
Ruling planet: The Sun
Planet in detriment: Saturn or Uranus
Planet in exaltation: None or Neptune
Planet in fall: None or Pluto.

The performers of the zodiac, they are self-expressive, confident, charming and somewhat dominating. They like the undivided attention of others and aim to stand out. Their image is the projection of their personality, and in contrast to most people, they are most 'themselves' when playing a role. In the negative, they can steamroll other quieter personalities.

Leo teaches Cancer self-expression and learns organisation and discipline from Virgo.

Virgo ♍

Date: 23 August–22 September
Polarity: Passive
Quality: Mutable
Element: Earth
Tarot card: The Hermit
Season: End of summer
Ruling planet: Mercury
Planet in detriment: Jupiter or Neptune
Planet in exaltation: Mercury
Planet in fall: Venus

These are practical, detail-focused people who like order. They are hardworking, like to have their own way of doing things, can have very high standards and little patience for those who don't live up to them. They are intellectuals like Geminis but are more likely to have fixed, well thought-out opinions, compared with Geminis who like to understand every point of view. They are analytical and critical and make excellent debuggers. To emotional personalities they can seem untactful and blunt.

Virgo, like a good ballet teacher, teaches Leo technique, and learns diplomacy from Libra.

Libra ♎

Date: 23 September–23 October
Polarity: Active
Quality: Cardinal
Element: Air
Tarot card: Justice

Season: Beginning of autumn
Ruling planet: Venus
Planet in detriment: Mars
Planet in exaltation: Saturn
Planet in fall: Sun

As the middle of the zodiac, this is the sign of balance, Libras are relationship-focused, diplomatic, obliging and fair. They generally dislike conflict and strive for peace and compromise. They are sharp to recognise the social dynamics of groups and take it on themselves to maintain order. They tend to take the side of the underdog, towards the quickest solution. They can frustrate idealistic people such as Sagittarius, as they are most comfortable maintaining the status quo. When combined with a strongly egotistic personality, Libras may switch from being fair to being very manipulative, playing people off of each other, though this is rare. Aleister Crowley was a Libra of the latter type.

Libra teaches Virgo diplomacy and negotiation, and learns from Scorpio how to repurpose one's hidden qualities.

Scorpio ♏

Date: 24 October–21 November
Polarity: Passive
Quality: Fixed
Element: Water
Tarot card: Death
Season: Middle of autumn
Ruling planet: Mars or Pluto
Planet in detriment: Venus
Planet in exaltation: None or Uranus
Planet in fall: Moon

Driven to uncover secret things, Scorpios are fascinated by mysteries, mysterious people, and 'dark' subjects such as death. They are private, passionate, subversive, and sometimes perverse, thriving in situations that other people find emotionally uncomfortable, and can be impish. They are attracted to the forbidden, and underground or exclusive subcultures. Scorpio is associated with sex and death, dramatic tension, fermentation, occulted activities, mining, espionage and engaging with one's 'shadow' nature.

Scorpio teaches the power of one's hidden nature to Libra and is taught to reach for a higher potential by Sagittarius.

Sagittarius ♐

Date: 22 November–21 December
Polarity: Active
Quality: Mutable
Element: Fire
Tarot card: Temperance
Season: End of autumn
Ruling planet: Jupiter
Planet in detriment: Mercury
Planet in exaltation: None or Venus
Planet in fall: Mercury

Sagittarius is the archer. They are idealistic and motivated people who set and work towards lofty goals. They are progressives, who are always concerned with how things can be improved with a focus on perfection. As far-reaching people, they can seem separated from reality in their enthusiasm for what could be. They are optimistic and require challenges to work towards. They will often bite off more than they can chew but are good at picking themselves up from failure. They don't enjoy naysayers or critics. While they are idealists like Aquarians, Sagittarius' mission is more affirming to their own individuality and ego, where Aquarius would like to change the world, for humanity or a group of people.

They teach optimism and goal-setting to Scorpio and are taught logistics and planning by Capricorn.

Capricorn ♑

Date: 22 December–19 January
Polarity: Passive
Quality: Cardinal
Element: Earth
Tarot card: The Devil
Season: Beginning of winter
Ruling planet: Saturn
Planet in detriment: Moon
Planet in exaltation: Mars
Planet in fall: Jupiter

These are practical and prudent people, who are great at organising, understanding rules and complex systems, and logistics. They make good generals, and are excellent at spotting loopholes. To more idealistic personalities they can seem overly focused on 'the game'. They also make excellent economists. To others they can be obsessed with rules, and while they love getting away with things, they dislike cheating or breaking the law. In this way they can be morally ambiguous, and willing to 'sell out' to get ahead.

Capricorns are the generals and logistics people who teach or allow Sagittarius how to reach their larger goals. They learn morality and justice from Aquarius.

Aquarius ♒

Date: 20 January–18 February
Polarity: Active
Quality: Fixed
Element: Air
Tarot card: The Star
Season: Middle of winter
Ruling planet: Saturn or Uranus
Planet in detriment: Sun
Planet in exaltation: None or Pluto
Planet in fall: None or Neptune

The most idealistic, rebellious, and fiercely independent of all the signs, they like to do things their way, and are progressive and humanitarian. Ready to fight for a cause, they can also tend to be self-martyrs. In contrast to Sagittarius, they fight for the ideals of a group. They have little tolerance for the status quo and can be contrary just to move things forward. They tend to invert the values of their society and fight against what they see as 'unfairness'.

Aquarius teaches group morality to Sagittarius and is taught the liberating power of fantasy, imagination and the liminal by Pisces.

Pisces ♓

Date: 19 February–20 March
Polarity: Passive
Quality: Mutable
Element: Water

Tarot card: The Moon
Season: End of winter
Ruling planet: Jupiter or Neptune
Planet in detriment: Mercury
Planet in exaltation: Venus
Planet in fall: Mercury

These are dreamy, watery people who are hard to pin down. They fit in with their environment and can for this reason be hard to get to know. They have a nebulous, imaginative personality. In the negative, they can be prone to saying whatever people want to hear, and sometimes appearing gullible. Their relationship with the uncertain 'fringes' of reality can make them excellent poets and psychonauts, capable of noticing and valuing things that everyone else misses. The hippie culture of the 1960s was a high expression of Pisces, especially psychedelia and communes.

Pisces teaches Aquarius the spirituality at the fringes of reality and is taught to focus their ego and ambition by Aries.[9]

The houses

Though they are not core to Tarot, the house system is very important in astrological readings. I have included it here in summary as some people do Tarot spreads based on the houses.

Each house governs an aspect in the life of the Tarot querent, or the recipient of the astrological reading. There are twelve houses which relate to the twelve signs of the zodiac. Each house is a division of the ecliptic plane, the Sun's apparent movement around the Earth. The houses however are fixed in relation to the Earth and move in relation to the zodiac: a wheel moving inside another wheel. The house 'wheel' is measured from the ascendant, which is the position of the eastern horizon at the moment of one's birth. It signifies a person's persona, and their approach to getting things done in the world. It is the public face of the individual.

To calculate the houses, for an individual in a natal astrological reading, it is necessary to know their birth time within the hour, their birth date, and their approximate birth location.

---

[9] Arguably a major reason for the fall of the idealism of hippie culture in the public eye was the infiltration of cult leaders into communes, with the highest profile case being the Charles Manson murders. This is Aries energy in its worst relation to that of Pisces. The solution is to strengthen the ego of each individual.

House	Name	Meaning	Associated sign and planet	Description
1.	Vita. Life.	House of self	Aries. Mars.	One's sense of self, the person, how one operates in the world. It covers the ascendant.
2.	Lucrum. Gain/profit.	House of value	Taurus. Venus.	Money and possessions. Perseverance and self-worth.
3.	Fratres. Order/brethren.	House of sharing	Gemini. Mercury.	Siblings and cousins. One's close environment. The house and town that one lives in. Early education.
4.	Genitor. Parent/father.	House of home and family	Cancer. Moon.	Home. One's ancestry, heritage, roots. How one was raised. One's parents. Foundation and environment. One's sense of security.
5.	Nati. Children.	House of children	Leo. Sun.	All creative acts, art, self-expression and children. One's personal relationship with one's father. Love affairs.
6.	Valetudo. Health.	House of health	Virgo. Mercury.	Routine and duties. Work and employment. Employees. Skills and training. Health. The body.
7.	Uxor. Spouse.	House of the balance	Libra. Venus.	Partnership. Commitment. Contracts, oaths, agreements. One-to-one relationships and close friendships. Spouses, romantic partners and marriage. Diplomacy.

8.	Mors. Death.	House of transformation	Scorpio. Mars/ Pluto	Sexual relationships. Other people's money. Debts. Inheritances. Karma. Regeneration. Self-transformation. Repressed psychological influences.
9.	Iter. Passage.	House of purpose	Sagittarius. Jupiter.	Long-term goals. Travel. Wider culture. Law and ethics. Higher education. Philosophy. Beliefs. Initiations. Status. Membership to institutions. Personal dreams.
10.	Regnum. Kingdom.	House of enterprise	Capricorn. Saturn.	Career. Ambitions. Social status and prestige. One's father or family authority. Notoriety. Advantage. (Usually aligns to the midheaven.)
11.	Benefacta. Support.	House of blessings	Aquarius. Saturn/ Uranus.	Friends and acquaintances. Membership of social groups. Charity. Social life.
12.	Carcer. Rehabilitation.	House of sacrifice	Pisces. Jupiter/ Neptune.	Hidden parts of the personality. Intuition. Secrets. Taking time out to heal. Addictions. Mental health. Rejuvenation. Hospitals and prisons.

Southern hemisphere astrology

Astrologers traditionally rely on the system of seasons of the northern hemisphere, even if they live or are born in the southern hemisphere. If you want to rework the system for the south, the choice is either to reassign the star signs their opposite season, making Libra the beginning of spring, or else the more radical move of shuffling your star sign along by the equivalent of six months, turning Aries into Libras and Libras into Aries etc.

For Tarot this is completely unnecessary, unless you want to experiment. For astrology I've found it interesting, but have ultimately found the traditional system works best despite being out of sync in the south where I was born and live. As a general theme, most systems of magic have places where the system is 'forced', or imperfect, and astrology and Tarot are no exceptions. For the pedants this can result in a lot of arguing or pulling of the hair. To me they are missing the point. 'Making it work' is part of the magic. Magical excuses have magical effects. Tension in the system helps the system move. But then I would say that, I'm a Gemini!

Decans

The decans are thirty-six divisions of the ecliptic that date back to ancient Egyptian astrology, as far back as 2100 BCE. This is long before the classical period where we got most of our astrological ideas from. When mapped onto the zodiac, they divide each sign into three parts, creating three versions of each sign.

There are two systems for assigning meaning to the decans, one which uses the planets, and one which uses the other signs of the same 'triplicity' (element). In astrology the latter is more common, but for Tarot the planetary assignments are most common, and these are what we will be working with here. As usual, the planets are assigned cyclically in the 'Chaldean' order, which is the order from slowest (Saturn) to fastest (the Moon). As Aries is the 'first' sign at the beginning of spring, the order starts with Mars, the ruling planet of that sign.

In the Golden Dawn system, which was also used by Crowley, each decan is then assigned to one of the Minor Arcana from twos to tens, excluding the aces, amounting to the necessary thirty-six cards. Crowley relied heavily on these designations for his interpretation of the Tarot. These decans can then be used as three subtypes of each zodiacal sign, taking the attributes of the decan's planet in combination with the star sign.

The decans, which are assigned groups of nine or ten days of the year, can also be used in Tarot readings to predict timed events:

- First decans represent twos, fives and eights
- Second decans represent threes, sixes and nines
- Third decans represent fours, sevens and tens.

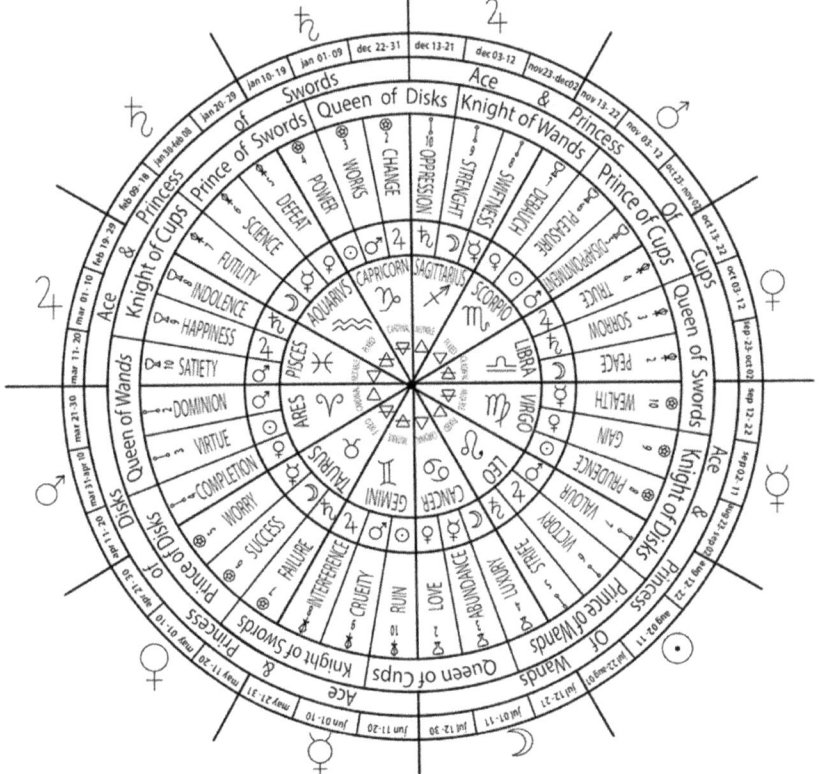

Figure 3. The decan system as it maps to Crowley's Thoth deck.

Card	Decan	Date	Ruling Planet
Two of Wands	First decan of Aries	21 March – 30 March	Mars (ruling)
Three of Wands	Second decan of Aries	31 March – 9 April	Sun (exalted)
Four of Wands	Third decan of Aries	10 April – 19 April	Venus (detriment)
Five of Pentacles	First decan of Taurus	20 April – 29 April	Mercury
Six of Pentacles	Second decan of Taurus	30 April – 10 May	Moon (exalted)
Seven of Pentacles	Third decan of Taurus	11 May – 20 May	Saturn
Eight of Swords	First decan of Gemini	21 May – 31 May	Jupiter (detriment)
Nine of Swords	Second decan of Gemini	1 June – 10 June	Mars
Ten of Swords	Third decan of Gemini	11 June – 20 June	Sun
Two of Cups	First decan of Cancer	21 June – 1 July	Venus
Three of Cups	Second decan of Cancer	2 July – 12 July	Mercury
Four of Cups	Third decan of Cancer	13 July – 22 July	Moon (ruling)
Five of Wands	First decan of Leo	23 July – 1 August	Saturn (detriment)
Six of Wands	Second decan of Leo	2 August – 12 August	Jupiter
Seven of Wands	Third decan of Leo	13 August – 22 August	Mars
Eight of Pentacles	First decan of Virgo	23 August – 2 September	Sun
Nine of Pentacles	Second decan of Virgo	3 September – 12 September	Venus (ruling, fall)
Ten of Pentacles	Third decan of Virgo	13 September – 22 September	Mercury (domicile)
Two of Swords	First decan of Libra	23 September – 3 October	Moon

Three of Swords	Second decan of Libra	4 October – 13 October	Saturn (exalted)
Four of Swords	Third decan of Libra	14 October – 23 October	Jupiter
Five of Cups	First decan of Scorpio	24 October – 1 November	Mars (ruling)
Six of Cups	Second decan of Scorpio	2 November – 11 November	Sun
Seven of Cups	Third decan of Scorpio	12 November – 21 November	Venus (detriment)
Eight of Wands	First decan of Sagittarius	23 November – 2 December	Mercury (detriment)
Nine of Wands	Second decan of Sagittarius	3 December – 12 December	Moon
Ten of Wands	Third decan of Sagittarius	3 December – 21 December	Saturn
Two of Pentacles	First decan of Capricorn	22 December – 31 December	Jupiter (fall)
Three of Pentacles	Second decan of Capricorn	1 January – 10 January	Mars (exalted)
Four of Pentacles	Third decan of Capricorn	11 January – 20 January	Sun
Five of Swords	First decan of Aquarius	21 January – 29 January	Venus
Six of Swords	Second decan of Aquarius	30 January – 8 February	Mercury
Seven of Swords	Third decan of Aquarius	9 February – 18 February	Moon
Eight of Cups	First decan of Pisces	19 February – 29 February	Saturn
Nine of Cups	Second decan of Pisces	1 March – 10 March	Jupiter (ruling)
Ten of Cups	Third decan of Pisces	11 March – 20 March	Mars

The decans show a structure of Tarot that was used by the Golden Dawn, Arthur Edward Waite, Pamela Colman Smith, and Aleister Crowley to inform the meanings of the decks they created.

Because each decan is assigned to a nine- or ten-day period, the cards can now be used for timings. This can as simple as asking a timing question and drawing a minor to find the nine- or ten-day period where something may occur. Or one can commence with a standard spread and note the dates that pop up as they come.

In the next section we will take a deep dive into the Kabbalah and its inclusion in Tarot readings. This section culminates with the Shem HaMephorash (the explicit name). This magical operation produces seventy-two Kabbalistic angels that are connected to each of the decans and their minor cards. These can then be used as the focus for spells.

Tarot Kabbalah

What is Kabbalah?

Kabbalah (קַבָּלָה) is a Jewish mystical tradition, magical practice, and system of meditation that formed a vital part of the core worldview of Western scholars, magicians and alchemists in the pre-Enlightenment era. It is central to a large part of the Western magical tradition, and has been incorporated into the practice of Christian mystics at least since Pico della Mirandola (1463–1494 CE).

A central theme of Kabbalah is the idea that the universe is made of language, that human beings participate in creation, and that therefore language—specifically Hebrew in this case—holds the secrets to understanding the universe. As the Hebrew alphabet is also a numerical system, and every word in Hebrew can also be reduced to a number, this idea is similar to (and was almost certainly influenced by) Pythagoras' idea that the world is made of numbers. Another way of saying this is that the world is made of information, which has become a dominant viewpoint in science today.[10]

Because of the special relationship for Kabbalists between words and creation, it became highly influential for the dominant Western streams

---

[10] As soon as energy becomes measured, the understanding of that measurement relies on numbers. As all energy is, in a sense, relationships between things or relationships between things and constants (like absolute zero), and numbers are measurements of relationships, saying that the universe is numbers, and saying that it is energy, are really two ways of looking at the same concept.

of magic, where spoken and written words are believed to produce magical effects. To begin understanding this, consider how the words you are reading now are affecting your concept of what is real.

The word Kabbalah can be translated as 'tradition', or 'reception'. As a practice, Kabbalah has some commonality in method and utility with the mystical practices of other traditions such as the Hindu and Buddhist chakra system, Sufism, Gnosticism, Pythagoreanism, Neoplatonism and Catholic angelology. However, it also has its own unique structure, and explanations that I find especially fascinating.

A history of Kabbalah

Within the Orthodox Jewish community, who represent the primary custodians of the original traditional Jewish Kabbalah, it is said that the first man, Adam, was the first Kabbalist, having received the wisdom from God or his angels.[11] Kabbalah's true historical origins are unclear. There were Kabbalistic schools in Southern France by 1100 CE, in Provence and Languedoc in particular. Kabbalah started to be influential on wider European culture from the thirteenth century CE onwards. Though it's hard to draw historical distinctions defining what strictly is and isn't Kabbalah, and what comes before it, it is clear that Kabbalah has its roots in the Jewish Merkabah tradition that goes back to at least the second century CE, and perhaps as far as 100 BCE.[12]

This period in Jewish history marked the gradual transition from the Pharisaic tradition of Judaism to the Rabbinic tradition, which is now by far the most dominant form. This change was marked by the breaking of the rite of the oral law, which was previously not to be written down. The Rabbinic movement broke this taboo, creating the Mishnah, a central text from the oral transmissions of the earlier initiatory Pharisees. This change took time to set in, and Rabbinic Judaism

---

[11] For those unfamiliar, it is important to note that Jews are almost never Bible literalists, or fundamentalists in the historical sense of the word. Both literalism and fundamentalism are actually very late developments that (for the most part) happened in Christianity first. For the history of this, refer to my first book, *Pragmatic Magical Thinking* (2023), in particular Chapter 16, 'The origins of Christian fundamentalism'. It is therefore safer to assume that Jewish thought contains layers of interpretation, rather than black and white messages. This is especially so in Kabbalah, as you will soon discover. As a case in point, the word Adam אָדָם is not only the name of the patriarch, but also a word for both 'human' and 'mankind'. Adam in turn comes from the root word 'adama' אֲדָמָה, meaning earth or soil.
[12] 'Merkabah' means 'chariot', referring to the holy chariot of God.

finally became the dominant form of Judaism by 600 CE, when the Talmud, comprising of the Mishnah and the Gemara, a collection of commentary texts, became codified as the canonical text of Judaism along with the Torah (Hebrew Bible).

Despite the somewhat muddy historical origins, it was in the thirteenth century CE when the term 'Kabbalah' was first used to refer to a specific group of practices, theology and spiritual philosophy. This came as a result of Spanish (Sephardic) Jews living in the Muslim caliphate of Al-Andalus, which at that time ruled what is now Spain. As 'people of the book', these Spanish Jews enjoyed a higher level of tolerance and freedom to practice their religion than other European Jews living under Christian rule, and this era was a golden age of Jewish scholarship.

In the struggle between Muslim and Christian control, the Jews were politically and theologically useful to both sides. This turned for the worst after the caliphate fell to the Catholics, and the Jews were first forced to convert to Catholicism, and then investigated under suspicion that they might still be practicing Judaism in secret.

The antisemitic factions of the Church and Christian society won out, culminating in a mass expulsion of all Jews from Spain in 1492 called the 'Alhambra Decree'. As a result of this, and the prior persecution, over 200,000 Jews converted to Catholicism and between 40,000 and 100,000 were expelled from Spain. This brought Jewish scholarship to the attention of the Christian thinkers in the countries they moved to. The two most important hubs, central to the Renaissance movement, were Italy and Germany. Other populations of Jews moved to Greece, Turkey and other countries.

Robert Wang, a Tarot artist, historian, and occult writer, has this to say about the effects of the migration and the spread of Hebrew scholarship:

> *Gentiles found it almost impossible to persuade the Jews to teach them Hebrew. Admittedly, there was no dearth of educated Jews in fifteenth-century Italy. By 1492, after their expulsion from Spain and Sicily, Italy was in fact the only country in Christian Europe open to them. [...] Christians, ordained and lay, began to employ Jews and converts from Judaism as teachers of Hebrew on a private basis. Two Renaissance popes, Nicholas V and Sixtus IV, made valuable collections of Hebrew manuscripts and commissioned Latin translations of Jewish works. The concern of prominent churchmen with Hebrew lore, however, was motivated*

by conversionist considerations rather than by a genuine academic interest. This was especially true of Spain where converts from Judaism attacked their former faith and sought to rationalize their own apostasy by quoting from Jewish works. Gradually the emphasis shifted from polemics to scholarship. Men of letters, especially those associated with the Platonist Academy in Florence, were anxious that Hebrew should be acknowledged as one of the three historic languages of the West and studied alongside Latin and Greek. Knowledge of the language would give the student access not only to the Old Testament in the original, but also to post-Biblical Jewish literature. The usefulness of the latter, especially the great medieval commentaries, would soon become apparent to the Christian exegete. Hence we find Marsilio Ficino, leader of the Academy, making use of rabbinic writings in his De Christiana religione *(1474).*[13]

Although beyond the scope of this book, the expulsion of the Jews from Spain was hardly the only time this happened. There have been numerous expulsions of Jews throughout history, especially from England and many European countries. The expulsion of Jews from Germany during the Second World War culminated in the Holocaust which exterminated 39% of the world's Jewish population. During the writing of this book in 2023/24, further expulsions of Jews are taking place in the Middle East and North Africa. Additionally, neo-Nazi factions on both sides of the Russia-Ukraine war are attempting the same with Ukrainian Jews. These pressures have contributed to the Israel-Hamas war which escalated on 7 October 2023.[14]

Isaac the Blind

The first scholar to define Kabbalah as a field of study was 'Isaac the Blind' (רַבִּי יִצְחָק סַגִּי נְהוֹר), Rabbi Yitzhaq Saggi Nihor (1160–1235 CE), from southern France. Isaac's writing focused on the analysis of the Sefer Yetzirah (סֵפֶר יְצִירָה 'Book of Formation') and the Sefer Bahir

---

[13] Robert Wang, 'Introduction,' in Johann Reuchlin, *On the Art of the Kabbalah, De Arte Cabalistica* (1517), tr. Martin Goodman and Sarah Goodman (Lincoln, NE: University of Nebraska Press, 1993), 8–9.

[14] Though it is not my primary concern to engage in politics, it is both tragic and fascinating that the Palestinian people owe a large part of their genetic heritage to Jews who were converted to Islam between 700–900 CE; the present war is therefore taking place between sister tribes.

(סֵפֶר הַבָּהִיר 'Book of Illumination'). These are two of the most important core Kabbalistic texts. Both are of uncertain authorship, though it has been hypothesised that Isaac the Blind may have written the Sefer Bahir himself, basing it on earlier works such as the Sefer Raza Rabba, of which complete copies unfortunately no longer exist.

Isaac the Blind instructs the reader on how to commune with God through meditation on the 'Tree of Life' (עֵץ חַיִּים 'ēṣ ḥayyim'), which we will explore further in its later relationship to Tarot later in this chapter. He was the first to write an explanation of the Tree of Life, especially the meanings of the sefirot. It is from Isaac's writings that all other existing Kabbalistic works descend.

Abraham ben Samuel Abulafia

Another important early Kabbalist is Abraham ben Samuel Abulafia (אברהם בן שמואל אבולעפיה (1240)–c. 1291), usually referred to as 'Abulafia'. He was born in Spain during Islamic rule, when it was called al-Andalus. Abulafia's works were amongst the first to be translated into Latin and Italian and were of great importance to the later Christian Kabbalists.

Abulafia developed a system of meditation based on the manipulation of Hebrew letters in order to create 'God-names', as suggested by the Bahir and Sefer Yeztirah, which developed into the Shem HaMephorash. This is a practice that started as a system of devotional prayer meditation, and was developed into a system of magic centring around the summoning of angels derived from passages of the Bible, especially Exodus. As this was incorporated into the Tarot tradition by the nineteenth-century magical order the Golden Dawn, we will explore it later in a dedicated section.

Abulafia taught that the most skilful and learned Kabbalists can perform a type of magic that manipulates the creation of the universe. Although he claimed to be against this practice, it of course caught the imagination of his readers, so that Kabbalah and Hebrew words have been used as a form of magic ever since.

Isaac ben Solomon Luria

Though there are many Jewish Kabbalists of note, the final one we will explore here, and perhaps the most revered into modern times, is Isaac ben Solomon Luria (1534–1572), also known as Yitzhak Ben Sh'lomo

Lurya (יִצְחָק בֶּן שלמה לוּרְיָא), as well as by the title 'Ha Ari', the Lion. Luria was the child of an Ashkenazi (Yiddish) father and a Sephardic (Spanish or North African Jewish) mother. Born in Jerusalem, he spent his early life in Egypt where he studied to become a rabbi, concentrating on the Zohar. He then moved to Galilee where he became the student of Moses ben Jacob Cordovero, another important Kabbalist. From these influences Luria developed his own system of Kabbalah, which has become the most influential. Most of Luria's work was recorded after his death by his initiated students, especially Hayyim Vital.

Lurianic Kabbalah proposes a theory of the creation and subsequent degeneration of the universe and a practical method of restoring the original harmony. In this system, humankind has a role as the co-creator and redeemer of the world; this is ripe ground for the development of magical systems based on Kabbalah.

In modern times, Jewish Kabbalah has its primary core within the 'Orthodox' Jewish Hasidic and Sephardic Haredim traditions. In the English-speaking world, the Hasidic tradition is most available to us, as a large proportion of Hasidim live in the USA, especially in New York City.

Kabbalistic texts

The most important books of Jewish Kabbalah are:

- The Sefer Yetzirah (Book of Formation), traditionally ascribed to the patriarch Abraham, although others attribute its writing to Rabbi Akiva ben Yosef (עֲקִיבָא בֶּן יוֹסֵף, c. 50–135 CE), or as mentioned earlier Isaac the Blind. Modern historians have not reached consensus on the dating of its composition but it is variously said to have been composed between 200 BCE and 400 CE.
- The Bahir (Book of Brightness), from approximately the first or second century CE; this is an anonymous mystical work, usually attributed to first-century rabbinic sage Nehunya ben HaKanah because it begins with the words, 'R. Nehunya ben HaKanah said:'.
- The Zohar (Book of Splendour), publicised by Moses de León (c. 1240–1305 CE), who claimed it was a Tannaitic[15] work recording the teachings of Simeon ben Yochai (c. 100 CE). This claim is

---

[15] The Tannaitic writings come from the rabbis who wrote the commentaries recorded in the Mishnah from 10–220 CE.

universally rejected by modern scholars, most of whom believe that de León, also an infamous forger of 'Geonic'[16] material, wrote the book himself between 1280 and 1286 CE. Despite the disputed status of de León's claims, the Zohar is considered a vital holy work, and is by far the longest of these three revered books, with one printed version spanning twelve volumes.

The Jewish Kabbalah comprises a vast amount of written material, and a tradition spanning in total more than two thousand years with a myriad of thinkers. Beyond a basic introduction, it is for the most part beyond the scope of a book about Tarot. However, I've found that even a small amount of Kabbalah can be life-changing and I consider it the most beautiful, ambitious and profound spiritual system that I have yet encountered.

For better or for worse, the Tarot draws from the Christian interpretation of Kabbalah far more than the Jewish tradition. If however you are drawn to Kabbalah, and because this book may well be your first introduction to this system of thought, I recommend you to include some of the Jewish Kabbalah in your studies. A great place to start is with Rabbi Yom Tov Glaser, a Hasidic Rabbi, who has videos for Kabbalah beginners on YouTube which are very well explained.[17]

Mythical Origins

Within traditional Hasidic lore, Kabbalah is said to have always existed since the first man, Adam, who is also said to have been the first Kabbalist. His teachings, which were divinely transmitted, are said to have been passed through the hands of a lineage of select spiritual teachers or 'tzadikim' (צדיקים, 'righteous ones'). Another legend says that the knowledge of the Kabbalah was transmitted later to Moses, from God, in the revelation on Mount Sinai around the thirteenth century BCE. Generally the important works of Kabbalah are claimed to be much older than historians have been able to date them, a common theme for almost all magical traditions, and in some cases they are attributed divine authorship, or are said to have been channelled from angels.

---

[16] The Geonic texts come from the Babylonian Jews who lived from roughly 589 CE to 1038 CE.
[17] See for example Rabbi Yom Tov Glaser, 'The Meaning of the Ten Sefirot' (2016), https://www.youtube.com/watch?v=Y1AH84vCoSo Last retrieved 3 December 2023.

Jewish, Christian and Hermetic Kabbalah

It has become popular to divide the practice of Kabbalah into three divisions, Jewish Kabbalah, Christian Cabala and Hermetic Qabala. Some historians use these different spellings in order to make clear the distinctions. As is usually the case in all human traditions, these divisions are less than perfect, as all thinkers are quick to grab and repurpose a good idea no matter the source. There is—for my purposes—no clear distinction between the Christian and Hermetic forms of Kabbalah, and the term 'Hermetic' is itself somewhat dubious as a scholarly category, as it is nearly impossible to clearly define with any separation from Christianity or other Abrahamic faiths. Nearly all, if not all, 'Hermeticists' before the modern era have been Christians, Muslims or Jews. The term 'Hermetic Qabala' is influenced in part by a tendency amongst modern occultists to want to remove themselves from Christian or Abrahamic faith, and often to position their 'occultism' in opposition to religion. These tendencies are in part influenced by 'anti-Christian' writers such as Aleister Crowley or the Church of Satan founder, Anton LaVey. The problem is that both of these figures draw from systems of magic that were designed by extremely pious Christian magicians such as John Dee, or from quasi-Christian syncretic orders such as the Golden Dawn. The separation of 'Hermeticism' from Christian, Jewish, or Muslim roots is in my opinion therefore not fully possible.

I do however draw a distinction between Jewish Kabbalah and the rest. The Jewish core is the realm of Jewish scholars of the Hebrew language, and has remained a more or less separate tradition. It is also extremely clear as one begins a study of Kabbalah, that the Jewish Kabbalah is significantly more complex, and its scholarship significantly more vast. As such, for my purposes in this book, I will be referring to 'Kabbalah' for the multicultural practice, and the 'Jewish Kabbalah' for the parent tradition. Though I am a Kabbalist in the general sense, and I have the deepest regard for the Jewish Kabbalah, here I am mostly teaching the Kabbalah in its wider sense. I am not fluent in Hebrew nor claim Jewish culture, though I have some Jewish ancestry, for what it is worth. If you are interested in my take on Jewish Kabbalah, there is an introduction to it in my first book, *Pragmatic Magical Thinking*, as well as a careful cross analysis with the Tantric Chakra system.

Kabbalah and the Tarot

The historical application of Kabbalah for Tarot comes entirely from the Christian Kabbalah and it comes quite late, specifically through the writings of Éliphas Lévi (1810–1875 CE).[18] From here, the Kabbalah and Tarot were made the core structure of the teachings of the Hermetic Order of the Golden Dawn, from which nearly all modern Tarot decks outside of the Marseilles tradition are designed.

The core principles of Kabbalah

Here I will use the word 'God'. There are many people in our modern era who are unfortunately suspicious of this word. For this reason, I have often found it useful in teaching magic and spirituality to define God not as an entity, like a person as such, but as the very principle of 'creativity' itself. This creative principle can, in my opinion, be observed as a scientific fact. The universe is always creating itself, seemingly out of 'nothing' (for instance, 'quantum foam', zero-point energy, the big bang). This property of 'creativity' in the universe is what I mean by 'God' from here out.

One thing I especially like about this conception is that it is beyond the restriction of 'faith', which is so often a perceived hurdle for the unreligious. If you are willing to shed your preconceptions of God, and get on board with 'creativity', then you will very likely start to find theology much more useful, and universal. If your experience is anything like mine, then eventually the identity badge 'atheist' might become so superfluous that you might put it away and start to get along a lot better with your religious and spiritual friends. Don't let me talk you out of it, just see what happens.

Some of the principles of Kabbalah are as follows:

- The creation of the universe is an ongoing process.
- Human beings are both a part of this creation, and are able to participate in creation.

---

[18] The first writers to link the Tarot to Kabbalah, specifically the twenty-two Major Arcana trumps to the Hebrew alphabet, were Comte de Mellet and Antoine Court de Gébelin, in Gébelin's *Le Monde primitif, analysé et comparé avec le monde moderne* ('The Primeval World, Analysed and Compared to the Modern World'), Volume VIII, 1781.

- Creation flows 'down' from a universal Godhead, 'Ein Sof', beyond our direct experience. Likewise individual experience flows upward back to the Godhead.
- God, though often referred to as a 'person', transcends our understanding of time, will, morality, gender and intelligence. Rather than considering God to be outside the universe, it is more useful to consider the universe as being 'inside' God. Note that something similar to this understanding of a universal Godhead can be found in nearly all other Eurasian traditions including the Hindu concept of 'Brahman', the Orphic 'Night' (Nyx), the Polynesian 'Te Po' (or 'Te Kore'), the Gnostic 'Monad', and the 'Singularity' described in the Big Bang theory in physics. As such, the idea of an undivided godhead which is the source of endless potential is an extremely old idea that is common to all European, Asian, Pacific, North African and Native American cultures. The last time all these cultures had a common ancestor was approximately 40,000 years ago. Perhaps this mytheme is that old.[19]
- As the universe is created 'downward' from the Godhead, and through the world of concepts towards matter, influence also flows 'upward' from manifestation to the universal Godhead. Put simply, just as God affects us, so we affect God. This is a great dynamic chain of influence. The Godhead is an active part of the cosmos and not truly separated from it.
- The universe's propensity to create itself can be considered the manifestation of this divine 'will'.
- The world of concepts, imagination and intellect has a reality which, though different, is just as 'real' as the world of objects.
- There is a relationship between the concept of language, especially the Hebrew language, spoken and written, and creation, which can be understood as the 'language of God'. For this reason, we too, in our own more limited way, affect manifestation through language, will and intent. This is the core tenet from which Kabbalistic magic draws.[20]

---

[19] For further information, read E. J. Michael Witl,'s *The Origins of the Wold's Mythologies* (Oxfo13). Oxford University Press, 2013).
[20] While Kabbalistic texts and Kabbalists often say that Hebrew is literally language of God and creation, it is enough to me to consider the fundamental property of creation to be information. In this way the universe can be said to be structured like a language.

- The many aspects of creation, and the corresponding states of consciousness available to human beings, can be 'mapped'. While no map is perfect, I have found Kabbalah's 'map', namely the Etz Hayim עץ חיים, aka the 'Tree of Life' and the 'Four Worlds', to be the most useful and complex map of this type that I have come across.
- The interacting points and paths of this Tree of Life map of creation are to be understood as a highly animated system. Each point is called a sefirah (plural, sefirot). This simply means 'numeration'. There are ten such points and one additional pseudo-sefirah which marks the experience of understanding the whole system in its entirety, a type of 'enlightenment'. Each sefirah has particular connections to other sefirot. Each of these 'paths' marks an interaction of two sefirot, which corresponds to a type of experience which joins them. Each path is marked by a letter of the Hebrew alphabet. There are ten sefirot and twenty-two connecting paths. In older Kabbalistic texts, the ten sefirot are considered paths themselves, and these ten plus the twenty-two marked by letters are referred to as the thirty-two paths.
- The Hebrew alphabet is considered to be the vehicle (literally or figuratively) by which the Godhead creates the whole universe. The Tree of Life maps the ways in which creation can unfold. This is considered an ongoing process.
- In later versions of Kabbalah, especially in the system used by Tarot, each of the Sefirot are assigned particular astrological planets, angels, god-names, and Tarot cards. The Golden Dawn developed its own particular system for this and this is the one normally used by Tarot readers.

Key figures of Christian Kabbalah and the Western magical tradition
Pico della Mirandola

The first Christian Kabbalist was the Italian philosopher, Giovanni Pico della Mirandola (1463–1494 CE). Pico was introduced to the Jewish Kabbalah in Perugia, central Italy, while recovering from nearly fatal wounds received as punishment for a love affair with the wife of a tax official of the powerful Medici family. His tutor was Rabbi Johanan Alemanno (c. 1430–c. 1510), who along with being a scholar was a magician of the techniques taught in the sometimes forbidden 'practical Kabbalah'. This was the part of Kabbalah where spells and magic were used and discussed. Within Judaism, Kabbalistic spells were only considered 'kosher' for Jewish Rabbis of the most pure intent. As the forbidden is often enticing, this is of course exactly the part of Kabbalah that the gentile magicians were most interested in.

In his works, starting with the humanist manifesto *900 Theses (Conclusiones Nongentae publicae disputandae*, 1486 CE) Pico della Mirandola sought to syncretise physics, Platonism, Neoplatonism, Aristotelianism, Hermeticism, Orphism, Catholicism and Kabbalah as evidence for a 'perennial philosophy', albeit one that was entirely about proving Catholicism 'right'. Despite this, Pico's attempts were ultimately rejected by the Catholic church, and considered a minor heresy by the Pope.

While deeply enamoured with Jewish teachings, one of Pico della Mirandola's core stated purposes for incorporating the Jewish teachings was to convert Jews to Christianity:

> 9>9. *There is no science that assures us more of the divinity of Christ than magic and Cabala. 11>5. Every Hebrew Cabalist, following the principles and sayings of the science of the Cabala, is inevitably forced to concede, without addition, omission, or variation, precisely what the Catholic faith of Christians maintains concerning the Trinity and every divine Person, Father, Son, and Holy Spirit. Corollary: Not only anyone who denies the Trinity, but anyone who proposes it in a different way than the Catholic church does, like the Arians, Sabellians, and similar men, can be clearly refuted if the principles of the Cabala are admitted.*[21]

From the Jewish perspective, this is of course complete nonsense. However, the overarching power of the Catholic Church, bristling at the 'heretical' and equally antisemitic protestant movements, may have created a situation where the only way to get any book on Jewish lore published was to repackage it as evidence for Christianity.

Despite Pico's statement of intent to use Kabbalah to convert the Jews, his *900 Theses* was eventually condemned by the Pope as a minor heresy and he was ordered to renounce it. The charge was that he was placing magic and Kabbalah above the gospels. This was not a time of freedom

---

[21] Pico della Mirandola, *Syncretism in the West: Pico's 900 Theses* (1496), tr. S. A. Farmer (Tempe, AZ: Arizona State University, 1998), 523.

of speech or religious freedom. However, Pico never fully renounced his ideology, and after the condemnation by the Pope, he fled to France, where he continued to write. In 1488 he was arrested. With the intervention of some princes, the Pope relented and allowed Pico to return to Florence. When Pope Innocent VIII died in 1492, Cardinal Borja was elected as Pope Alexander VI. The new Pope was deeply interested in magic and the occult, and pardoned Pico for his transgressions.

Pico was fascinated by the Kabbalistic idea that Hebrew is the language of creation that God used to create the world, and that therefore Hebrew could be used to modify nature by acts of magic:

> 9>22. *No names that mean something, insofar as those names are singular and taken per se, can have power in a magical work, unless they are Hebrew names, or closely derived from Hebrew.*[22]

The scholar Francis Yates makes an interesting observation on the status of Hebrew among occultists today:

> *Pico based his version of magic on the natural magic of Ficino, although he believed that Ficino's magic was quite weak by itself, and that nothing much could really be achieved with it. It was by merging of Ficino's natural magic with that of the Kabbalah that Pico claimed to be able to create a serious magical force. And in this regard, Pico made one demand of the magician which was to influence the entire history of magic and the occult. He said that in order for a name to assume power in a magical incantation it must be in Hebrew, and he is thus responsible for the fact that even today practitioners of Christian Kabbalist magic call upon gods and archangels in a language which may be meaningless to them.*[23]

Although Pico's take on Kabbalah was not detailed, his proposal was highly influential and was quickly taken up by other 'Christian Kabbalists' who had a much better understanding of the Hebrew source texts and the Kabbalistic techniques. Despite the antisemitism of the Church, some of Pico's ideas about adapting Kabbalah to Christianity

---

[22] Pico della Mirandola (1998), 501.
[23] Quoted in Robert Wang, *How the Modern Occult Movement Grew Out of Renaissance Attempts to Convert the Jews* (Marcus Aurelius Press, 2003), 32.

came from Jewish converts to Catholicism. This is hardly an endorsement, but shows the complexity of the issue. As Robert Wang writes,

> One must ask, however, how it could have happened that Christians were able to derive arguments against Judaism from manuscript documents written largely in complicated Mishnaic Hebrew. The answer is that the originators of this movement were Spanish Jews who had converted to the Christian faith. The first to apply the Jewish mystical tradition was Moshe Sefardi, who on being baptized about 1106 took the name Pedro Alfonso and whose Dialogus argued that the Trinity was inherent in the sacred name YHVH.[24]

Johann Reuchlin

Pico's most important follower was the German Catholic humanist Johann Reuchlin (1455–1522 CE). Reuchlin's understanding of Hebrew and Kabbalah was a world above Pico's, and while he had a deeper respect for the Hebrew texts and methods, his stated mission was the same, to find a validation for Christianity in Kabbalah, in order to convert the Jews. His most overt manoeuvre was to alter the Tetragrammaton from YHVH to YHSVH, 'Yahshuah' (יהשוה) a new spelling for 'Jesus' (Yeshuah יֵשׁוּעַ). He called this brazen move, of putting Jesus into the holiest Hebrew name of God, the 'Pentagrammaton'. This can be found in his work *De verbo mirifico*.

Reuchlin and Pico met for the first time at Florence in 1490, while Reuchlin was on a diplomatic visit to Italy. Pico showed Reuchlin his enthusiasm for all things Hebraic, and urged him to master the Hebrew language. Reuchlin had true passion for studying Hebrew and became an expert. At the time, due to deep prejudices, Hebrew was not respected as a language of Biblical study, despite being the language of the Old Testament. Reuchlin fought hard for Hebrew as a scholarly language for the study of the Bible, and he was ultimately successful. Amongst his tutors was Jacob Loans, private physician to Emperor Frederick III and Obadiah ben Jacob Sforno who was renowned for his exegetical and philosophical writings, having founded a Talmudic school at Bologna.

In 1506 Reuchlin published a Hebrew grammar and dictionary, the *De rudimentis hebraicis*. This was intended as a manual for beginners.

---

[24] Wang (2003), 24.

He went on to publish two more works in the instruction of Hebrew: *In septem psalmos poenitentiales* and the *De accentibus et orthographia linguae hebraicae*, published four years before his death.

His most famous work however remains *De arte cabalistica*, an apologia on the importance of Christian study of Biblical and Kabbalistic Hebrew, published at a time when even the study of the Hebrew Bible was treated with deep suspicion and calls were made to the Catholic authorities by extremists to burn all Jewish texts. In this work Reuchlin made the claim that Kabbalah and Pythagoreanism draw from a common knowledge and concept:

> *If I declare that Kabbalah and Pythagoreanism are of the same stuff, I will not be departing from the facts.*[25]

Indeed Reuchlin believed that the Kabbalah was the source of the Pythagorean teachings. This cannot be the case historically, as the earliest Kabbalistic writings are much more recent than Pythagoras' life, 570–495 BCE. In his own time, Pythagoras was reported to have learned from scholars in Egypt and magi in Persia. In any case, there are similarities between Kabbalah and ancient Greek thinkers, especially Pythagoreanism and Platonism. Either Kabbalah and previous Jewish schools of mysticism were influenced by the Greek knowledge or both Jewish and Greek thought come from a common root. I believe the most likely answer is a bit of both. As important as they were to history, the Greeks made no claim to being the first philosophers, and both cultures have very ancient roots. The ancestors of the Jews, the Phoenicians, were the source for the first alphabet, from which the Greek writing system (and those of all other Europeans) derives.[26] There are also many similarities between Kabbalah and all other Eurasian mysticisms. This suggests that parts of Kabbalah are older than history.[27]

For Reuchlin's Hebrew studies and his championing of the language and Rabbinic works, he stands as an important figure in the history

---

[25] Johann Reuchlin, *On the Art of the Kabbalah, De Arte Cabalistica* (1517), tr. Martin Goodman and Sarah Goodman (Lincoln, NE: University of Nebraska Press, 1993), 147.

[26] The term Phoenician is a name for the Canaanites who lived on the coast of the Mediterranean. The Jews are descendants of Canaanites also.

[27] If you want to go down the wormhole of how old Eurasian mythology is, and the idea that it may come from a common root, you ought to read *The Origins of the World's Mythologies*, by Michael Witzel (2013). In it he makes a strong evidential case for a 40,000-year-old tradition.

of Biblical scholarship as well as the history of Kabbalah's inclusion in the canon of Western magic. He was responsible for the preservation of major Hebrew texts in Christian Europe, which may not have survived otherwise.

The Christian Kabbalah emphasised the magical applications of the practical Kabbalah, which is a thread in Jewish Kabbalah but not the primary focus. Each successive Christian writer seems to have built upon this fascination resulting in our current situation where the Hebrew language is deeply embedded into the Western magical tradition of Tarot reading, spell craft and theurgy.[28] The concept of 'angelic magic', and the incorporation of the Tree of Life as central to the spell-working and structure of the Golden Dawn and subsequent magical societies, is a testament to the fascination started by Pico and Reuchlin.

Henricus Cornelius Agrippa von Nettesheim

Henricus Cornelius Agrippa von Nettesheim (1486–1535) was the next important Christian Kabbalist to pick up the torch. His *Three Books of Occult Philosophy* are considered the most influential of all the Renaissance grimoires,[29] and a primary source for later Golden Dawn rituals. He was born to a minor noble family in Cologne, Germany, and displayed an extraordinary intelligence from an early age, especially for languages. A legend about him states that he attracted the attention of scholars as a boy when he refused to speak any language but Latin.

Agrippa shifted the focus of Kabbalah from using it as tool to convert Jews to a system of magic for its own sake. This focus on the practical magic side of Kabbalah has remained in the Western Occult tradition until this day.

After earning degrees in canon law, civil law, medicine (by his own reporting) and a licentiate in Arts (similar to a modern Master's Degree in Liberal Arts), Agrippa moved on to the University of Paris at the young age of twenty. It was here that he gathered around himself a group of occult scholars, which some historians interpret as being a premodern precursor to later Victorian secret magic societies such as the Golden Dawn, Ordo Templi Orientis (OTO) and Crowley's later

---

[28] The intersection of prayer and spells; techniques of persuading or compelling deities to do one's bidding.
[29] A 'grimoire' is simply a fancy name for a spell book.

magic society, the A∴A∴. There is also conjecture in this period that he may have performed espionage on behalf of the Holy Roman Emperor Maximillian I as well as covert military missions. The Holy Roman Empire was a major Western governmental power which saw itself as a the Roman Empire reborn.

He was appointed as a professor at the University of Dole, in France, in his early twenties after a series of publicly acclaimed lectures on Reuchlin's work *De verbo mirifico*. Agrippa is known to have learned much of his Kabbalah from the books of Reuchlin, in particular *De verbo mirifico* and Reuchlin's Hebrew Grammar and dictionary.

It is around this time, 1509–1510, that Agrippa wrote the first draft of his *Three Books of Occult Philosophy* (*De occulta philosophia libri tres*), a magnum opus that he would continue to work on until its publishing in complete form in 1533 in Cologne. As a side note, he also wrote in 1509 a proto-feminist treatise on the equality of women called *Declamatio de nobilitate et praecellentia foeminei sexus* (Declamation on the Nobility and Pre-eminence of the Female Sex), which was eventually published in 1529.

In 1518, while serving as town advocate at Metz, France, he successfully defended a woman in a trial against an accusation of witchcraft by an inquisitor. Donald Tyson writes that

> *So persistent, and so lucid was Agrippa that the Inquisitor fell into discredit and was removed from the case. The accused woman received absolution from the vicar of the church of Metz. Her accusers were fined 100 franks for unjust accusation.*[30]

Despite winning this trial, this was the end of Agrippa's career in Metz, due to angering those suspicious of witches, and he moved to Cologne. Throughout his life, Agrippa worked variously as a scholar, a soldier, a lecturer, a professor, a physician and, in 1529 in Antwerp, a plague doctor (the plague had taken his own wife).

Despite his endorsement of Jewish writings and magic, Agrippa remained deeply Christian. He followed Pico's idea of the Pentagrammaton YHSVH, and he claimed a disbelief in Kabbalah: 'Therefore this Cabala of the Jews is nothing else than a most pernicious

---

[30] Agrippa, *Three Books of Occult Philosophy* (1533), ed. Donald Tyson (Rochester, VT: Inner Traditions, 1993), xxv.

superstition.'³¹ As he includes Kabbalistic workings in his writings it seems likely that this was a protection against censors.

Agrippa equated the Kabbalah to the Orphic Mysteries:

> ...whosoever understandeth truly the Hymns of Orpheus, and the old magicians, shall find that they differ not from the Cabalistic secrets and orthodox traditions; for whom Orpheus calls Curetes and unpolluted gods, Dionysius names Powers; the Cabalists appropriate them to the numeration Pahad, that is to the divine fear: so that which is En Soph in the Cabala, Orpheus calleth Night; and Typhon is the same with Orpheus, as Zamael in the Cabala.³²

By combining alchemy, astrology and Kabbalah into a system of magic, Agrippa set the template for the next five hundred years of Western occult practice. As such, he marks the major junction where Kabbalah, as understood by Western occults, split off from the Jewish tradition.

Athanasius Kircher

After Agrippa, the next most mentioned Christian Kabbalist is Athanasius Kircher (1602–1680) and his is a curious and somewhat mysterious case. Although he is frequently mentioned as a major influence on the Western occult movement, and was a highly regarded scholar in his own time, his magnum opus *Oedipus Aegyptiacus* (1652–54), remains untranslated into English, and deals primarily with what is in retrospect an outrageously misguided and defunct attempt to translate Egyptian hieroglyphics and syncretise them into a 'rediscovered' syncretic philosophy with texts from Greek, Hebrew, Aramaic, Armenian, Ethiopian and other languages. Though he is often mentioned in occult history as an important thinker, from what I can tell, people were most excited by Kircher's fantastic mystical diagrams, especially those dealing with Kabbalah and angel magic, while completely ignoring his actual writing.

Kircher claimed to have found the key to translating hieroglyphics which he considered to be a source of perennial Eurasian wisdom and the source of Kabbalah. Though he was a respected scholar amongst Catholics, his ideas were controversial even at the time, and since the

---

[31] Agrippa, ed. Tyson (1993), 701.
[32] Agrippa, ed. Tyson (1993), 467.

Rosetta Stone was deciphered in 1822 by Jean-François Champollion, Kircher's translations look quite bizarre. Kircher's diagram of the Sefirot, which will be explained in detail in this chapter, appears to be the source used in the Golden Dawn's interpretation of Kabbalah, and is therefore the origin of the system used by most Tarot readers who include the Kabbalah in their readings.

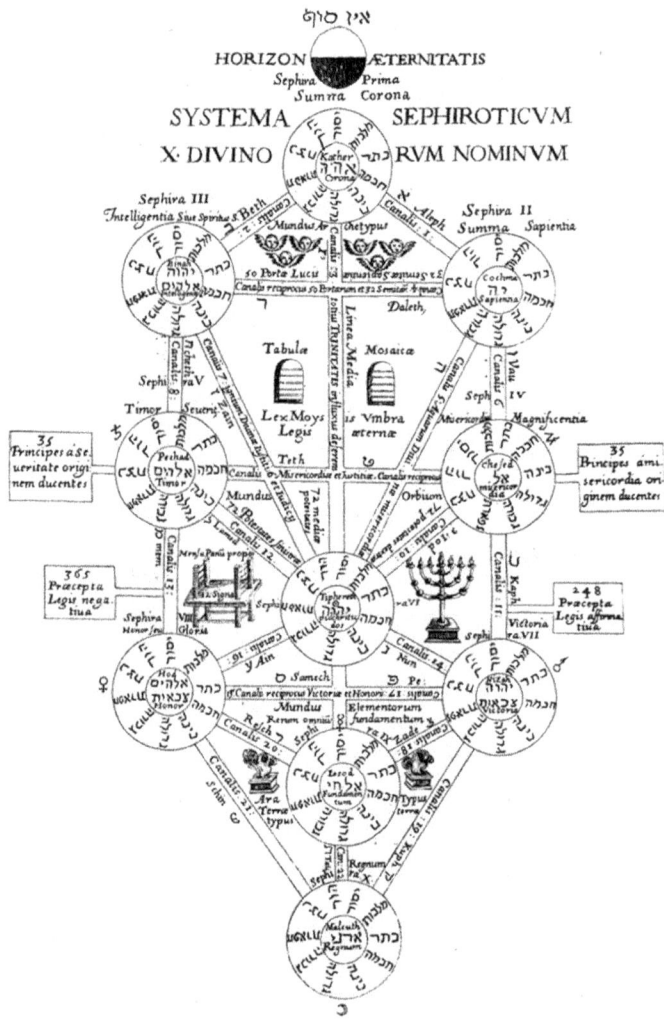

Figure 4. Athanasius Kircher's Tree of Life diagram, which become the template for the Golden Dawn diagram, also used by modern Tarot readers.

Censorship of Kabbalah

It can be hard to ascertain exactly how much of the Christianisation of Kabbalah came from the opinions of these authors and how much was a response to censorship. Perhaps they truly respected the Jewish tradition and had to dress their writings up as a tool for converting the Jews in order to get their works published. Or perhaps they were actually enthusiastic about the antisemitic idea that Kabbalah was more rightfully Christian than Jewish.

Kircher, as a Jesuit in Rome, had to have all of his writings pass under the censorship of a committee of Catholics who were deeply orthodox, suspicious of Jewish and Muslim thought and most of all against any magic or theology that wasn't their own. Pico had his *900 Theses* banned, and most of the copies were burned. He died aged thirty-one in 1494. In 2007 his body was exhumed and high levels of arsenic in his corpse suggest that he was probably murdered by poisoning.

Agrippa escaped most of the persecution that Kircher and Pico faced in Rome, allowing him to write more freely on magic and Kabbalah, but was still ousted from his professorship at the University of Dole by the Catholic establishment, for being a 'Judaising heretic'. This was despite his popularity amongst his students and colleagues. He continued his occult writings and activities behind the scenes. He seems to have been gifted at escaping persecution, even when the Inquisition took exception to the printing of the *Three Books of Occult Philosophy*. Perhaps Agrippa's magical writings represent what Pico and Kircher's may have looked like if they weren't so heavily censored?

Later figures and organisations in Hermetic Kabbalah

Éliphas Lévi

I have written of Éliphas Lévi in the 'History of Tarot' section of the first book *Tarot for Sceptics*. Lévi is important to us, not only for reinfusing Kabbalah into modern magic, but most importantly for combining it with Tarot, which via Kabbalah, he considered to be a lost book of Egyptian wisdom, which was transmitted first to Moses, then to the Gypsies.

> ALL religions have preserved the remembrance of a primitive book, written in hieroglyphs by the sages of the earliest epoch of the world. This book, attributed by the Hebrews to Enoch, seventh master of the world

> *after Adam; by the Egyptians to Hermes Trismegistus; by the Greeks to Cadmus, the mysterious builder of the Holy City: this book was the symbolical summary of primitive tradition, called subsequently Kabalah or Cabala, meaning reception.*[33]

Lévi's 1854 visit to London introduced Tarot cards to English society for the first time. Unlike in Europe, where the cards have always been used for games as well as divination, the English were for the most part unfamiliar with this context and the cards were immediately impressed upon them as something magical.

Europe and Britain were in the middle of an Egypt craze at the time, due to renewed interest due to the decipherment of the Rosetta Stone by Jean-François Champollion, allowing translations of hieroglyphics for the first time. People couldn't wait for the data to be released, and many predictions were made about what wisdom the hieroglyphs might contain, including the idea that they were a precursor to the Kabbalah. Lévi's story bought into this speculation with the added firework of real fortune-telling demonstrations. Given that for many, Lévi would have also been their introduction to Kabbalah, this event, and the mysterious story, was the perfect spark to ignite an occult revival.

Lévi was influenced by Francis Barrett's *The Magus*, which itself was plagiarised from Agrippa, and like Agrippa only mentions the Kabbalah very briefly. Although he was a Christian, many historians mark Lévi's work as a turning point away from the mission to incorporate, or appropriate, Jewish teaching into Christian (usually Catholic) theology, and instead see this as a rebellious departure into 'occultism'. While Lévi was definitely heterodox, these categories are not so clear cut as many would like them to be, given the mass movement away from Christianity in our modern times.

The Golden Dawn

The Golden Dawn brought all of these aforementioned influences under the banner of their secret society, which was inspired in part by the secret society started by Agrippa centuries earlier. Central to the structure of their rituals and hierarchy was a combination of Freemasonry

---

[33] Éliphas Lévi, *Transcendental Magic, its Doctrine and Ritual* [*Dogme Et Ritual de la Haute Magie*, 1856], tr. A.E. Waite (London: Rider & Company, 1896), 45.

and Kabbalah, with Tarot being seen, as put forth by Lévi, as the key to understanding the latter.

The Golden Dawn used Kircher's diagram of the Sefirot throughout their material, especially the particular letters assigned to the paths, which has a few differences to the diagram of Isaac Luria and other Jewish Kabbalists. (Even within Jewish Kabbalah there are however multiple versions.) This Golden Dawn/Kircher version of the diagram is the one most widely used by Tarot readers, and therefore the one I will use in this book.

Kabbalah explained

The Three Veils

These are three preconditions which must exist before anything reaches the realm where humans are able to relate to things. They are in a sense the preconditions for creation itself. They are also the Kabbalistic concept of God and his qualities. They are:

- Ein: Nothing
- Ein Sof: No End
- Ein Sof Aur: Endless Light.

These are called the Three Veils because they are beyond human experience. This attempt to describe the ultimately indescribable is something that I deeply admire about Kabbalah.

Ein is the potential for there to be something. Ein Sof is the fact that if there is something, there must be a place for it to be in, and that as there is nothing yet to limit this space, it must be an infinity. If there is infinite space, then there are potentially infinite concepts and things which may fill it. This potentiality is the Endless light, Ein Sof Aur. To try and see all things all at once means that there is no opportunity to see 'difference' or 'details' and this overwhelming sense is compared to an infinite field of light. In Kabbalah, 'light' is used as a term to understand God's will. When humans sense this, it is called the Shekhinah (שְׁכִינָה), which is understood to be feminine, and corresponds to the Christian 'Holy Spirit'.

In the Kabbalist cosmology, qualities appear before things, concepts follow from qualities and physical things follow from concepts. In this sense it is like Plato's universe and his ideas of 'forms'. This may seem 'backwards' to a materialist, where qualities are often considered to be emergent from the building blocks of matter, except that nothing can be understood without appealing to qualities. Even the materialist model for reality relies on mathematics to measure things and maths is the realm of concept, not in physicality. If this is still a roadblock, then it is enough to consider Kabbalah and by extension all magical models to be descriptions of how we perceive 'reality', and not necessarily descriptions of the 'source code' of reality that is beyond our perception. Of course, this only pushes the problem of materialism downstream, with the logical endpoint being that the idea of a reality before or without perception may be nonsensical. In any case, this is not a problem we have to solve here.

The Three Veils can also be considered the qualities that persist when one tries to rid the universe of all qualities. If one had to reduce the universe to a single quality, the one that must precede all existence, then that quality is surely 'creativity'. Creation in Kabbalah is considered to be an ongoing process, not necessarily something that started once and then produced a chain reaction. From all scientific explorations this seems to be the case. If one takes a container, and tries to remove all matter from it, one still doesn't end up with 'nothing' inside. Instead, at least at the tiniest scales, bits of energy pop in and out of existence. These are known to science by terms like 'quantum foam' and 'zero-point energy'. My conclusion from this is that the universe does not allow a true state of 'nothing'. It is always bubbling away, creating itself. This quality of 'creativity', which fills all voids, is a nearly perfect understanding of God as described in Kabbalah.

The Four Worlds

These are four layers, from the realm of the most abstract qualities to the sphere of human sensory experience and the world of objects. Each of these corresponds to one of the four letters of the Tetragrammaton, YHWH (יהוה), the holiest name of God in Judaism. In Tarot we also attribute each of these to one of the suits and one of the types of court card.

The four worlds are:

- Atzilut: Emanation.
  The realm of the most abstract concepts. It is beyond time and space. It is assigned the letter Yod י. In Tarot it is the suit of Wands and the King cards. In the Tree of Life it is the first three sefirot, Keter,

Chokmah and Binah, which are three aspects of the mind: will, inspiration and understanding. In Kabbalah the universe is understood to also have a mind, which is structured in a way that relates directly to the human mind. Therefore Keter, Chokmah and Binah, as well as the concept Atzilut, are both 'inside' and 'outside' of the human mind.

- Briah: Creation.
  This is the world of 'forms', where ideas can be combined, compared, related, felt and modified. It is assigned to the first Heh ה in YHWH. In Tarot it is the suit of Cups, and the Queens. This is the realm of emotions, feelings and relationships as well as the active parts of the imagination. It is the sefirot Chesed, Geburah and Tiferet. In Jewish Kabbalah this is where the 'neshamah' resides, the intellectual part of the soul.
- Yetzirah: Formation.
  This is the place where plans become detailed. It is assigned the letter Vav ו. In Tarot it is the suit of Swords and the Knight cards. In this realm things are worked upon, ready to be finished, manifested or communicated in the next 'world'. It is the sefirot Netzach, Hod and Yesod. Yetzirah is the realm of 'types' where things can be categorised. It is the space of our 'mind's eye', where things can be visualised. In Jewish Kabbalah it is the dwelling place of the 'ruach', the emotional and intuitive part of the soul.
- Assiah: Action.
  This is the realm of the physical world, the world of the senses and also the realm of shared human experiences. It is manifestation. It is assigned the final letter Heh ה. In Tarot it is the suit of Pentacles and the Page cards. In the Tree of Life it is the sefirah Malkut. In Jewish Kabbalah it is the place where the 'nepesh' part of the souls resides, which is the animating force which is shared by all living things.

To understand these four 'worlds', one can use an example of a house:

- Atzilut would be the pure concepts of 'dwelling', 'enclosed space', and 'safety'. These are the needs of all living things, that precede the notion of a house.
- Briah would be the rough categories of living places: caves, mansions, castles, tents, bungalows etc. Here things are properly differentiated. In this case we will choose 'cottage'. Some details about the house are also decided here. Whether it is tall, wide, full of windows, etc.

- In Yetzirah we draw up a blueprint for the cottage. Here every detail allowing the construction of the house is measured and worked out.
- In Assiah the cottage is finally worked upon and then built. Here we can finally move in.

Etz Hayim, the Tree of Life

The Tree of Life, or Etz Hayim (עֵץ הַחַיִּים), is the title of a book by Isaac Luria. The Tree of Life is often referred to as the 'Sefirot', which is also the name for its ten parts. The symbol of the Tree comes from the myth of the Garden of Eden where there were said to be two trees, the tree of eternal life, and the tree of knowledge of good and evil. The term sefirah comes from the Hebrew for 'sapphire', or 'illumination'. It also means 'numeration'. Sefirot is the plural.

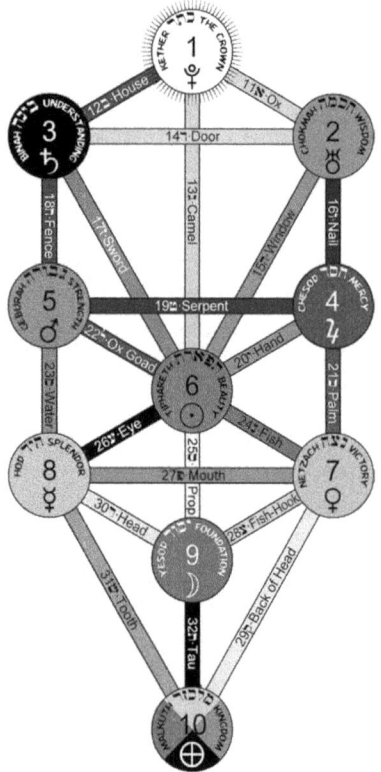

Figure 5. The Tree of Life as used by the Golden Dawn.

The Three Pillars

These divide the Tree of Life diagram into three columns. They are symbolised by the mythical pillars of justice of the Temple of Solomon: Boaz ('Strength') and Jachin ('He will establish'), and a third, 'middle pillar', representing the balance of these two forces.[34]

- The right pillar is 'mercy', 'intimacy' and 'flow'.
- The left pillar is 'severity', 'strength', 'discipline', 'restriction' or 'containment'.
- The middle pillar is 'mildness' but can also be understood as 'balance'.

In the Solomonic symbolism, which is also a big part of Freemasonry, these are the qualities required for morality. In a more cosmic sense, they are the qualities required in order that the universe can exist, and in order that anything can be perceived. In Kabbalah the right pillar is deemed masculine, the left pillar is feminine and the middle pillar as their offspring is neutral. This can seem like an inversion to the typical Western framing of the intuition as feminine, and the rational as masculine. I have found that these types of inversions can be very useful thought experiments.

In philosophical terms, the right pillar is the movement of information or the movement of energy. It is also the ability for one thing to relate to another. Without this quality, no information would reach the observer, so nothing could be known. The left pillar would be 'logos', or 'difference', the ability to be able to tell one thing from another. Without this, nothing could be understood, nor acted upon. The middle pillar is therefore comprehension, understanding, order, and the ability for one thing to act upon another.

Put another way, in electrical terms, the right pillar is current, the power of the electrical force to move. The left pillar is a wire and its insulation, a channel through which the electricity is able to be directed, and the middle pillar is the completion of a circuit allowing one to use the electricity, for instance to power a light bulb. Without the channel of

---

[34] The 'middle pillar' is also the name of a magical meditation created by Israel Regardie based on the Tree of Life.

the wire the electricity would be like a lightning bolt; unable to move in a predictable direction.

In another analogy, the right pillar is water, the left is a container, for instance a bucket, and the middle pillar is the ability to move the water in the bucket without it being spilled. Too much flow is represented in Biblical symbolism by the flood. In this state all difference is wiped out and everything becomes like a body of water, without form. Too much containment is like a dam. There is nowhere for the flow to move and the system becomes blocked.

All things in the universe and the world of concepts are considered to have this relationship, to be a balance (or imbalance) of these qualities.

On the Tree of Life, the right pillar of 'mercy' consists of the sefirot Chokhmah, Chesed and Netzach. The middle pillar consists of the sefirot Keter, (Da'at), Tiferet, Yesod and Malkut.

The right pillar consists of the sefiro: Binah, Gevurah and Hod.

The Sefirot

The Tree of Life consists of ten sefirot in total. The first three sefirot form a trinity pertaining to personal experiences of the individual mind which cannot be shared. These are in the world of Atzilut.

1. Keter: Crown

This is the first spark of divine will that is the pre-condition for existence. It is considered to be beyond human experience and is sometimes described as 'the most hidden of all hidden things'. Keter is the potential for all being, before differentiation. It can be thought of as the state of things preceding the Big Bang, or the first stirring of a void before a concept is born. It is the gulf of the edge of what is knowable. It can also be thought of as the pure consciousness of the mind of the universe, and the most abstract of all abstractions. In the Hermetic system, Keter is associated with the Primum Mobile (the prime mover or first cause).

2. Chokhmah: Wisdom

Here we have the first inkling, and the sphere of the intuition. This corresponds to the first flashes of consciousness, where a concept can first be imagined. Chokhmah in Hebrew means the 'potential of what is'.

This can be understood as the right brain and its associative thinking. It is also where we experience 'flow states', the idea of 'being in the zone'. It is the feeling of transcendence in meditation and is called the 'Abba', or supernal father, that which seeds all experience: the divine masculine.

Put another way, it is the core of consciousness itself. Chokhmah as an instigating active power, considered masculine. Two is the first number that allows a relationship between concepts. Too much Chokhmah is an inability to discern and a tendency to only see relationships, and not differences. In the Hermetic system Chokhmah is associated with the zodiac.

3. Binah: Understanding

This is the sphere where things can be related, compared and understood. It corresponds to the left side of the brain and to rational processes. Because it receives the message rather than forming them, it is considered receptive, or 'feminine'. Three is the first number in geometry that can enclose a space, so here we have the first understanding of territory and of categories: what is and what isn't. It is called the 'Imma' or supernal mother, the divine feminine. Too much Binah in an individual is over-analysis. In the Hermetic system Binah is associated with the planet Saturn.

Da'at: Knowledge

Da'at is an event rather than a sefirah, but when it is depicted on the tree, it lies in the position just below the highest three 'supernal' sefirot. Da'at marks the event where one is finally able to experience the whole tree directly as a dynamic, animated system. In this way it is a type of enlightenment. To have this experience, it is said that one must 'cross the abyss'. That is, that one must temporarily dissolve the ego and one's sense of self in order to experience what lies beyond. This correlates to the experience that psychonauts refer to as 'ego-death'. Beyond that is pure awareness, and a relation to the mind of the universe, the super-consciousness that in mysticism is said to pervade all things.

The following three sefirot form another trinity which can be thought of as a lower reflection of the first. These allow interpersonal experiences which can be shared by more than one person. They are the world of Briah.

4. Chesed: Mercy

Though often translated as 'kindness', I prefer the more Jewish conception which is that of 'intimacy'. Chesed is pure giving, selflessness and flow. While these are often considered positive concepts, in Jewish morality too much Chesed is also associated with promiscuity and hedonism. As Chesed is also 'flow', it is also like a force not yet directed. In this sense, a river overflowing its banks is too much Chesed, while too little Chesed is a dry riverbed.

In a musical performance, a feed-backing electric guitar is an overabundance of Chesed, whereas a lacklustre, dull performance would be too little Chesed. Chesed is like energy. It is necessary for existence, but too much can be destructive. In the Hermetic system, Chesed is associated with the planet Jupiter.

5. Gevurah: Strength

Gevurah can be understood as overcoming, bravery, discipline, limitation, protection and fighting. It is that which guards or pushes back against unfettered flow. It is containment, allowing things to keep their form, their place and their position in a hierarchy. It is associated with the law, and with strict morality. It is the bravery to confront one's enemies and to withhold kindness from those deemed undeserving. Too much Gevurah is restraining, and can be cruel. In balance with Chesed however, Gevurah allows love and kindness to be properly meted out and experienced. In parenting, too much Chesed is spoiling the child, while Gevurah is the discipline which, in balance, allows the child to grow up feeling safe and able to function in a society. In the Hermetic system, Gevurah is associated with Mars.

6. Tiferet: Beauty

Tiferet is love experiences, and the ego, in the sense of that which normally separates one person's experiences from another. In this sense Tiferet is both the boundary of the ego, and the ability to let other people into that boundary. It can also be the extension of the boundary, for instance as is the case with group experience, like being at one with the crowd at a rock concert or a rave. Implicit in this type of experience though, is that it is led by a performer who extends their ego to the group. This can be a beautiful and affirming experience, but it can also be misused by charismatic leaders. Tiferet can also be one-on-one experiences such as sex and/or intimacy with a partner.

There is a bliss experience in the sphere of Tiferet that is sometimes misunderstood as enlightenment. Unlike the more intense type of enlightenments associated with Da'at and Keter however, the Tiferet experience does not allow one to truly transcend one's ego in any meaningful sense. Finally, Tiferet is beauty. That is, the qualities of order, symmetry and perfection. In the Hermetic system, Tiferet is associated with the Sun.

The next three sefirot are another layer and reflection of the higher trinities. They are in the world of Yetzirah, which is just above the physical or sensory realm.

7. Netzach

This is the sefirah of group-mind and group experiences at a more earthly level. Here lies the ability to lead and charm groups of people. More mundane love experiences such as family bonds, friendships, and everyday romantic attachments happen here. Here is the experience of compassion and bonding. In conversation, this is the intuitive aspect where what the other person is saying is 'felt'. This is also the sphere of perseverance. Here lies the ability to motivate oneself or others. It is the rationing of energy that allows one to go the distance. In sports, Chesed would be sprinting whereas Netzach would be marathon running. Netzach is associated with leaders and the ability to talk people into getting a job done. It is a 'call to action'. Netzach and Hod relate to how we must act in order to manifest our will. In the Hermetic system, Netzach is associated with Venus.

8. Hod: Splendour

Hod is getting work done. It is the sefirah of learning and study. It is the ability to function in a group and the movement and sorting of information to the right places. It is associated with the intellect, especially as it relates to details and processing. Where Netzach is motivation, Hod is that motivation directed into getting things done. Hod is focused attention. In the Hermetic system, Hod is associated with Mercury.

9. Yesod: Foundation

Yesod is the sefirot where communication happens. It relates to direct subjective experience. It is the balance of Netzach and Hod that allows things to properly manifest. In Jewish Kabbalah it is associated with the sexual organs and reproduction, with the final sefirah, Malkut, as its offspring. A great orator or teacher communicates through Yesod, with the right balance of charm (Netzach) and detail (Hod). Yesod is also associated with manifestation magic, the final stage before the will affects the physical or sensory realm. It can also be any other act of creativity, such as writing, sculpture, singing etc. In the Hermetic system, Yesod is associated with the Moon.

The final sefirah is in the world of Assiah.

10. Malkut: Kingdom

This is the sensory realm where we interact with objects and relate to things through our bodies. It is the realm of shared experience where real exchanges of information take place, and it is the 'dispatch' area of the sefirot. It is the recipient of all the other sefirot as they descend to the physical realm and to matter. Malkut gives tangible form to the other sefirot.

Malkut is in the world of Assiah; from here there is no further place to go other than back up the Tree. In this way it serves as the opposite pole to Keter which is divine will.

The interaction between Malkut and the higher sefirot in the Tree is described by the alchemical adage: 'Solvé et Coagula'. Solvé is the ability to understand things by breaking them up into their component parts, or by relating to each of their details conceptually. In philosophy this is 'analysis'. Seeing an object and understanding it to be a 'chair' is Solvé. Coagula is the bringing together of parts to form a thing. Building a chair from other materials is Coagula. This represents an ongoing cycle, and so does the Tree of Life. Just as something is manifest, so it is experienced, and that interaction leads us back up the tree to the world of concepts. In Kabbalah it is said that the spiritual realm 'needs' the physical and vice versa.

In the realm of concepts, opposites—for example 'good' and 'evil'—can never come together. Only in Malkut, the manifest realm, can something be both 'good' and 'evil' at the same time. Thus, concepts act upon us as if they desire to be manifested and we relate to the world around us through concepts.

In Tarot, the ten sefirot relate to the numbers one to ten in each suit:

>Aces: Keter
>Twos: Chokhmah
>Threes: Binah
>Fours: Chesed
>Fives: Gevurah
>Sixes: Tiferet
>Sevens: Netzach
>Eights: Hod
>Nines: Yesod
>Tens: Malkut

The Numerology of Creation

This my own take on what is called 'The Naples Arrangement' by Crowley. It is in turn based on the ideas of Pythagoras, the foundation of our mathematics. Pythagoras was himself trained in Egypt and in Persia, though the details of these earlier systems and how they influenced classical Greece are somewhat lost to time. Despite this, we can infer that this way of thinking is very ancient.

- Zero symbolises the void of potentiality. This is Ein Sof.
- One symbolises 'position'. Though it has no measurements, it is a thing separated from the void. This is the precondition for the idea of 'space'. This is Keter.
- Two symbolises difference. The first true concept of 'space'. One point can now be compared to another point. A line can be drawn between them, creating the first dimension. This is Chokhmah.
- Three gives us two dimensions, and the idea of 'surface'. Now we can have basic geometry. We can say 'one is more like two than it is like three'. This allows the first analysis. This is Binah.
- Four is the breaking through to a new stage. We now have 'depth' and the third dimension. This for the first time allows a direct correlation between our imagination and the world of matter that we see. This is Chesed.

- Five in Crowley's description is the idea of motion. With motion we can now understand 'change', and with 'change' we now have 'time'. Time is a restricting quality. This is Gevurah.
- Six in Crowley's system is the idea of 'self', as now our object can have a past, present and future. To us, what is being described is the idea of 'narrative'. We can now explain the change from one position, or one form, to another. Crowley describes this as 'self', because there is now an experience that can be described, and the experiencer must be, in some way, a 'self'. This is Tiferet.
- Seven, eight, and nine are said by Crowley to be 'Being, Thought, and Bliss'. These he drew from the Hindu 'Rishis': Sat, Chit, and Ananda. They are conceptualised as the three preconditions for consciousness. In a sense they are one's recognition of oneself, one's ability to relate to 'not-self', and the ability to be motivated by feeling. Implicit in the idea of 'bliss' is the idea of 'more bliss' and 'less bliss' (pain) and now we have the tension and release that motivates all things. These are Netzach, Hod and Yesod.
- Ten is the comprehension of all these parts working together: a system. It is therefore the 'world' or the 'universe'; the conceptual containment of 'all'. This is Malkut.

A fractal system

Though I have discussed how the four worlds relate to specific sefirot, it is also understood—especially in Jewish Kabbalah—that each world can contain a complete Tree of Life itself. In Tarot, as each of the four worlds has a suit, each suit has ten numbers and each of these is one of the sefirot. Each of the four worlds can have four more worlds inside it as well: this relates to the four Court Cards of each suit in the Tarot. Finally, in the Kabbalah it is understood that each tree of ten sefirot has inside it another complete tree of ten more sefirot. This can then be understood as an infinite recursion.

In this way the system is reflected at every level of reality and in every concept. If this gives you a headache, feel free to move on; it is perfectly fine to leave this to the most conceptual of thinkers. I describe it here only to point out how far Kabbalistic thinkers have gone with their system.

The following is a table of how the four worlds and ten sefirot map to the Tarot:

REALLY ADVANCED TAROT READING

	Wands: Atzilut	Cups: Briah	Swords: Yetzirah	Pentacles: Assiah
Kings: Atzilut	Atzilut of Atzilut	Azilut of Briah	Atzilut of Yetzirah	Atzilut of Assiah
Queens: Briah	Briah of Atzilut	Briah of Briah	Briah of Yetzirah	Briah of Assiah
Knights: Yetzirah	Yetzirah of Atzilut	Yetzirah of Briah	Yetzirah of Yetzirah	Yetzirah of Assiah
Pages: Assiah	Assiah of Atzilut	Assiah of Briah	Assiah of Yetzirah	Assiah of Malkut
Tens: Malkut	Malkut of Atzilut	Malkut of Briah	Malkut of Yetzirah	Malkut of Assiah
Nines: Yesod	Yesod of Atzilut	Yesod of Briah	Yesod of Yetzirah	Yesod of Assiah
Eights: Hod	Hod of Atzilut	Hod of Briah	Hod of Yetzirah	Hod of Assiah
Sevens: Netzach	Netzach of Atzilut	Netzach of Briah	Netzach of Yetzirah	Netzach of Assiah
Sixes: Tiferet	Tiferet of Atzilut	Tiferet of Briah	Tiferet of Yetzirah	Tiferet of Assiah
Fives: Gevurah	Gevurah of Atzilut	Gevurah of Briah	Gevurah of Yetzirah	Gevurah of Assiah
Fours: Chesed	Chesed of Atzilut	Chesed of Briah	Chesed of Yetzirah	Chesed of Assiah
Threes: Binah	Binah of Atzilut	Binah of Briah	Binah of Yetzirah	Binah of Assiah
Twos: Chokhmah	Chokhmah of Atzilut	Chokhmah of Briah	Chokhmah of Yetzirah	Chokhmah of Assiah
Aces: Keter	Keter of Atzilut	Keter of Briah	Keter of Yetzirah	Keter of Assiah

Here each of the Minor Arcana can represent a state of human consciousness and a part of the process of creation.

The Hebrew alphabet

Kabbalah has many uses for the letters of the Hebrew alphabet. For Tarot readers, the most important use is for the paths that each link two sefirot on the Tree of Life. Each of these is assigned a letter.

The Hebrew alphabet is divided into three categories. The three mother letters, the seven double letters and the twelve single letters.

The three mother letters

These represent Awareness.

א Aleph: Air, Concept, Thesis, the Fool.
This is either unpronounced or it produces a glottal stop: the sound 'aa' or sometimes 'e'.

מ Mem: Water, Space, Antithesis, the Hanged Man.
This produces the sound 'm'.

ש Shin: Fire, Will, Synthesis, Judgement.
This produces the sound 's' or 'sh'.

In Kabbalah, the element of Earth is understood to be a combination of the other three elements.

The seven double letters

These represent space, and each has a dichotomy of meaning. Each also produces two sounds in Hebrew. The numerology of seven gives us the seven classical planets, the days of the week, and the gates of the soul (two eyes, two ears, two nostrils and mouth).

ב Bet: Mercury, Wisdom/Folly, the Magician.

ג Gimel: Moon, Grace/Indignity, the Priestess.
This produces the sounds 'b' and 'v'.

ד Dalet: Venus, Fertility/Solitude, the Empress.
This produces the sounds 'd' and 'th' (as in the word 'this').

כ Kaf: Jupiter, Life/Death, the Wheel of Fortune.
This produces the sounds 'k' and the guttural 'kh'.

פ Peh: Mars, Power/Servitude, the Tower.
This produces the sounds 'p' and 'f'.

ר Resh: Sun, Peace/War, the Sun.
This produces the sounds 'r' and the guttural 'rh' (as used in French, German and Yiddish).

ת Tav: Earth, Wealth/Poverty, the World.
This produces the sounds 't' and 'th' (as in the word 'thought').

Twelve Simple Letters

These reflect the twelve signs of the zodiac and represent Time.

ה Heh: Aries, Sight, the Emperor.
This is pronounced 'h' (though breathier than in English) or on the end of words is unpronounced.

ו Vav: Taurus, Hearing, the Hierophant.
This is the consonant 'v', or the vowels 'oo', 'oh' or 'ow'.

ז Zayin: Gemini, Smell, the Lovers.
This produces the sound 'z' as pronounced in English.

ח Chet: Cancer, Speech, the Chariot.
This produces the guttural 'kh' sound.

ט Tet: Leo, Taste, Strength.
This is the consonant T.

י Yod: Virgo, Eros, the Hermit.
This is the consonant 'y' and the vowel 'ee'.

ל Lamed: Libra, Work, Justice.
This is the sound 'L'.

נ Nun: Scorpio, Movement, Death.
This is the sound 'n'.

ס Samekh: Sagittarius, Anger, Temperance.
This is the sound 's'.

ע Ayin: Capricorn, Mirth, the Devil.
Like Alef, this is pronounced as a glottal stop or as the vowel 'aa'.

צ Tsaddi: Aquarius, Imagination, the Star.
This is the consonant 'ts'.

ק Qoph: Pisces, Sleep, the Moon.
Like Kaf, this is pronounced 'k' or the guttural 'kh'.

Letters as numbers

The Hebrew letters also serve double duty as a numbering system, and therefore every word spelled in Hebrew can be deduced to a number. These numbers can then be used to associate words together mathematically or numerologically. This practice is called Gematria. It can be used as a teaching aide for learning Hebrew, for a type of numerical symbolism, or for linking concepts together in the creation of spells. The numbering system is as follows:

Alef	א	1
Bet	ב	2
Gimel	ג	3
Dalet	ד	4
Heh	ה	5
Vav	ו	6
Zayin	ז	7
Chet	ח	8
Tet	ט	9
Yod	י	10
Kaf	כ	20
Lamed	ל	30
Mem	מ	40
Nun	נ	50
Samech	ס	60
Ayin	ע	70
Peh	פ	80
Tsaddi	צ	90

(Continued)

(Continued)		
Qof	ק	100
Resh	ר	200
Shin	שׁ	300
Tav	ת	400

Gematria doesn't come into the Tarot tradition much so I will not explain it in depth, but if you are interested it works like this:

The Hebrew greeting is שָׁלוֹם 'shalom'. It means 'peace'.

Broken down to its letters we have

Shin	300
Lamed	30
Vav	6
Mem	40

This adds up to 376.

In Gematria, one could then associate it with other words that add up to 376.

The thirty-two paths of the sefirot

In traditional Kabbalah, from the Sefer Yetzirah, there are said to be thirty-two paths, which relate to thirty-two categories of experiences of creation. The first ten are simply the sefirot themselves as we have already explored. Paths eleven to thirty-two are the paths that connect two sefirot. While there are multiple ideas about which order these come in, here as before, we will use the system most often utilised by Tarot readers, which is the system as taught by the Hermetic Order of the Golden Dawn.

After the sefirot, the remaining paths are then thus:

Path Eleven: Alef. Keter to Chokhmah. 0 The Fool.
This is a transmission from the Primum Mobile (first cause) to the first concept, associated with the fixed stars and zodiac. This is the experience of being 'one with everything'. In Hinduism it is the experience of Brahman of the Sahasrara Chakra.

Path Twelve: Bet. Keter to Binah. I The Magician.
The Primum Mobile to the first understanding. Saturn. This is communication with the Godhead or messages from God.

Path Thirteen: Gimel. Keter to Tiferet. II The High Priestess.
Divinity relating to selfhood. Primum Mobile to Sun. This is the experience of feeling the divine.

Path Fourteen: Dalet. Chokhmah to Binah. III Empress.
Inspiration to understanding. Right brain to left. Concept to discernment. This is the path of thought and the experience of having thoughts.

Path Fifteen: Heh. Chokhmah to Tiferet. IV Emperor.
Inspiration to emotion. Transcendence to group experience (e.g. artist to audience). This is the experience of intuitively understanding inspiration through another person or through a group of people.

Path Sixteen: Vav. Chokhmah to Chesed. V Hierophant.
Inspiration to flow or transcendence. This is the experience of spiritual and social 'energy'.

Path Seventeen: Zayin. Binah to Tiferet. VI The Lovers.
Discernment, recognition and understanding to emotion or self. This is the experience marked by a decision to love one instead of many. It is the experience of love between two people.

Path Eighteen: Chet. Binah to Gevurah. VII Chariot.
Understanding of restriction, separation, withholding or discipline. This is the experience marked by a decision to compete, fight or conquer. It is judgement. It is an act of defence to mark one's territory, conceptual or physical.

Path Nineteen: Tet. Chesed to Gevurah. VIII Strength.
This is the balance of give and take. Love and discipline. It is flow directed (a river, Chesed, and its banks, Gevurah). It is the path where we communicate and regulate our emotions. It is also general motivation channelled towards getting work done.

Path Twenty: Yod. Chesed to Tiferet. IX The Hermit.
This is the experience of unconditional love, and the feeling that 'everything is love'. It is the feeling of deepest connection to others. The drug MDMA often provides an experience of this pathway, one of overflowing love or love without proper containment.

Path Twenty-one: Kaf. Chesed to Netzach. X Wheel of Fortune.
This is the path of charm. It is where we can be persuaded by others. It is the rallying cry and the pep talk. It is also the path where we feel beauty in art and aesthetics.

Path Twenty-two: Lamed. Gevurah to Tiferet. XI Justice.
This is the path of discipline out of love. It is the experience of separation in order to affirm one's self or to affirm what is unique. It is the path where one fights for oneself.

Path Twenty-three: Mem. Gevurah to Hod. XII Hanged man.
This is fighting for the group, and for group identity. It is also the path of intellectual arguments and opinions. It is restriction in order to allow intellectualisation.

Path Twenty-four: Nun. Tiferet to Netzach. XIII Death.
This is the path where one experiences the radiant charm of the individual. It is the experience of beauty in the individual. The love of the one.

Path Twenty-five: Samekh. Tiferet to Yesod. XIV Temperance.
This is the path of personal experiences had by oneself. It is the realm of creativity of the individual, be it writing, music, or speaking. It is the shining of light in the dark. The making explicit what was implicit.

Path Twenty-six: Ayin. Tiferet to Hod. XV Devil.
This is the beauty of the individual as perceived by the group. It is the experience of idols, celebrities. It is the transmission of the self and of self-expression to the group.

Path Twenty-seven: Peh. Netzach to Hod. XVI The Tower.
This is the path of leadership towards group action. It is a balancing of power and work in relation to the group.

Path Twenty-eight: Tsadi. Netzach to Yesod. XVII The Star.
This is the path of motivation. Here one feels a desire to get work done and then acts it out. It is a path of participation, and it can be individual or experienced as part of a group. This path is also that of a talented speaker, teacher or lecturer communicating to a class or a student.

Path Twenty-nine: Qof. Netzach to Malkut. XVIII The Moon.
Here art is manifested. It is the everyday experience of beauty.

Path Thirty: Resh. Hod to Yesod. XIX The Sun.
This is the experience of communicating or understanding what was occulted. It is direct experience of the esoteric. It is the place where we form words and decide what we want to say.

Path Thirty-one: Shin. Hod to Malkut. XX Judgement.
This is the experience of calculating, recording the intellect, and naming the world around us. It is our rationalisation of the world of objects.

Path Thirty-two: Tav. Yesod to Malkult. XXI The World.
This is the path of manifestation magic. It is the channel between the human experience and the world around us. Here words become action, and plans become objects and things. It is the path of conversation where we talk to each other.

As it is very hard to find explanations of the paths anywhere these are my own summaries based on my current knowledge. There is no truly 'correct' way to interpret these, and one never stops being a student of Kabbalah. As such you may form your own relationship with and understanding of the paths over time.

Angels in Tarot

'Wait, what is an angel?' you may ask.

Our modern conception of what angels are has really lost its way from the original Jewish conception, and the way they are understood in Kabbalah. First, it's important to drop all your conceptions of angels as winged humanoids, and especially the non-Biblical folk-belief that angels are the spirits of dead humans.

In Greek the word Angelos (ἄγγελος) merely means 'messenger'; in Hebrew the word Mal'akh (מַלְאָךְ) has the same meaning. Even within the Bible itself the words Angelos and Mal'akh are used to refer to both human messengers and a wide range of spirit messengers, in particular those who relay information to humans from God.

In Kabbalah a Mal'akh or angel can be anything from a kind of 'spiritual email', a message carrying an intent, like those generated through prayer, to an incorporeal spirit 'person' who can be summoned and communicated with. Angels are said by Kabbalists such as Aryeh Kaplan to be created with every intentional act and most are destroyed once that ambition is carried out. For this reason, the idea of summoning or even creating angels out of language is quite normal within Kabbalah.

The idea that angels are the souls of dead humans is not Biblical, though sometimes humans are compared to angels in the Bible, and sometimes angels are said to appear as humans. Despite this, angels are not normally seen, and when they are they are not always human-shaped. Angels are spirits that relay messages. In Jewish Kabbalah, the emphasis is more on the message than the being, and angels can be thought of as a kind of 'living information'. In Renaissance magic, including Kabbalah, where the entire universe was considered conscious, angels were the agents connected to every concept. In this way every object or concept had an angel and if one knew how, one could have a conversation with that being. This was a conception of the universe where everything could be personified. In this way, angels are what happens when one treats concepts as if they are 'people'. One may therefore understand angels as spiritual beings, or simply heuristics that behave 'as if' they have will and intent. In my experience the outcome is more or less the same, and in any case, due to the subjective nature of angel experiences one will never have objective evidence one way or another. Here I will offer an explanation of some of the angels that are used in Tarot imagery.

Chayot and the Merkabah

Described in chapter ten of the Book of Ezekiel, where they appear to Ezekiel in a vision, these are the strangest descriptions of angels in the Bible. The term used, Chayot (or Hayyot), means 'living creatures' and they are further described as 'Cherubim', which are guardian deities. In this case, they guard and hold up the throne of God, which is in the form of a chariot. The Chayot each have four faces, that of a man, a lion, an ox, and an eagle. These are widely assumed by esotericists, astrologers and occultists to refer to the fixed signs of the zodiac: Aquarius, Leo, Taurus, and Scorpio. The Chayot each have four wings with four hands under them. They are also covered in eyes (possibly an old Hebrew metaphor for stars). Accompanying them are four pairs of spoked wheels called Ophanim. The pairs of wheels intersect with each other, and are also covered in 'eyes'. In the Kabbalah, the Ophanim are of the sefirah of Chockhmah, which is the realm of the firmament of fixed stars. These 'eyes' are therefore probably a reference to these stars. The Ophanim are the wheels of God's chariot, the 'Merkabah'.

This unusual imagery, and the concept of Ezekiel's vision, led to a movement of mysticism also called 'Merkabah'. In this tradition, direct experience and visions of angels and of God are sought, with stories of visionaries rising to the 'throne of God' in order to get direct access to the divine. Merkabah literature is considered the direct ancestor of Kabbalah, which explores direct experience of the ongoing creation of the universe and our place in relation to the divine. These traditions spawned a great deal of visionary and practical magic techniques and were central to later forms of Jewish, Christian and Islamic magic.

Cherubim/Kerabim

These are guardian spirits which date right back to Babylonian times (early 1700s BCE), where they were known as lamassu, or shedu. They took a sphinx-like form, possessing the wings of an eagle, the body of a lion or bull, and the head of a human, sometimes a king. These were represented as carvings in wood or stone to protect relics or temples. Babylon was a dominant culture that had a big influence on Judaism and the Hebrew cultures that preceded it. Another related source is the Assyrian 'kāribu', thought to be the source of the Hebrew word Kerabim. This shows that the Cherubim are a remnant or an evolution of a mythology far older than the oldest versions of the Bible. These Cherubim were said to have been depicted on the 'Ark of the Covenant', the legendary chest containing the Ten Commandments: Moses' contract with God that he brought to the Hebrews, and which really marks the beginning of the Jews as a people.

Cherubim were only much later conflated with the child angels known as 'Putti' who are derived from the winged, child archer god Cupid. This later use of the term cherub is not commonly used in the Western magic tradition that includes Tarot.

Gabriel

Depicted in the Judgement card, his name means 'God is my man'. Gabriel appears in the Old Testament in Daniel 8:15–26 and 9:21–27 to explain Daniel's visions to him. He also appears in the apocryphal Book of Enoch.

With the archangel Michael, Gabriel is described as the guardian angel of Israel. Gabriel appears several times in the New Testament, first announcing the birth of John the Baptist. John's father Zechariah, a priest of the course of Abia (Luke 1:5–7),[35] was childless because his wife Elisabeth was barren. Gabriel appeared to Zechariah announcing that Elizabeth was to have a son after all. This story is also repeated in Luke 1:11–20, then later in Luke 1:26–38, Gabriel appears to Mary to announce that she will give birth to Jesus the Messiah. In Christian tradition, Gabriel is usually considered the archangel who will sound the trumpet of end times. Thus, he is depicted on the Tarot card Judgement. In the Islamic tradition it is Israfil—often equated with Raphael—who will sound the trumpet. Gabriel, as Jibril, is also venerated as one of the primary archangels and as the Angel of Revelation in Islam. He provides Mohammed with verses of the Koran.

In the Lesser Ritual of the Pentagram, the core ritual of the Hermetic Order of the Golden Dawn, Gabriel is the angel of the west and of the element water.

Holy Guardian Angel

This is a concept that comes to us through Aleister Crowley and which is sourced from *The Book of Abramelin*, attributed to Abraham of Worms (c. 1362–c. 1458).[36] This book was translated by Samuel Liddell MacGregor Mathers, the compiler of most of the Golden Dawn's syllabus. Within his translation there is a description of a six-month ritual of prayer, fasting and purification which culminates in knowledge and conversation with one's Holy Guardian Angel. This being is variously described by others as a guardian being or the highest aspect of one's own self or spiritual will. This operation is supposed to put the adherent on their true righteous path.

A more recent translation from the original German has stretched the ritual to eighteen months long, and this is now considered by scholars to be the more correct version. To my knowledge nobody has performed

---

[35] A 'course' was a division or rotation system among the priestly classes in ancient Israel, installed by King David to share the priestly power. Each division was named after a Patriarch. Abia or Abijah is a descendant of Aaron.
[36] Worms here refers to the city in Germany, rather than a collection of invertebrates.

the eighteen-month version, though the six-month version has brought prestige to the few who have succeeded at it.[37]

The Holy Guardian Angel is central to Aleister Crowley's idea of 'true will', which he called 'Thelema'. His writings are ambiguous as to whether the angel is part of one's self or a separate being, and he seems to have changed his mind about this over time. While at his 'Abbey of Thelema' in Cefalù, Italy, Crowley wrote his book *Liber Samekh* based on the 'Bornless Ritual', a ritual designed as an example of how one may attain knowledge and conversation with one's Holy Guardian Angel. The Bornless Ritual was derived from the Greek Magical Papyri, specifically PGM V. 96–172: 'Stele of Jeu the Hieroglyphist in his letter'. Oddly it was originally an exorcism, and not a summoning.

In Tarot the Holy Guardian Angel represents the higher self and one's true path.

Michael

This is the angel depicted in the card Temperance. In Catholicism he is also called Saint Michael the Archangel, or the Archangel Michael. He is often considered to be the chief of the angels and of the archangels, and he is the guardian of Israel (along with Gabriel). In Revelation 12:7–12 he does battle with Satan in the 'end times'. The earliest surviving mention of Michael is in the third-century BCE apocryphal Book of Enoch. In Catholic art, Michael is often depicted in medieval armour and wielding a sword.

In the Lesser Ritual of the Pentagram used by the Golden Dawn, Michael is the angel of the south and of the element fire. This ritual is derived from the Jewish Kriat Shema, or bedtime prayer. It is common in Judaism to invoke the four archangels after one recites the Shema before going to bed: with Michael by your right side, Gabriel by your left side, Uriel before you, and Raphael behind you. This later became the Lesser Banishing Ritual of the Pentagram and a template for many other similar rituals in the magic of the Golden Dawn, who were influenced by Éliphas Lévi.

---

[37] I asked Lionel Snell—one of the original Chaos magicians, who performed the six-month Abramelin ritual in his youth and wrote a book about it in 2019 called *The Abramelin Diaries* (using his pseudonym Ramsey Dukes)—, if he knew of anyone who had performed the eightee- month ritual. He replied that he did not. Since then, I've come across a couple of people online who claim to have completed the long version.

Raguel

His name means 'God shall shepherd'. He is a Jewish angel of justice, punishment, vengeance and redemption. In the apocryphal but influential Book of Enoch, he is the angel that punishes fallen angels and restricts demons. He can be associated with the card Justice.

Raphael

He is the angel depicted in the Lovers card. His name means 'God has healed' and he is an archangel of healing mentioned in the Book of Tobit, which is canonical to Catholic and Orthodox Christians but not to Jews. In Tobit he acts as a physician and expels and binds demons with magic. He is also mentioned in the apocryphal Book of Enoch.

In *Reshit Chochmah* (the Beginning of Wisdom), an introduction to Kabbalistic thought composed by Rabbi Aharon Meir Altshuler (1835–1905), Raphael is said to correspond to the Sefirah of Tiferet. For this reason, he is the angel depicted in the Lovers card. In Catholicism, Saint Raphael is the patron of travellers, the blind, nurses, physicians, matchmakers, and marriage. In the Lesser Ritual of the Pentagram, used by the Golden Dawn, Raphael is the angel of the east and of the element air.

Uriel

Uriel is not mentioned in the canonical books of the Bible, but is in the Second Book of Esdras in the Biblical apocrypha (sometimes also called Esdras IV) when God sends Uriel to answer the prophet Ezra's questions. In the Golden Dawn's Lesser Ritual of the Pentagram, Uriel is the angel of the north and of the element earth.

The Shem HaMephorash

In this section we will embark on a seriously heady, and perhaps 'over the top' esoteric application of the Tarot. There are two reasons for my inclusion of this section in this book. One is for a sense of completion, as there are a small minority of you who really get off on this stuff, the weirder the better. The other is to show how many systems were syncretised into Tarot, by practitioners such as the Golden Dawn. For those who have read my first book, *Pragmatic Magical Thinking*, the chapter entitled 'Smart People Traps' should forewarn you before spending too much time on this chapter. Let's just say if you came here for quick results then skim read it and move on.

It will however still benefit you to get a feel for this operation, by showing how a magical system like Tarot can act as a foundation for more and more layers. Later we will explore how one can construct one's own layers in Tarot, and I recommend focusing on those that one likes rather than simply piling on as many as possible.

Finally, this chapter is here to prove that I have done the thing so that you don't have to. For those really serious elite magicians amongst you who are going to try this anyway, get ready to take notes!

Kabbalistic Secrets

In Jewish scholarship there is a system for the analysis of Biblical texts called PaRDeS, which is an abbreviation of the following:

- Peshat (פְּשַׁט)—'surface'. This is the literal and obvious meaning of the text.
- Remez (רֶמֶז)—'hints'. This is a secondary layer of symbolic meaning, just beneath the literal.
- Derash (דְּרַשׁ) –'inquire'. A context of meaning acquired through the comparison with other similar texts or other parts of the scripture.
- Sod (סוֹד)—'secret'. The esoteric and mystical meanings underlying a text, as given through inspiration, revelation, rearrangement or magical methods.

The Shem HaMephorash operation which is explained in this chapter belongs to the fourth category.

Kabbalistic Angels

The Shem HaMephorash is a 'Sod' method for contacting (or creating) angels from Old Testament texts. It means 'the explicit name'. In Kabbalah it is believed that God generated the universe by condensing pure 'concept', specifically language. That is, God (YHWH), who is conceived of as a universal creativity beyond direct human experience, 'speaks' or 'writes' the universe into being. Unlike some other theologies, this isn't a 'one and done' process, but an ongoing one. Because it is the language of the Jewish people and the language of the Torah, it is thought by Jewish Kabbalists, either literally or figuratively, that God speaks and writes Hebrew.

Because human beings are created in God's likeness, and because we have language, we have since Adam[38] had the ability to participate in creating the universe by our own use of holy language, and because Jews use Hebrew, it is considered by Kabbalists to be the language of creation, and therefore the language of magic. If this sounds odd to you, remember that many people today believe that mathematics is the source code or 'language' of the universe, and that the Hebrew alphabet is a number system as well as a phonetic one. In this way, to Kabbalists, all maths can be accessed through Hebrew. This idea was then taken up by the previously mentioned Christian Kabbalists, especially Johann Reuchlin in his work *De Arte Cabbalistica* (*On the Art of Kabbalah*, 1517 CE) and his predecessor Giovanni Pico della Mirandola in his *900 Theses* (1486 CE).

As previously explored, the concept of 'Christian Cabala' as a separate entity to 'Jewish Kabbalah' (some insist on the spelling difference) is certainly a controversial one. Though Pico and Reuchlin undoubtably had a deep respect for Kabbalah, their appropriation of it for their own Christian interpretations has led some to reject their scholarship. It is beyond the scope of this book, or my interest, to apply modern morality to 500-year-old magic, however if one is squeamish about 'cultural appropriation', then magic, including Tarot reading, may not be the right field for you. Magic has always been cross-cultural in its influences and there is no way to 'purify' it without dumping the whole thing. There's 'cultural appropriation' at every level, for better or for worse. Magicians, like artists, are always borrowing from other cultures. Because since Reuchlin the Western tradition, both in magic and in the beginnings of science, has incorporated Kabbalah, a study of Western magic makes it essential. This includes the Kabbalah written by Christians.

The Shem HaMephorash is a method to derive seventy-two 'god names', later interpreted as 'angel names' from three verses of the book of Exodus (14:19–21) in the Old Testament. These three verses have exactly seventy-two letters each, and each of the three-letter names are

---

[38] In Hebrew the word 'Adam' (אָדָם), means both 'man' and 'mankind'.

constructed from one letter from each of these verses. I will be showing exactly how this is done later in this chapter. The earliest source for the seventy-two name Shem HaMephorash is in the *Bahir*, paragraph 110, attributed to Nehunya ben HaKanah, a Rabbi who is said to have lived around 100 CE. Some scholars put its composition much later at around the thirteenth century, by either Isaac the Blind (1160–1235 CE) or one of his students. This is however debated.

Renaissance occultists who used the Shem HaMephrorash include Roger Bacon, Johann Reuchlin, Heinrich Cornelius Agrippa, Athanasius Kircher, Thomas Rudd[39], and Blaise de Vigenère. De Vigenère's system, which included sigils or 'seals' for each angel and descriptions of their powers, was used by MacGregor Mathers who expanded it for use in the Hermetic Order of the Golden Dawn, and from him it remains a respected part of the Western occult 'syllabus' today.[40] Athanasius Kircher's system included Latin names and astrological attributions for each name. His Kabbalistic diagrams were also a major influence on the Golden Dawn. As with many other systems they adopted, the Golden Dawn sought to unify it with as many of its source materials as possible, applying it to 5° sections of the zodiac, each ruled by an angel (derived from Kircher), which was applied to the minor cards of the Tarot from twos to tens, and the fixed stars in astrology.

It is an interesting turn of history that non-Hebraists became interested in the Shem HaMephorash and other magical letter rearrangements from Hebrew. For the fluent Hebrew speaker, the lack of vowels (with the exception of Aleph, Ayin and in some cases Vav) in Biblical Hebrew would cause each written letter cluster to allude to multiple possible words and pronunciations, creating a web of meanings, akin to the techniques of poetry and metaphor. What is lost in direct meaning seems to be made up for by the imaginations of later magicians. That is, the lack of understanding creates an open space which direct meditative experience is allowed to fill, in a way that we don't normally allow in regular experience.

---

[39] As well as using the seventy-two names for angels, Rudd paired them with the seventy-two Demons of the Goetia. Each angel is used to control one demon.

[40] Since you asked, the types of magic and magical rituals I see most discussed by Western magicians are: Tarot, astrology, geomancy, the middle pillar, the qabalistic cross, the pentagram rituals, the analysis of the keyword, the hexagram rituals, Enochian magic, the consecration of magical tools, the gnostic mass, the star ruby, the Abramelin ritual, and the Shem (HaMephorash) operation.

According to Pico della Mirandola,

> 9>20. *Every voice has power in magic insofar as it is shaped by the voice of God. 9>21. Voices that mean nothing are more powerful in magic than voices that mean something. And anyone who is profound can understand the reason for this conclusion from the preceding conclusion.*[41]

Reuchlin paraphrases this as:

> *Meaningless sounds have more magical power than meaningful ones. Any sound is good for magic in so far as it is formed from the word of God.*[42]

One can take this in a number of ways, some more cynical than others, but if we take them at their word, as the writers of numerous books of Western occultism did, there was found a use in allowing a space for either the associative mind of the magician, an intuition, or, if you like, a spirit to fill in a meaning for a word. If we are honest with ourselves, as we work with Tarot and other divination, something similar is going on. That is, the creative act of 'filling the gaps' is a large part of what divining is.

What is the Shem HaMephorash?

Meaning 'the explicit name', the term Shem HaMephorash (שֵׁם הַמְפֹרָשׁ) comes originally from the Mishnah (הַמִּשְׁנָה), a collection of Jewish literature derived from oral law, referred to as the 'Oral Torah' and compiled from roughly 10–220 CE. Before this time, the Oral Torah was not written down, and is said to have been handed down from generation to generation. The word Mishnah means 'study by repetition'. Together with a commentary text called the Gemara (גמרא), the Mishnah makes up the Talmud, the central text of Rabbinic Judaism, the most common form of Judaism today.

The term Shem HaMephorash originally referred to the Tetragrammaton יהוה (YHWH). Over time however, it came to be an exploration of other God-names comprising of four, twelve, twenty-two, forty-two, or seventy-two letters, or in this case groups of three letters.

---

[41] Pico della Mirandola, *Syncretism in the West: Pico's 900 Theses* (1496), tr. S. A. Farmer (Tempe, AZ: Arizona State University, 1998), 501.
[42] Johann Reuchlin, *On the Art of the Kabbalah, De Arte Cabalistica* (1517), tr. Martin Goodman and Sarah Goodman (Lincoln, NE: University of Nebraska Press, 1993), 271.

These names became important for Jewish Kabbalah, which explains that the world was spoken or engraved into existence by God, using the Hebrew alphabet and spoken and rearranged sacred God-names. There is a whole wing of Jewish magic that relies on the study and use of language and gematria—the application of numerical values and numerology to words. As God created the world, it is thought that nature can be manipulated through the correct use of the alphabet and holy words. These God-names were later borrowed by the Golden Dawn and became an integral part of their rituals.

The Seventy-two-fold Name

For most occultists and Tarot readers, the relevant form of the Shem HaMephorash is the 'Seventy-two-fold Name', which as mentioned before is first attested in the *Bahir*, though not in great detail. After the *Bahir*, an expansion of the Seventy-two-fold Name was written in a Jewish Aramaic grimoire, called the Sefer Raziel HaMalakh (the Book of the Angel Raziel), which is of uncertain authorship, but was probably produced by the German Orthodox Jews of the Hasidim movement. While it cannot be proven to be written any earlier than the thirteenth century CE, it claims to be a revelation to Adam himself from the angel Raziel, the 'angel of mysteries'. The contents draw from earlier Kabbalistic works, especially the Sefer Yetzirah and the Sefer HaRazim.

Gematria of the Tetragrammaton

As we have seen, the Hebrew alphabet is also used as a numbering system. This adds a layer of numerological meaning to written Hebrew, and the esoteric use and manipulation of these number values is called 'gematria'. Gematria is used for all sorts of things, from magic to theology to poetry. We have explored Neo-Pythagorean numerology, as outlined by Papus and Crowley, in earlier sections of this book, and the logic of Gematria is similar. As Kabbalists like to bring everything back to the supreme Godhead, the number seventy-two, which we will be exploring, can be derived from YHVH as follows:

י Yod = ten.
ה Heh = five.
ו Vav = Six.

Y = 10

YH = 15

YHV = 21

YHVH = 26

10+15+21+26 = 72

The writing of a word in this pyramid fashion is an occult tradition. For example, other magical words such as 'abracadabra' are used similarly. Abracadabra is a word from the second century CE Roman text *Liber Medicinalis*, written by the physician and magician Quintus Serenus Sammonicus. In chapter fifty-two, Sammonicus explains that malaria sufferers could be treated by wearing an amulet containing the word written in the form of a triangle:

ABRACADABRA
ABRACADABR
ABRACADAB
ABRACADA
ABRACAD
ABRACA
ABRAC
ABRA
ABR
AB
A

The modern occultist and writer Aaron Leitch says that the thinking behind these word pyramids is that one can build up and manifest a power from a single letter, or reduce a power by reducing the triangle to a single letter. Therefore in the earlier example above, the YHVH triangle is designed to draw in the power of the supreme Deity and therefore the triangle is built up, while in the case of the ABRACADABRA triangle, the word is reduced in order to reduce the power of an illness.[43]

---

[43] Aaron Leitch, *Shem ha-Mephoresh, The Divine Name of Extension* (1998), https://cdn.preterhuman.net/texts/religion.occult.new_age/occult_library/Leitch_A-Shem_Ha-Mephoresh.pdf Last retrieved 5 December 2023.

Uses of the Shem HaMephorash in the Tarot

As well as giving a further level of meaning to each of the Minor Arcana cards, the Shem HaMephorash attaches a spirit 'intelligence' to each card, which can be used for spells, with the corresponding Tarot card acting as their 'key' or 'spirit link'. This is considered by magicians to be a bit like generating a phone-line to an angel helper. This of course takes the application of Tarot far beyond mere fortune telling. Now you are negotiating with manifestation itself, and interacting with angels!

How did it get attributed to Tarot?

The magic names of the Sefer Raziel HaMalakh really tickled the fancy of Johann Reuchlin, who in learning Kabbalah from the Renaissance philosopher and writer of magic Giovanni Pico della Mirandola decided that Kabbalah was a perfect system for marrying theology with alchemy and philosophy. We have discussed Pico previously as the founder of 'Christian Kabbalah', which became a central part of the philosophy of Renaissance esotericism, especially hermetic philosophy, alchemy and magic. Put bluntly, without 'Christian Kabbalah', the West may not have developed its own sciences. Along with astrology and Platonism, Kabbalah was central to the alchemical worldview. Alchemy in turn was the mother of chemistry, physics, and psychology. It also massively influenced medicine.

From there the Shem HaMephorash was used in the *Lesser Key of Solomon*, in Agrippa's *Three Books of Occult Philosophy*, in Athanasius Kircher's *Oedipus Aegyptiacus*, and eventually by the Hermetic Order of the Golden Dawn, who were directly influenced by these earlier texts.

As we have explored before, Éliphas Lévi (1810–1875 CE) was the writer who connected the Tarot with Kabbalah, especially the twenty-two letters of the Hebrew alphabet, though he got the idea from Antoine Court de Gébelin and Comte de Mellet's earlier writings. From there it was a natural progression of one-upmanship by later writers to apply more and more Kabbalistic concepts onto Tarot's sturdy frame. Éliphas Lévi also assigned the Shem HaMephorash angel names to the Tarot in his 1895 book *Clefs Majeures et Clavicules de Salomon (Major Keys and Minor Keys of Solomon)*.

Suffice to say, when MacGregor Mathers (1854–1918 CE), the primary founding member of the Golden Dawn, started his great act of syncretism that he compiled from his readings at the library of the British Museum, he absorbed all of this stuff. From a variety of sources, he created an admirably vast and well-functioning magical system. Well-functioning that is, despite being cobbled together like some Rube Goldberg machine.

Biblical verse

Nowadays it is popular to think of the occult as being in opposition to religion; historically however, the opposite was the norm. Most magicians and occultists who wrote books were religious and often were clergy. Even in the preeminent Victorian occult society, the Hermetic Order of the Golden Dawn, the magic is explicitly Christian, albeit with many additions and influences from 'pagan' polytheisms, ancient Egyptian mythology, Hinduism and Buddhism. The modern confusion can perhaps be blamed on Aleister Crowley, who—along with being the person most responsible for leaking the core material of the Golden Dawn secret society—was also on a self-appointed mission to invert the moral values of the Christian culture around him, and especially—like a man perpetually committed to teenage rebellion—those of his Plymouth Brethren parents. There were of course precursors in the witch trials, and you can bet that even back in the Renaissance, rebellious teenagers were flirting with forbidden magic, at least in their games.

So, given that most occult material was also religious, one of the primary texts used for Western magic throughout history has been the Bible. Jewish Kabbalists, Islamic scholars, and Christian esotericists have all explored the Bible for magical material. In the *Bahir* and the books that were influenced by it, the Seventy-two-fold Name is derived from Exodus 14, Chapters 19–21. In the original Hebrew, each of these chapters have exactly seventy-two letters each. The original Hebrew text is as follows:

Exodus 14:19

ויסע מלאך האלהים ההלך לפני מחנה ישראל וילך מאחריהם ויסע עמוד הענן מפניהם ויעמד מאחריהם:

Exodus 14:20

ויבא בין מחנה מצרים ובין מחנה ישראל ויהי הענן והחשך ויאר את הלילה ולא קרב זה אל זה כל הלילה:

Exodus 14:21
ויט משה את ידו על הים ויולך יהוה את הים ברוח קדים עזה כל הלילה וישם את הים לחרבה ויבקעו המים:
The English translation from the King James Bible is:

Exodus 14:19
'And the Angel of the Elohim that went before the camp of Israel removed and went behind them, and the pillar of cloud went from before their face and stood behind them.'

Exodus 14:20
'And it came between the camp of the Egyptians and the camp of Israel; and it was a cloud of darkness to them, but it gave light by night to these: so that one came not near the other all the night.'

Exodus 14:21
'And Moses stretched out his hand over the sea, and the Lord caused the sea to go back by a great east wind all that night, and made the sea dry land, and the waters were divided.'

Using the original Hebrew, the lines of this text are then read 'boustrophedonically',[44] alternating right to left and left to right, or 'as the ox ploughs'. When these three lines are laid on top of one another, this generates the seventy-two names of three letters each, read in downwards columns. When spoken together, these names are said by Kabbalistic legend to allow magical powers such as the power to cast out demons, heal the sick, prevent natural disasters, kill enemies, or—as Moses was able to do—divide the waters.

Leitch writes:

> The technique of deriving Names, descriptions, functions, etc from Scripture is a long established Qabalistic Tradition. For instance, if an unnamed Angel delivers a message, simply take the first letter of each word He speaks and you will have the Angel's Name. Take a description of an Angel and add up the numeric value of the entire phrase, then see what Hebrew words and phrases have the same value, and you will get a clue into the function of the Angel. The possibilities are endless.[45]

---

[44] If you can ever find an opportunity to use this word again, I will be impressed.
[45] Leitch (1998).

In the following, I have done the Shem HaMephorash operation on the text (so you don't have to). To my knowledge this has not been laid out this methodically anywhere else. These are derived by writing the letters of the three verses, with no vowel points, spaces, or punctuation marks (and in my case the letters which were in their final forms have been returned to initial forms, for ease).[46]

The first chapter, 19, from right to left (as Hebrew is normally written):

<<<   <<<
כ ל ה ה מ י ה ל א ה כ א ל מ ע ס י ו
מ כ ל י ו ל א ר ש י ה נ ח מ י נ פ ל
נ נ ע ה ד ו מ ע ע ס י ו מ ה י ר ח א
מ ה י ר ח א מ ד מ ע י ו מ ה י נ פ מ

The second chapter, 20, from left to right (reverse order than normal):

>>>   >>>
ה ל י ל כ ה ז ל א ה ז ב ר ק א ל
ו ה ל י ל ה ת א ר א י ו כ ש ח ה ו נ
נ ע ה י ה י ו ל א ר ש י ה נ ח מ נ י
ב ו מ י ר צ מ ה נ ח מ נ י ב א ב י ו

---

[46] Some Hebrew letters have final forms if they are the final letter in a word. Though this is extra to our uses in Tarot, the final form letters are:

> Final Kaf: ך
> Final Mem: ם
> Final Nun: ן
> Final Peh: ף
> Final Tsadi: ץ

The other small dots and marks indicate vowels. These are not used at all by magicians, but are useful as a pronunciation guide when learning to speak or read Hebrew. Expert and native speakers often omit them entirely. Though this makes the writing system more vague than with European languages, it also allows many more words to be associated together. This is part of the reason Hebrew has been used as a magical language over other writing systems. It offers many more options than English.

And the third chapter, 21, from right to left:

<<<																	<<<
י	ו	מ	י	ה	ל	ע	ו	ד	י	ת	א	ה	ש	מ	ט	י	ו
ד	ק	ח	ו	ר	ב	מ	י	ה	ת	א	ה	ו	ה	י	כ	ל	ו
ת	א	מ	ש	י	ו	ה	ל	י	ל	ה	כ	ה	ז	ע	מ	י	
מ	י	מ	ה	ו	ע	ק	ב	י	ו	ה	ב	ר	ח	ל	מ	י	ה

The lines are then arranged on top of each other with the first verse being the top row, the second verse the second row and the third verse the third row. As Hebrew is written right to left I have numbered them in that direction. This generates our seventy-two angel names of three letters each which are read in each column from top down:

18	17	16	15	14	13	12	11	10	9	8	7	6	5	4	3	2	1
כ	ל	ה	ה	מ	י	ה	ל	א	ה	כ	א	ל	מ	ע	ס	י	ו
ל	א	ק	ר	ב	ז	ה	א	ל	ז	ה	כ	ה	ל	י	ל	ה	ה
י	ו	מ	י	ה	ל	ע	ו	ד	י	ת	א	ה	ש	מ	ט	י	ו
36	35	34	33	32	31	30	29	28	27	26	25	24	23	22	21	20	19
מ	כ	ל	י	ו	ל	א	ר	ש	י	ה	נ	ח	מ	י	נ	פ	ל
נ	ו	ה	ח	ש	כ	ו	י	א	ר	א	ת	ה	ל	י	ל	ה	ו
ד	ק	ח	ו	ר	ב	מ	י	ה	ת	א	ה	ו	ה	י	כ	ל	ו
54	53	52	51	50	49	48	47	46	45	44	43	42	41	40	39	38	37
נ	נ	ע	ה	ד	ו	מ	ע	ע	ס	י	ו	מ	ה	י	ר	ח	א
י	נ	מ	ח	נ	ה	י	ש	ר	א	ל	ו	י	ה	י	ה	ע	נ
ת	א	מ	ש	י	ו	ה	ל	י	ל	ה	כ	ה	ז	ע	מ	י	
72	71	70	69	68	67	66	65	64	63	62	61	60	59	58	57	56	55
מ	ה	י	ר	ח	א	מ	ד	מ	ע	י	ו	מ	ה	י	נ	פ	מ
ו	י	ב	א	ב	י	נ	מ	ח	נ	ה	מ	צ	ר	י	מ	ו	ב
מ	י	מ	ה	ו	ע	ק	ב	י	ו	ה	ב	ר	ח	ל	מ	י	ה

Below are the seventy-two three-letter names with their Latin alphabet equivalents. I have used Reuchlin's transliterations. In this case ' refers to a glottal stop, such as in the outburst 'uh oh'.

1. והו	VHV	19. לוו	LVV	37. אני	ANY	55. מבה	MBH
2. ילי	YLY	20. פהל	PHL	38. חעם	H'M	56. פוי	PVY
3. סיט	SYT	21. נלכ	NLK	39. רהע	RH'	57. נממ	NMM
4. עלמ	'LM	22. יי	YYY	40. יז	YYZ	58. ייל	YYL
5. מהש	MHsH	23. מלה	MLH	41. ההה	HHH	59. הרח	HRH
6. ללה	LLH	24. חהו	HHV	42. מיכ	MYK	60. מצר	MSR
7. אכא	AKA	25. נתה	NGH ?	43. וול	VVL	61. ומב	VMB
8. כהת	KHTh	26. האא	HAA	44. ילה	YLH	62. יהה	YHH
9. הזי	HZY	27. ירת	YRT	45. סאל	SAL	63. ענו	'NV
10. אלד	ALD	28. שאה	SAH	46. ערי	'RY	64. מחי	MHY
11. לאו	LAV	29. ריי	RYY	47. עשל	'ShL	65. דמב	DMB
12. ההע	HH'	30. אומ	AVM	48. מיה	MYH	66. מנק	MNQ
13. יזל	YZL	31. לכב	LKB	49. והו	VHV	67. איע	AY'
14. מבה	MBH	32. ושר	VShR	50. דני	DNL	68. חבו	HBV
15. הרי	HRY	33. יחו	YHV	51. החש	HHSh	69. ראה	RAH
16. הקמ	HQM	34. להח	LHH	52. עממ	'MM	70. יבמ	YBM
17. לאו	LAV	35. כוק	KVQ	53. ננא	NNA	71. היי	HYY
18. כלי	KLY	36. מנד	MNR	54. נית	NYT	72. מומ	MVM

From here, Reuchlin adds the suffixes 'yah' or 'el', two Biblical names for God, also used for angels (and in Hebrew names). His precise reasoning for applying one rather than the other is somewhat lost to time outside of this quote: 'the Jewish nation call their god Yah because of his kindnesses and El because of his strength and virtue'.[47] Later the Golden Dawn associated 'Yah' with Chesed the sefirah of 'mercy', and 'El' with Gevurah the sefirah of 'strength'. In this way 'Yah' is the active power, and 'El' is its container, or modulating controller.

Reuchlin has also added vowels as he sees fit, and again his reasoning is not clear. The original Kabbalistic pronunciations use the same vowels as the name of the letter. Here are Reuchlin's spellings:

1. Vehuiah	4. Elemiah	7. Achaiah	10. Aladiah
2. Ieliel	5. Mahasiah	8. Cahethel	11. Laviah
3. Sitael	6. Lelahel	9. Haziel	12. Hahaiah

---

[47] Reuchlin, tr. Goodman (1993), 273.

13. Iezalel	28. Saeehiah	43. Veualiah	58. Ieialel
14. Mebahel	29. Reiaiel	44. Ielahiah	59. Harahel
15. Hariel	30. Omael	45. Sealiah	60. Mizrael
16. Hakamiah	31. Lecabel	46. Ariel	61. Umabel
17. Loviah	32. Vasariah	47. Asaliah	62. Iahhael
18. Caliel	33. Iehuiah	48. Mihael	63. Anavel
19. Levuiah	34. Lehahiah	49. Vehuel	64. Mehiel
20. Pahaliah	35. Chavakiah	50. Daniel	65. Damabiah
21. Nelchael	36. Manadel	51. Hahasiah	66. Manakel
22. Ieiaiel	37. Aniel	52. Imamiah	67. Eiael
23. Melahel	38. Haamiah	53. Nanael	68. Habuiah
24. Haiviah	39. Rehael	54. Nithael	69. Roehel
25. Nithhaiah	40. Ieiazel	55. Mebahiah	70. Iabamiah
26. Haaiah	41. Hahahel	56. Poiel	71. Haiaiel
27. Ierathel	42. Michael	57. Nemamiah	72. Mumiah

The Zodiac and the Names

As previously discussed in the section, in astrology the twelve signs of the zodiac can be divided into three decans for each sign. This produces thirty-six divisions in total, each being 10° of the circle.

These can further be divided into pairs of 'quinences', 5° each, for a total of seventy-two, which is where our angel names come in.[48] Each quinence lasts approximately five days, and these are metaphorically called the 'day' and 'night' of each decan. Another way to look at it would be to assign the angels in pairs to each decan, and have the first govern the days of that decan and the second govern the nights of that decan. If these variations seem a bit imprecise to you, this is par for the course in the occult.[49]

The Minor Arcana from twos to tens in the four suits are then applied to these 5° quinences and Shem angel names. The aces, which are left out, can be allocated to the four archangels as follows:

- Ace of Wands – Michael, guardian of the Element of Fire
- Ace of Cups – Gabriel, guardian of the Element of Water

---

[48] Leitch (1998).
[49] See the section 'Making it work might be the point of the exercise', near the end of my *Tarot for Sceptics* (2025), and the final chapter 'Bullshit that works', for my justification and scepticism of this tendency.

- Ace of Swords – Raphael, guardian of the Element of Air
- Ace of Pentacles – Uriel, guardian of the Element of Earth.

There are a couple of ways to assign the names to the cards. Some apply the names in order from Aries to Pisces. The Golden Dawn instead starts with Leo. Their reasoning is that this is the position of the fixed star Cor Leonis, the 'heart of the lion', also known as Regulus. Regulus is the brightest star in the constellation of Leo, and one of the brightest objects in the night sky. It is also the brightest star falling on the ecliptic[50] and is traditionally associated with kingship. Astrologically it is said to impart a 'regal' quality that combines the attributes of Mars and Jupiter. Mathers gave an explanation of his reasoning in a paper called 'The Tree of Life as Projected in a Solid Sphere':

> *Another very important note of difference is that, throughout the true tarot, the teaching assigns the commencing point of the zodiac to the bright star Regulus, which is in Leo. And it measures right ascension and longitude from that point, and not from a suppositious point divided by the equinox and called 0° of Aries (though in reality now far removed from the constellation of that name) which has been adopted by modern or Western astronomy or astrology.*[51]

As we can see, it was important to Mathers to work directly to the constellations, rather than the tropical zodiac, which due to the precession of the equinoxes, no longer lines up the twelve zodiacal divisions of the sky with the constellations they are named after. The original zodiac was named by the Babylonians around 1000 BCE, and in our era things have slipped.

Here we will use the Golden Dawn attributions as they are the most widely followed by Tarot readers.[52] The cards are counted from the twos to the tens, from Aries with each suit matching the element of its corresponding sign of the zodiac. The astrological decan correspondences for the Shem angels come from Athanasius Kircher (1602–1680 CE), in his book *Oedipus Aegyptiacus* (1652–1655 CE).

---

[50] The Sun's apparent path around the Earth from our vantage point.
[51] Israel Regardie, *The Golden Dawn: The Original Account of the Teachings, Rites, and Ceremonies of the Hermetic Order* [1940], 7th edition, ed. John Michael Greer (Woodbury, MN: Llewellyn Publications, 2016), 749.
[52] These can be found on page 104 (for the Shem angels) and page 685 (for the card attributions) of Regardie, ed. Greer (2016).

Card	Sign	Decan	Quinance	Angel name	Angel name	
5 of Wands	**Leo**	Saturn	July 23	והויה	Vehuiah	Day
			July 28	יליאל	Ieliel	Night
6 of Wands		Jupiter	August 2	סיטאל	Sitael	Day
			August 7	עלמיה	Elemiah	Night
7 of Wands		Mars	August 12	מהשיה	Mahasiah	Day
			August 17	ללהאל	Lelahel	Night
8 of Pentacles	**Virgo**	Sun	August 23	אכאיה	Achaiah	Day
			August 28	כהתאל	Cahethel	Night
9 of Pentacles		Venus	September 2	הזיאל	Haziel	Day
			September 7	אלדיה	Aladiah	Night
10 of Pentacles		Mercury	September 12	לאויה	Laviah	Day
			September 17	ההעיה	Hahaiah	Night
2 of Swords	**Libra**	Moon	September 23	יזלאל	Iezalel	Day
			September 28	מבהאל	Mebahel	Night
3 of Swords		Saturn	October 3	הריאל	Hariel	Day
			October 8	הקמיה	Hakamiah	Night
4 of Swords		Jupiter	October 13	לאויה	Loviah	Day
			October 18	כליאל	Caliel	Night

Card	Sign	Planet	Date	Hebrew	Name	Day/Night
5 of Cups	**Scorpio**	Mars	October 23	לויה	Levuiah	Day
			October 28	פהליה	Pahaliah	Night
6 of Cups		Sun	November 2	נלכאל	Nelchael	Day
			November 7	ייאי	Ieiaiel	Night
7 of Cups		Venus	November 12	מלהאל	Melahel	Day
			November 17	חהויה	Haiviah	Night
8 of Wands	**Sagittarius**	Mercury	November 22	נתהיה	Nithhaiah	Day
			November 27	האאה	Ha'aiah	Night
9 of Wands		Moon	December 2	ירתאל	Ierathel	Day
			December 7	שאהיה	Saeehiah	Night
10 of Wands		Saturn	December 12	ריאל	Reiaiel	Day
			December 17	אומאל	'Omael	Night
2 of Pentacles	**Capricorn**	Jupiter	December 22	לכבאל	Lecabel	Day
			December 27	ושריה	Vasariah	Night
3 of Pentacles		Mars	January 1	יחויה	Iehuiah	Day
			January 6	להחיה	Lehahiah	Night
4 of Pentacles		Sun	January 11	ככויה	Chavakiah	Day
			January 16	מנדאל	Manadel	Night
5 of Swords	**Aquarius**	Venus	January 20	אניאל	Aniel	Day
			January 25	חעמיה	Haamiah	Night

(Continued)

(Continued)

Card	Sign	Decan	Quinance	Angel name		
6 of Swords		Mercury	January 30	האאל	Rehael	Day
			February 4	ייאל	Ieiazel	Night
7 of Swords		Moon	February 9	ההאל	Hahahel	Day
			February 14	מכאל	Michael	Night
8 of Cups	Pisces	Saturn	February 19	וויל	Veualiah	Day
			February 24	ילהיה	Ielahiah	Night
9 of Cups		Jupiter	March 1	סאליה	Sealiah	Day
			March 6	עריאל	Ariel	Night
10 of Cups		Mars	March 11	עשליה	Asaliah	Day
			March 16	מיהאל	Mihael	Night
2 of Wands	Aries	Mars	March 21	והואל	Vehuel	Day
			March 26	דניאל	Daniel	Night
3 of Wands		Sun	April 1	ההשיה	Hahasiah	Day
			April 6	עממיה	Imamiah	Night
4 of Wands		Venus	April 10	ננאל	Nanael	Day
			April 15	נתאל	Nithael	Night
5 of Pentacles	Taurus	Mercury	April 20	מבהיה	Mebahiah	Day
			April 25	פואל	Poiel	Night

6 of Pentacles		Moon	April 30	נממיה	Nemamiah	Day
			May 5	ייאל	Ieialel	Night
7 of Pentacles		Saturn	May 10	הרחאל	Harahel	Day
			May 15	מצראל	Mizrael	Night
8 of Swords	Gemini	Jupiter	May 21	ומבאל	Umabel	Day
			May 26	יההאל	Iahhael	Night
9 of Swords		Mars	May 31	ענואל	Anavel	Day
			June 5	מחיאל	Mehiel	Night
10 of Swords		Sun	June 10	דמביה	Damabiah	Day
			June 15	מנקאל	Manakel	Night
2 of Cups	Cancer	Venus	June 21	איעאל	Eiael	Day
			June 26	חבויה	Habuiah	Night
3 of Cups		Mercury	July 1	ראהאל	Roehel	Day
			July 6	יבמיה	Iabamiah	Night
4 of Cups		Moon	July 11	היאיאל	Haiaiel	Day
			July 16	מומיה	Mumiah	Night

Another earlier system can be created with the order beginning from Aries. This was used by Athanasius Kircher. He goes through the names in order of element, starting with fire, cardinal (Aries), fixed (Leo), mutable (Sagittarius). This time, to demonstrate the variety that one may introduce, I have used the angel names as written by Agrippa who has a different pronunciation of the names than Reuchlin. The card attributions in this table are those of Éliphas Lévi who uses the cards from aces through to nines, and leaves out the tens. Lévi's Tarot attributions predate the Golden Dawn, but Agrippa comes after Reuchlin. Lévi's spellings of the names are divergent from the Hebrew letters. As you can see there are a few ways to put this information together, and if this annoys you, all I can say is that all esoteric traditions seem to have this trait of there being multiple, conflicting ways to do the same thing. Choose one or compile your own and test it. In my experience they all seem to work despite the steam rising off the pedants. As Lévi didn't himself assign the Shem angels to the zodiac, the elements here do not line up as they did in the Golden Dawn table.

Card	Sign	Decan	Quinance	Angel name	
Ace of Wands	**Aries**	Mars	March 21	הויאל	Vehuiah
2 of Wands			March 26	ילאי	Yeliel
3 of Wands		Sun	April 1	סיטאל	Sitael
Ace of Wands			April 6	עלמיה	Aulemiah
2 of Wands		Venus	April 10	מהשיה	Mahasiah
3 of Wands			April 15	ללהאל	Lelahel
4 of Wands	**Taurus**	Mercury	April 20	אכאיה	Akaiah
5 of Wands			April 25	כהתאל	Kahathel
6 of Wands		Moon	April 30	הזיאל	Heziel
4 of Wands			May 5	אלדיה	Eladiah
5 of Wands		Saturn	May 10	לאויה	Laviah
6 of Wands			May 15	הההעיה	Hahauah
7 of Wands	**Gemini**	Jupiter	May 21	יזלאל	Yezalel
8 of Wands			May 26	מבהאל	Mebahel
9 of Wands		Mars	May 31	הריאל	Hariel
7 of Wands			June 5	הקמיה	Haqemiah
8 of Wands		Sun	June 10	לאויה	Leviah
9 of Wands			June 15	כליאל	Keliel

(Continued)

(Continued)

Card	Sign	Decan	Quinance	Angel name	
Ace of Cups	**Cancer**	Venus	June 21	לויה	Levoiah
Two of Cups			June 26	פהליה	Paheliah
Three of Cups		Mercury	July 1	נלכאל	Nelakel
Ace of Cups			July 6	ייאל	Yiaiel
Two of Cups		Moon	July 11	מלהאל	Melahel
Three of Cups			July 16	חהויה	Chaihuiah
Four of Cups	**Leo**	Saturn	July 23	נתהיה	Nethhaiah
Five of Cups			July 28	האאיה	Ha'aiah
Six of Cups		Jupiter	August 2	ירתאל	Yerathel
Four of Cups			August 7	סאהיה	Sheahiah
Five of Cups		Mars	August 12	ריײל	Riyiel
Six of Cups			August 17	אומאל	Aumel
Seven of Cups	**Virgo**	Sun	August 23	לכבאל	Lekabel
Eight of Cups			August 28	ושריה	Vesheriah
Nine of Cups		Venus	September 2	יחוה	Yechoiah
Seven of Cups			September 7	להחיה	Lehachiah
Eight of Cups		Mercury	September 12	כוקיה	Keveqiah
Nine of Cups			September 17	מנדאל	Menadel

REALLY ADVANCED TAROT READING 101

Card	Sign	Planet	Date	Hebrew	Angel
Ace of Sword	Libra	Moon	September 23	אניאל	Aniel
Two of Swords			September 28	חעמיה	Chaumiah
Three of Swords		Saturn	October 3	רהעאל	Rehauel
Ace of Swords			October 8	ייזאל	Yeizel
Two of Swords		Jupiter	October 13	ההההאל	Hahahel
Three of Swords			October 18	מיכאל	Mikael
Four of Swords	Scorpio	Mars	October 23	ווליה	Vevaliah
Five of Swords			October 28	ילהיה	Yelahiah
Six of Swords		Sun	November 2	סאליאה	Saeliah
Four of Swords			November 7	עריאל	Auriel
Five of Swords		Venus	November 12	עשליה	Aushaliah
Six of Swords			November 17	מיהאל	Miahael
Seven of Swords	Sagittarius	Mercury	November 22	והואל	Vehuel
Eight of Swords			November 27	דניאל	Daniel
Nine of Swords		Moon	December 2	החשיה	Hachashiah
Seven of Swords			December 7	עממיה	Aumemiah
Eight of Swords		Saturn	December 12	נגאל	Nanael
Nine of Swords			December 17	ניתאל	Neithael
Ace of Pentacles	Capricorn	Jupiter	December 22	מבהיה	Mabehiah
Two of Pentacles			December 27	פואל	Poiel

(*Continued*)

(Continued)

Card	Sign	Decan	Quinance	Angel name	
Three of Pentacles		Mars	January 1	נממיה	Nememiah
Ace of Pentacles			January 6	ייאל	Yeilel
Two of Pentacles		Sun	January 11	הרחאל	Harachel
Three of Pentacles			January 16	מצראל	Metzerel
Four of Pentacles	Aquarius	Venus	January 20	ומבאל	Umabel
Five of Pentacles			January 25	יההאל	Yehahel
Six of Pentacles		Mercury	January 30	עניאל	Aunuel
Seven of Pentacles			February 4	מחיאל	Mechiel
Eight of Pentacles		Moon	February 9	דמביה	Damebiah
Nine of Pentacles			February 14	מנקאל	Menaqel
Seven of Pentacles	Pisces	Saturn	February 19	איעאל	Aiauel
Eight of Pentacles			February 24	חבויה	Chebuiah
Nine of Pentacles		Jupiter	March 1	ראהאל	Raahel
Four of Pentacles			March 6	יבמיה	Yebemiah
Five of Pentacles		Mars	March 11	האיאל	Haiaiel
Six of Pentacles			March 16	מומיה	Moumiah

Get better imaginary friends

Some of you are scowling at this book now. 'I thought this was a sceptic-friendly guide to Tarot, not some woo-woo angel fantasy!'

Okay, bear with me. Have you ever had an argument with yourself in the space of your own mind? In our 'modern' worldview we consider this an ordinary case of one part of the self talking to another. In the pre-modern world this was usually framed differently, as a discussion with a daemon (or a demon).[53] Put another way, people used to (and still do) attribute 'personhood' to thoughts. Or put another way, spirits were thought to occupy the same space as the mind, and to be made of the same 'stuff' as thoughts. Because this mind-space, which was also called 'the heavens' was thought to be more real than matter, a lot of importance was put on these 'thought entities'. Likewise, the human mind was considered to be a smaller reflection of 'the mind of the universe'. This was the space where both concepts and spirits existed, and both of these were considered real.

Have you ever felt inspired? The word 'inspired' originally meant to invoke a spirit into oneself. Amused? This originally meant to be influenced by a muse (a demigoddess of the arts). 'Enthusiastic' about something? This word originally literally meant to channel a god into oneself. These things that we now, arguably poorly, define via psychology, and frame in terms of a 'self' which is entirely contained or even imprisoned in a bony skull, used to be described in terms of a vibrant engagement with a huge number of entities, or, if you prefer, 'conceptual personifications'. In the past, concepts, ideas, archetypes and memes were all personified as 'spirits' who were trying to get things done through human beings and their environment. Some of these spirits made good deals with humans, and some took more than they gave.

Now we are so used to the idea that we are 'closed off' from the outside conceptual environment (the spirit world) that we fail to see that this is, in fact, wrong. As Carl Jung said, 'People don't have ideas, ideas have people.'

By framing a sub-personality that is nagging at you to lie in bed all day, smoke cigarettes, or binge watch Netflix, as a 'part of yourself', you may have robbed yourself of the opportunity to overcome it. How do you get rid of yourself? By framing it as a 'demon', you have made a

---

[53] The word daemon was a neutral name for a spirit, without the negative connotation of the later word demon.

clear distinction between the habits you want to exorcise and the ones you want to nurture. Looked at pragmatically, this is arguably a more sensible way of making sense of your 'mind-space' than by constantly arguing with 'yourself'.

Who better to help you defeat a 'procrastination demon' than an angel? Call them imaginary friends if you will, or a 'trick of the mind', but try it, and see if your new angelic 'sub-personality' doesn't help you get out of bed, go for a run, call your mum, do your homework, vacuum your floor, or learn Esperanto... Try it and see!

'No way Ari, imaginary friends are childish!'[54] Okay then, put down this book. You will never be a wizard with that attitude. Instead go pick up a copy of the Richard Dawkins Delusion, and read his rant about how memes (spirits) are invading your mind-space like viruses.[55] After that you can go bother some Christians on Facebook and feel smug.

For those I have convinced, let's give it a go. What's the worst that could happen? (Just letting you know that I take absolutely no responsibility for how this goes for you.)

Angel-summoning methods

The Kabbalistic method for invoking the names relies only on the trigrams, without the suffixes 'el' or 'iah'. In this approach, all seventy-two names are called and work their magic as a group.

Aryeh Kaplan gives instructions for meditating on the words as follows:

> *Clear your mind completely.*
>
> *Then, with complete concentration and with a proper, pleasant, sweet melody, pronounce the Name [of Seventy-two].*
>
> *Using the natural vowels of each letter [begin by pronouncing these six triplets]:*
>
> *VaHeVa YoLaYo SaYoTe EaLaMe MeHeShi LaLaHe*
>
> *These six triplets of the Holy Name pronounce with eighteen breaths.*
>
> *If the divine influx does not force you to stop, continue pronouncing the Name in this manner until you reach the triplet MVM [the last of the seventy-two].*[56]

---

[54] This is me summoning the sceptic demon.
[55] Seriously though, page 193 of *The Selfish Gene* (1976), where Dawkins first introduced the idea of 'memes', is also a very good explanation of spirits. I also explore this more thoroughly in my first book *Pragmatic Magical Thinking* (2023), page 89.
[56] Aryeh Kaplan, *Meditation and Kabbalah* (Newburyport, MA: Weiser, 1982), 98.

The full chant would then be:

VaHeVa, YoLaYo, SaYoTe, AaLaMe, MeHaShi, LaLaHa, AaKaAa, KaHeKhe, HaZaYo, AaLaDa, LaAaVa, HaHaAa, YoZaLa, MeBeHA, HaReYo, HaQoMe, LaAaVa, KaLaYo, LaVaVa, PeHaLa, NuLaKa, YoYoYo, MeLaHa, HaHaVa, NuTaHa, HaAaAa, YoReTa, ShiAaHe, ReYoYo, AaVaMe, LaKaBe, VaShiRe, YoKheVa, LaHaKhe, KaVaQo, MeNuDa, AaNuYo, KheAaMe, ReHaAa, YoYoZa, HaHaHa, MeYoKa, VaVaLa, YoLaHa, SaAaLa, AaReYo, AaShiLa, MeYoHa, VaHaVa, DaNuYo, HaKheShi, AaMeMe, NuNuAa, NuYoTa, MeBeHa, PeVaYo, NuMeMe, YoYoLa, HaReKhe, MeTzaRe, VaMeBem YoHaHa, AaNuVa, MeKheYo, DaMeBe, MeNuQo, AaYoZa, KheBeVa, ReAaHe, YoBeMe, HaYoYo, MeVaMe

(Khe represents a guttural. Represented by /x/ in the International Phonetic Alphabet.)

In the *Sixth and Seventh Books of Moses* (an eighteenth- or nineteenth-century magical text of unknown authorship purporting to be the lost writings of Moses), the Shem HaMephorash becomes associated with verses from Bible Psalms. The seventieth angel Iabamiah is the exception, getting the first verse of the Bible, Genesis 1:1. This verse contains the trigram of the seventieth name. The addition of the Psalms was put forth by Thomas Rudd (c. 1583–1656) who was expanding on Blaise de Vigenère's approach (1523–1596), who in turn was basing his Shem HaMephorash on Reuchlin's.

Thomas Rudd also combined the system with the seventy-two demons of the grimoire, the *Ars Goetia*, and stated that the angels could be used to control the demons which in turn could be used to get stuff done for the magician who correctly summoned them. This is its own long tradition based upon the legend that King Solomon from the Bible used demons to build his temple. A side note: demons were not always considered evil, so in this case they are neutral spirits, albeit chaotic ones who certainly need a careful approach.

The Angelic approach to invoking the Shem HaMephorash is to slowly intone the name of an individual angel of your choice then recite an associated verse from Psalms in the Bible. All these psalm verses contain the four letters of the Tetragrammaton. Kabbalistically, the Psalms would be chanted in their original Hebrew, but I have offered the King James Versions here. (I feel you have come with me out on this branch far enough. I will not force you to also learn Hebrew pronunciation.) I've also included each angel's job prescription based on the tradition.

	Angel		Qualities	Verse	King James Translation
1.	יהואל	Vehuiah	Subtle spirit. Endowed with great wisdom, enthusiastic for science and the arts, capable of undertaking and accomplishing the most difficult things.	Psalms 3:3	But thou, O Lord, art a shield for me; my glory, and the lifter up of mine head.
2.	יליאל	Ieliel	To quell popular uprisings. To obtain victory over those who attack unjustly. Sprightly spirit, agreeable and courteous manners, passionate for sex.	Psalms 22:19	But be not thou far from me, O Lord: O my strength, haste thee to help me.
3.	סיטאל	Sitael	Against adversities. Protects against weapons and wild beasts. Loves truth, will keep his word, will oblige those in need of his services.	Psalms 91:2	I will say of the LORD, He is my refuge and my fortress: my God; in him will I trust.
4.	עלמיה	Elemiah	Against mental troubles and for the identification of traitors. Governs voyages, sea travels. Industrious, successful, keen for travel.	Psalms 6:4	Return, O Lord, deliver my soul: oh save me for thy mercies' sake.
5.	מהשיה	Mahasiah	To live in peace with everyone. Governs high science, occult philosophy, theology, the liberal arts. Learns easily, keen for honest pleasures.	Psalms 34:4	I sought the Lord, and he heard me, and delivered me from all my fears.

REALLY ADVANCED TAROT READING 107

6.	לְאלִיאֵל	Lelahel	To acquire knowledge and cure disease. Governs love, renown, science, arts and fortune. Features include ambition, fame.	Psalms 9:11	Moreover by them is thy servant warned: and in keeping of them there is great reward.
7.	אֲחָאיָה	Achaiah	Governs patience, secrets of nature. Loves learning, proud to accomplish the most difficult tasks.	Psalms 103:8	The LORD is merciful and gracious, Slow to anger, and plenteous in mercy.
8.	כָּהֵתֵאל	Cahethel	To obtain the benediction of God and to drive away evil spirits. Governs agricultural production. Inspires man to rise towards God.	Psalms 95:6	O come, let us worship and bow down: let us kneel before the Lord our maker.
9.	הָזִיאֵל	Haziel	Mercy of God, friendship and favour of the great, execution of a promise made. Governs good faith and reconciliation. Sincere in promises, will easily extend pardon.	Psalms 25:6	Remember, O Lord, thy tender mercies and thy lovingkindnesses; for they have been ever of old.
10.	אֲלָדִיָה	Aladiah	Good for those guilty of hidden crimes and fearing discovery. Governs rage and pestilence, cure of disease. Good health, successful in his undertakings.	Psalms 33:22	Let thy mercy, O Lord, be upon us, according as we hope in thee.

(Continued)

(Continued)

	Angel		Qualities	Verse	King James Translation
11.	לאויה	Laviah	Against lightning and for the obtainment of victory. Governs renown. Great personage, learned, celebrated for personal talents.	Psalms 18:46	The Lord liveth; and blessed be my rock; and let the God of my salvation be exalted.
12.	ההעיה	Hahaiah	Against adversity. Governs dreams. Mysteries hidden from mortals. Gentle, witty, discreet manners.	Psalms 110:1	The Lord said unto my Lord, Sit thou at my right hand, until I make thine enemies thy footstool.
13.	יזלאל	Iezalel	Governs friendship, reconciliation, conjugal fidelity. Learns easily. Adroit.	Psalms 98:4	Make a joyful noise unto the LORD, all the earth: Make a loud noise, and rejoice, and sing praise.
14.	מבהאל	Mebahel	Against those who seek to usurp the fortunes of others. Governs justice, truth, liberty. Delivers the oppressed and protects prisoners. Loves jurisprudence, affinity for law courts.	Psalms 9:9	The Lord also will be a refuge for the oppressed, a refuge in times of trouble.

15.	הריאל	Hariel	Against the impious. Governs sciences and arts. Religious sentiments, morally pure.	Psalms 94:22	But the Lord is my defence; and my God is the rock of my refuge.
16.	הקמיה	Hakamiah	Against traitors and for deliverance from those who seek to oppress us. Governs crowned heads, great captains. Gives victory. Frank, loyal, brave character, sensitive to points of honour, an affinity for Venus.	Psalms 88:1	O lord God of my salvation, I have cried day and night before thee:
17.	לואיה	Loviah	To be invoked while fasting. Against mental anguish, sadness. Governs high sciences, marvellous discoveries. Gives revelations in dreams. Loves music, poetry, literature and philosophy.	Psalms 8:9	O Lord our Lord, how excellent is thy name in all the earth!
18.	כליאל	Caliel	To obtain prompt aid. Makes truth known in law suits, causes innocence to triumph. Just, honest, loves truth, judiciary.	Psalms 35:24	Judge me, O LORD my God, according to thy righteousness; and let them not rejoice over me.
19.	לוויה	Levuiah	To be invoked while facing South. To obtain the grace of God. Governs memory, human intelligence. Amiable, lively, modest, bearing of adversity with resignation.	Psalms 40:1	I waited patiently for the Lord; and he inclined unto me, and heard my cry.

(Continued)

(Continued)

	Angel		Qualities	Verse	King James Translation
20.	פהליה	Pahaliah	Against enemies of religion, for the conversion of nations to Christianity (!) Governs religion, theology, morality, chastity, purity. Ecclesiastical vocation.	Psalms 120:1–2	In my distress I cried unto the Lord, and he heard me. Deliver my soul, O Lord, from lying lips, and from a deceitful tongue.
21.	נלכאל	Nelchael	Against calumniators (slanderers) and spells and for the destruction of evil spirits. Governs astronomy, mathematics, geography and all abstract sciences. Loves poetry, literature, avid for study.	Psalms 31:14	But I trusted in thee, O Lord: I said, Thou art my God.
22.	ייאל	Ieiaiel	Governs fortune, renown, diplomacy, commerce, influence on voyages, discoveries, protection against storms and shipwreck. Loves business, industriousness, liberal and philanthropic ideas.	Psalms 121:5	The Lord is thy keeper: the Lord is thy shade upon thy right hand.
23.	מלהאל	Melahel	Against weapons and for safety in travel. Governs water, produce of the earth, and especially plants necessary for the cure of disease. Courageous, accomplishes honourable actions.	Psalms 121:8	The Lord shall preserve thy going out and thy coming in from this time forth, and even for evermore.

24.	היויה	Haiviah	To obtain the grace and mercy of God. Governs exiles, fugitives, defaulters. Protects against harmful animals. Preserves from thieves and assassins. Loves truth, the exact sciences, sincere in word and deed.	Psalms 33:18	Behold, the eye of the Lord is upon them that fear him, upon them that hope in his mercy.
25.	נתהיה	Niththaiah	For the acquisition of wisdom and the discovery of the truth of hidden mysteries. Governs occult sciences. Gives revelations in dreams, particularly to those born on the day over which he presides. Influences those who practise the magic of the sages.	Psalms 9:1	I will praise thee, O Lord, with my whole heart; I will shew forth all thy marvellous works.
26.	האאיה	Ha'aiah	For the winning of a lawsuit. Protects those who search after truth. Influences politics, diplomats, secret expeditions and agents.	Psalms 119:145	I cried with my whole heart; hear me, O Lord: I will keep thy statutes.
27.	ירתאל	Ierathel	To confound wrong-doers and liars and for deliverance from one's enemies. Governs propagation of light, civilization. Love, peace, justice, science and arts; special affinity for literature.	Psalms 140:1	Deliver me, O Lord, from the evil man: preserve me from the violent man.

(Continued)

(Continued)

	Angel		Qualities	Verse	King James Translation
28.	שאהיה	Saeehiah	Against infirmities and thunder, protects against fire, the ruin of buildings, falls and illnesses. Governs health, simplicity. Has much judgement.	Psalms 71:12	O God, be not far from me: O my God, make haste for my help.
29.	ריאל	Reiaiel	Against the impious and enemies of religion; for deliverance from all enemies both visible and invisible. Virtue and zeal for the propagation of truth, will do his utmost to destroy impiety.	Psalms 54:4	Behold, God is mine helper: the Lord is with them that uphold my soul.
30.	אומאל	Omael	Against sorrow and despair, and for the acquisition of patience. Governs animal kingdom, watches over the generation of beings. Chemists, doctors, surgeons. Affinity for anatomy and medicine.	Psalms 71:5	For thou art my hope, O Lord God: thou art my trust from my youth.
31.	לכבאל	Lecabel	For the acquisition of knowledge. Governs vegetation and agriculture. Loves astronomy, mathematics and geometry.	Psalms 71:16	I will go in the strength of the Lord God: I will make mention of thy righteousness, even of thine only.
32.	ושריה	Vasariah	Against those who attack us in court. Governs justice. Good memory, articulate.	Psalms 33:4	For the word of the Lord is right; and all his works are done in truth.

REALLY ADVANCED TAROT READING

33.	יהוה	Iehuiah	For the identification of traitors.	Psalms 94:11	The Lord knoweth the thoughts of man, that they are vanity.
34.	להחיה	Lehahiah	Against anger. Known for his talents and acts, the confidence and fervour of his prayers.	Psalms 131:3	Let Israel hope in the Lord from henceforth and for ever.
35.	כוקיה	Chavakiah	To regain the favour of those one has offended. Governs testaments, successions and all private financial agreements. Loves to live in peace with everyone. Loves rewarding the loyalty of those in his service.	Psalms 116:1	I love the Lord, because he hath heard my voice and my supplications.
36.	מנדאל	Manadel	To retain one's employment and to preserve one's means of livelihood. Against calumny (slander) and for the deliverance of prisoners.	Psalms 26:8	Lord, I have loved the habitation of thy house, and the place where thine honour dwelleth.
37.	אניאל	Aniel	To obtain victory and stop the siege of a city. Governs sciences and arts. Reveals the secrets of nature, inspires philosophers, sages. Distinguished savant.	Psalms 80:3	Turn us again, O God, and cause thy face to shine; and we shall be saved.

(Continued)

(Continued)

	Angel		Qualities	Verse	King James Translation
38.	החמיה	Haamiah	For the acquisition of all the treasures of heaven and earth. Against fraud, weapons, wild beasts and infernal spirits. Governs all that relates to God.	Psalms 91:9	Because thou hast made the Lord, which is my refuge, even the most High, thy habitation.
39.	רהאל	Rehael	For the healing of the sick. Governs health and longevity. Influences paternal and filial affection.	Psalms 30:10	Hear, O Lord, and have mercy upon me: Lord, be thou my helper.
40.	יאזל	Ieiazel	For the deliverance of prisoners, for consolation, for deliverance from one's enemies. Governs printing and books. Men of letters and artists.	Psalms 88:14	Lord, why castest thou off my soul? why hidest thou thy face from me?
41.	ההההל	Hahahel	Against the impious, slanderers. Governs Christianity. Greatness of soul, energy. Consecrated to the service of God.	Psalms 120:2	Deliver my soul, O Lord, from lying lips, and from a deceitful tongue.
42.	מיכאל	Michael	For safety in travel. For the discovery of conspiracies. Concerned with political affairs, diplomatic.	Psalms 121:7	The Lord shall preserve thee from all evil: he shall preserve thy soul.

REALLY ADVANCED TAROT READING 115

43.	והיו	Veualiah	For the destruction of the enemy and deliverance from bondage. Love glory and the military.	Psalms 88:13	But unto thee have I cried, O Lord; and in the morning shall my prayer prevent thee.
44.	יהיה	Ielahiah	Success of a useful undertaking. Protection against magistrates. Trials. Protects against armies, gives victory. Fond of travel and learning. All his undertakings are crowned with success; distinguished for military capabilities and courage.	Psalms 119:108	Accept, I beseech thee, the freewill offerings of my mouth, O Lord, and teach me thy judgments.
45.	סאליה	Sealiah	To confound the wicked and the proud, to exalt the humiliated and the fallen. Governs vegetation. Loves learning, much aptitude.	Psalms 94:18	When I said, My foot slippeth; thy mercy, O Lord, held me up.
46.	עריאל	Ariel	To procure revelations. To thank God for the good he sends us. Discovers hidden treasure, reveals the greatest secrets of nature, causes the object of one's desire to be seen in dreams. Strong subtle mind, new and sublime thoughts, discreet, circumspect.	Psalms 145:9	The Lord is good to all: and his tender mercies are over all his works.

(Continued)

(Continued)

	Angel		Qualities	Verse	King James Translation
47.	עשליה	Asaliah	For the praising of God and the growing towards him when he enlightens us. Governs justice, makes the truth known in legal proceedings. Agreeable character, avid for the acquisition of secret knowledge.	Psalms 92:5	O Lord, how great are thy works! and thy thoughts are very deep.
48.	מיהאל	Mihael	For the preservation of peace and the union of man and wife. Protects those who address themselves to him, gives premonitions and secret inspirations. Governs generation of beings. Avid for love, fond of walks and pleasures in general.	Psalms 98:2	The Lord hath made known his salvation: his righteousness hath he openly shewed in the sight of the heathen.
49.	והואל	Vehuel	Sorrow, contrariness. For the exaltation of oneself for the benediction and glory of God. Sensitive and generous soul. Literature, jurisprudence, diplomacy.	Psalms 145:3	Great is the Lord, and greatly to be praised; and his greatness is unsearchable.
50.	דניאל	Daniel	To obtain the mercy of God and consolation. Governs justice, lawyers, solicitors. Furnishes conclusions to those who hesitate. Industrious and active in business, loves literature and is distinguished for eloquence.	Psalms 145:8	The Lord is gracious, and full of compassion; slow to anger, and of great mercy.

REALLY ADVANCED TAROT READING   117

51.	הָשִׁיָה	Hahasiah	For the elevation of the soul and the discovery of the mysteries of wisdom. Governs chemistry and physics. Reveals the secret of the Philosopher's Stone and universal medicine. Loves abstract science. Devoted to the discovery of the properties of animals, plants and minerals. Distinguished in medicine.	Psalms 104:31	The glory of the Lord shall endure for ever: the Lord shall rejoice in his works.
52.	עממיה	Imamiah	Destroys the power of enemies and humbles them. Governs voyages in general, protects prisoners who turn to him and gives them the means of obtaining their freedom. Forceful, vigorous temperament, bears adversity with patience and courage. Fond of work.	Psalms 7:17	I will praise the Lord according to his righteousness: and will sing praise to the name of the Lord most high.
53.	נַנְאֵל	Nanael	Governs the high sciences. Melancholy humour, avoids rest, meditation, well-versed in the abstract sciences.	Psalms 119:75	I know, O Lord, that thy judgments are right, and that thou in faithfulness hast afflicted me.
54.	נִיתאֵל	Nithael	To obtain the mercy of God and live long. Emperor, king, and prince. Renowned for writings and eloquence, of great reputation among the learned.	Psalms 103:19	The Lord hath prepared his throne in the heavens; and his kingdom ruleth over all.

(*Continued*)

(Continued)

	Angel		Qualities	Verse	King James Translation
55.	מבהיה	Mebahiah	Beneficial for obtaining consolation and compensations. Governs morality and religion. Distinguished by good deeds and piety.	Psalms 102:12	But thou, O Lord, shall endure for ever; and thy remembrance unto all generations.
56.	פויאל	Poiel	For the fulfilment of one's request. Governs renown, fortune and philosophy. Well esteemed by everyone for his modesty and agreeable humour.	Psalms 145:14	The Lord upholdeth all that fall, and raiseth up all those that be bowed down.
57.	נממיה	Nemamiah	For general prosperity and the deliverance of prisoners. Governs great captains. Drawn to the military; distinguished for activity and the courageous bearing of fatigue.	Psalms 115:11	Ye that fear the Lord, trust in the Lord: he is their help and their shield.
58.	ייאל	Ieialel	Protects against sorrow and care and heals the sick, especially afflictions of the eyes. Influences iron and those in commerce. Brave, frank, affinity for Venus.	Psalms 6:3	My soul is also sore vexed: but thou, O Lord, how long?
59.	הראל	Harahel	Against the sterility of women and to make children obedient to their parents. Governs treasure and banks. Printing, books. Love of learning, successful in business (especially money market).	Psalms 113:3	From the rising of the sun unto the going down of the same the Lord's name is to be praised.

60.	מצראל	Mizrael	For the cure of mental illness and deliverance from those who persecute us. Virtuous, longevity.	Psalms 145:17	The Lord is righteous in all his ways, and holy in all his works.
61.	ומבאל	Umabel	To obtain the friendship of a given person. Fond of travel and honest pleasures; sensitive heart.	Psalms 113:2	Blessed be the name of the Lord from this time forth and for evermore.
62.	יההאל	Iahhael	For the acquisition of wisdom. Governs philosophers, illuminati. Loves tranquillity and solitude, modest, virtuous.	Psalms 119:159	Consider how I love thy precepts: quicken me, O Lord, according to thy lovingkindness.
63.	ענואל	Anavel	For the conversion of nations to Christianity. Protects against accidents, heals the sick. Governs commerce, banking. Subtle and ingenious, industrious and active.	Psalms 100:2	Serve the Lord with gladness: come before his presence with singing.
64.	מחיאל	Mehiel	Against adversities. Protects against rabies and wild beasts. Governs savants, professors, orators and others. Distinguished in literature.	Psalms 33:18	Behold, the eye of the Lord is upon them that fear him, upon them that hope in his mercy.

(*Continued*)

(Continued)

	Angel		Qualities	Verse	King James Translation
65.	דמביה	Damabiah	Against magic spells, for obtaining wisdom and the undertaking of successful ventures. Governs seas, rivers, springs, sailors. Amasses a considerable fortune.	Psalms 90:13	Return, O Lord, how long? and let it repent thee concerning thy servants.
66.	מנקאל	Manakel	For the appeasement of the anger of God and for the healing of epilepsy. Governs vegetation, aquatic animals. Influences dreams. Gentleness of character.	Psalms 38:21	Forsake me not, O Lord: O my God, be not far from me.
67.	איעאל	Eiael	To obtain consolation in adversity and for the acquisition of wisdom. Influences occult science. Makes the truth known to those who call on him in their work. Enlightened requirements of the spirit of God. Fond of solitude, distinguished in higher sciences.	Psalms 37:4	Delight thyself also in the Lord: and he shall give thee the desires of thine heart.
68.	חבויה	Habuiah	For the preservation of health and the healing of the sick. Governs agriculture and fecundity. Fond of the countryside, hunting, gardens and all that is related to agriculture.	Psalms 106:1	Praise ye the Lord. O give thanks unto the Lord; for he is good: for his mercy endureth for ever.

REALLY ADVANCED TAROT READING 121

69.	ראהאל	Roehel	To find lost or stolen objects and discover the person responsible. Distinguished in the judiciary, morals and customs of all peoples.	Psalms 16:5	The Lord is the portion of mine inheritance and of my cup: thou maintainest my lot.
70.	יבמיה	Iabamiah	Governs the generation of beings and phenomena of nature. Protects those who wish to progress spiritually. Distinguished by genius; one of the great lights of philosophy.	Genesis 1:1	In the beginning God created the heaven and the earth.
71.	הייאל	Haiaiel	To confound the wicked and for deliverance from those who seek to oppress us. Protects those who call upon him. Influences fire. Brave.	Psalms 109:30	I will greatly praise the Lord with my mouth; yea, I will praise him among the multitude.
72.	מומיה	Mumiah	A divine talisman should be prepared under favourable influences with the name of the spirit on the reverse side. Protects in mysterious operations, brings success in all things. Governs chemistry, physics and medicine. Influences health and longevity. Doctor.	Psalms 116:7	Return unto thy rest, O my soul; for the Lord hath dealt bountifully with thee.

Though too involved to adequately teach here, there are many other methods magicians have come up with for summoning the Shem angels. One method is to attach them to the Golden Dawn Hexagram rituals. This is shown in the book *Self-Initiation into the Golden Dawn Tradition*.[57] These can be used with the Greater Ritual of the Hexagram where six angels are attached to each point of a six-pointed star with their corresponding zodiacal sign in the centre.[58]

Another approach is to inscribe an angel name on a talisman and wear it for that angel's influence. Certain magicians have created elaborate seals for this purpose.

Tarot cards as keys

One way to interact with the angels is to draw a minor card at random and invoke that angel (or pair of angels) to aide you or your querent in their life task. One can also draw a minor to help decide what kind of approach, or aid, one might seek in order to solve one's problem. This can be done as an addition to a regular reading if you querent is onboard with the concept. The card corresponding to an angel one is interested in might also be chosen as a focal point for meditation while doing the summoning ritual.

Alternatively a Tarot card could be treated as a talisman in its own right and worn on the person in order to connect to the angel or pair of angels that correspond to that card.

Using the Shem names in a Tarot reading

There's no right or wrong way to do this, but I would suggest these types of uses:

- Draw a minor card after a reading and use the corresponding angel's description to suggest how one would approach a situation, or invoke an angel to help with the situation.

---

[57] Chic Cicero and Sandra Tabatha Cicero, *Self-Initiation into the Golden Dawn Tradition* (Woodbury, MN: Llewellyn Publications, 2002), 475.
[58] I thank Marcus Mattern, a Golden Dawn magician and teacher for his information on this.

- Draw a minor card after a reading to suggest a timing for when something would take place or to elect an optimal time to act. Each card has a ten or nine day period, and each a day angel and a night angel.
- During a reading, look up each angel associated with each minor card in order to better understand the type of help one will need with a situation.

Generating your own angels from your own name or text of your choosing

For fun, it occurred to me to try the Shem operation method on other bits of text. Here I have generated some angel names from my own name. With this method one can generate some personal angel helpers to help do your shopping, study for a driver's licence or get laid.

ARI
EERF
MAN

A	R	I
EE	R	F
M	A	N

Angel 1: AaEeMeYah
Angel 2: ReReAaEl
Angel 3: IeFaNaYah

There you go. I suggest summoning the angels from your own name rather than mine, otherwise I will get laid instead of you.

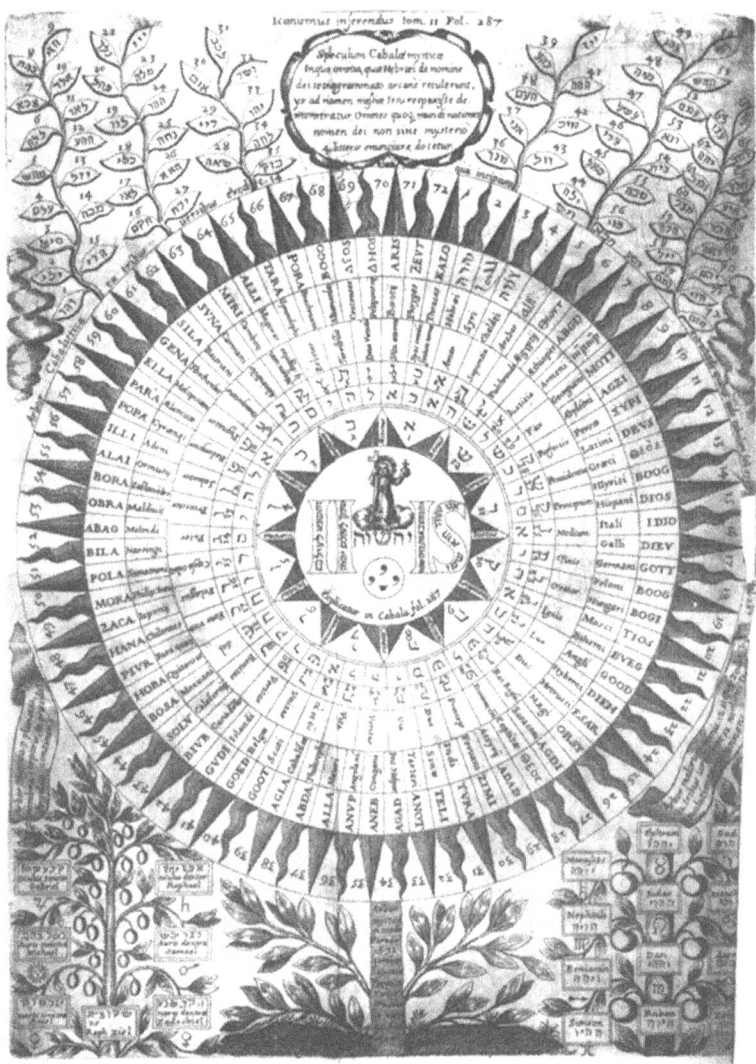

Figure 6. *Athanasius Kircher's Shem HaMephorash diagram from* Oedipus Aegyptus.

High information decks

If the art of Tarot reading is to be understood as the creation of narratives relevant to a prompting question, using randomised symbols as prompts, then the question could be asked, 'What happens when we increase the number of symbols'? To answer this, one must grapple with what the symbols do for us in the first place.

It is well understood by all expert creative people, that to have a new idea, one must first start with a narrowing of options. That is to say, it is very easy to think of an example of 'a vegetable',[59] and very hard to think of an example of 'an anything'. Therefore, the initial function of the cards is to provide us with a way to begin a story. The human imagination is excellent at joining the dots but becomes slowed down when it has nothing to grab on to.

Lower information Tarot decks like the Marseilles are therefore easier to start with. They present fewer options and are less overwhelming.

When teaching my beginner music students to improvise for the first time, they usually freeze if I ask them to play 'a solo in the key of A'. All of them however are able to improvise music on the spot if I give them only four notes to choose from. The four-note solo is very easy, but also limited. It's hard to say anything novel with only four notes, and therefore the next step is to add another four notes. Eventually the student develops a repertoire of 'signature moves' and if they continue this way, though they will massively improve, they will eventually become stuck in habit and will at some point, stop progressing. At this point, they have to try new things that are 'outside the box'.

This is where high information decks can help. They allow more ways to tell a story, but more importantly, they allow the reader to get off their well-beaten track. For this reason, they are most useful for experienced readers rather than beginners.

In music, the master improviser can find a way to play compelling music in any style, in any group setting, to any audience, and eventually with multiple instruments. Importantly, the master can make any note right, even if it is out of key.[60]

If you have made it this far in this book, this is where we leave most Tarot readers behind. The only way to progress beyond Tarot tradition,

---

[59] An extraordinary proportion of people will say 'a carrot'. You may now use this powerful piece of predictive magic to take over the world.

[60] There are twelve note names in music. In any given key there are seven that belong and sound harmonious. So if one was to play notes at random, one has a 58.333% chance of hitting 'right note'. If one finds a 'wrong note' there is always a right note next to it above or below. Furthermore, the human perception system is slow. So the audience will not hear a 'wrong note' if it is quickly resolved to a 'right note'. In this way a musician can fix any 'wrong note' by what they play after it. I see no reason why Tarot reading should be different.

is to push to a higher, more detailed art, using 'outside of the box' methods. One way to do this is to increase the amount of information. This is the necessary step to progress in any art form, when all the 'low hanging fruit' has already been picked.

An example of this happened in jazz, when the famous saxophone player, Charlie Parker, had a transcendent moment which motivated him to invent bebop, a style of fast jazz improvisation and melody writing that pushes musicians to their human limit. This event happened at Clark Monroe's Uptown House, New York, in early 1942:

> I'd been getting bored with the stereotyped changes that were being used … and I kept thinking there's bound to be something else. I could hear it sometimes. I couldn't play it…. I was working over 'Cherokee', and, as I did, I found that by using the higher intervals of a chord as a melody line and backing them with appropriately related changes, I could play the thing I'd been hearing. It came alive.[61]

Charlie Parker was talking about playing melodies using the higher harmonies or 'colour tones' of the chord, the 9th, 11th and 13th, instead of relying on the more explored and 'obvious' harmonies of the root note, 3rd 5th and 7th.[62] He connecting these higher harmonies by neighbouring chromatic passing notes that momentarily drifted outside of the key, and were then quickly resolved to scale tones. This happens so fast that the listener's ear is not given time to hear the 'wrong notes' and yet the music still sounds different than if these notes had never been placed. Parker changed the sound of jazz. It was as if earlier musicians had been using arithmetic, and he came in with calculus.

For those interested in how far an art form can go, this is the type of move that becomes necessary. Otherwise, the art will eventually become fenced in. These bounds are certainly just as possible to break through in Tarot as they are with music. Are you ambitious enough to try?

---

[61] Gerhard Kubik, 'The African matrix in jazz harmonic practices', *Black Music Research Journal* 25.1 (2005).

[62] These numbers mean notes of a scale. So if we have C major CDEFGAB, there are seven notes which can be numbered. Therefore the 3rd is E, the 5th is G, etc. The 9th, 11th, and 13th are the 2nd, 4th and 6th notes (D, F, A) spaced up an octave. This spacing allows them to harmonise where they would otherwise clash with the lower notes. These higher harmonies have a more challenging sound, which take training to be able to hear and incorporate.

As I have covered here and in the first book *Tarot for Sceptics*, the Rider Waite Smith and Crowley Thoth decks can be made even more complex by adding more associations such as Kabbalah, astrology, mythology, and the complicated Shem HaMephorash operation. These open up the Tarot toward being used for timed readings, states of consciousness, meditative techniques, and even spirit contact.

On the way, you may have noticed that I have snuck in pop culture references, mythological figures, TV characters and historical figures. Making a list of your own references can add new ways to read. I encourage you to make it interesting and make it fun.

The easiest way to get these results is to start using decks that have more complex correspondences built in, forcing different kinds of readings. Crowley's Thoth deck is a good early example, but there are many 'occult' decks on the market. One of my favourites is the 'Hermetic Tarot' by Godfrey Dowson, which is based upon the Tarot and magical teachings of the Golden Dawn, and includes as many of their correspondences on the cards as Dowson was able to fit, especially focusing on the Hebrew names of the angels of the Shem HaMephorash. Dowson's experiment has resulted in a beautiful and useful deck which offers new avenues for the reader.

The daring magician, like Charlie Parker, however, takes the development of their magic into their own hands. The first act may need to be one of irreverence. You can bet that Charlie Parker upset the jazz traditionalists, just as Crowley upset the Golden Dawn, with his works. Start modifying your cards with marker pens, assign them to creatures from a Dungeons and Dragons monster manual, or throw in some 'Magic the Gathering' game cards. Use the cards to generate a number system to look up I Ching hexagrams, or pages from Homer's Odyssey.[63] The results do not need to be perfect, the point is to 'break through' the wall. There's magic on the other side.

High information spreads

Although the trend in modern Tarot reading has been a push towards simple spreads, especially three- and six-card spreads, with the Celtic cross generally being considered a more 'complex' spread,

---

[63] There's a very long tradition of using the Odyssey for 'bibliomancy', which is divination by reading parts of books at random.

this has not always been the case. Early Tarot manuals often used many more cards. While they may not be your primary mode of reading, Tarot's full capabilities are not going to be well understood unless you have tried a couple of longer form, high information spreads.

Here is MacGregor Mathers' and Harriet Felkin's massive five-part spread from *Book T*.[64] It was plagiarised word for word by Crowley, in the back of the *Book of Thoth*.[65]

MacGregor Mathers' method of divination by the Tarot

This is longer than all the other spreads I've covered in the previous book, *Tarot for Sceptics*, and it's not clear that anyone, even Crowley, ever did a reading this large, but I have done it here anyway. In a world full of quick takes, it is worth understanding that in the past, Tarot readings were sometimes complex undertakings. I've done the difficult thing so you don't have to. If, like me, you wish to understand as many of the parameters of Tarot as possible, then I recommend trying at least one long spread at some point.

The set up

1. Choose the 'Significator'. This is a card to represent the querent. Use your knowledge or judgement of their character and role, given the nature of their question. Once you have chosen the card, take note of it, then put it back in the deck and shuffle. (Using Significators was a standard practice for Tarot readers in the past, but they seem to have fallen out of vogue in the last generation.)
2. Take the cards in your left hand. In the right hand hold the wand over them, and say, 'I invoke thee, I A O, that thou wilt send H R U, the great Angel that is set over the operations of this Secret Wisdom, to lay his hand invisibly upon these consecrated cards of art, that

---

[64] Israel Regardie, *The Golden Dawn: The Original Account of the Teachings, Rites, and Ceremonies of the Hermetic Order* [1940], 7th edition, ed. John Michael Greer (Woodbury, MN: Llewellyn Publications, 2016), 718.
[65] Aleister Crowley, *The Book of Thoth: A Short Essay on the Tarot of the Egyptians* [1944] (New York: Weiser, 1969), 249.

thereby we may obtain true knowledge of hidden things, to the glory of thine ineffable Name. Amen.'[66]
3. Hand the cards to the querent, bid the querent to think of the question attentively, and cut.
4. Take the cards as cut, and hold as for dealing.

First operation

This shows the situation of the querent at the time when they consult you.

1. The pack being in front of you, cut, and place the top half to the left.
2. Cut each pack again to the left.
3. These four stacks represent Y H V H, from right to left.
4. Find the Significator.
   - If it is in the 'Y' pack, the question refers to work, investment or business.
   - If in the first 'H' pack, to love, marriage, or pleasure.
   - If it is in the 'V' pack, to trouble, loss, scandal or quarrels.
   - If in the final 'H' pack, to money, goods, and such purely material matters.
5. Tell the querent what they have come for: if wrong, abandon the divination.
6. If correct, spread out the pack containing the Significator, face upwards.
   (In this section a system for counting up values of the cards is given, however it is never explained what to do with these values, so we have left this section out.)
   Make a 'story' of these cards. This story is that of the beginning of the affair.
7. Pair the cards on either side of the Significator, then those outside them, and so on. Make another 'story', which should fill in the details omitted in the first.

---

[66] IAO is a god-name representing a trinity of the Egyptian gods: Isis, the mother and restorer, representing beginnings; Apophis, the serpent god who represents destruction; Osiris, the god who dies and is resurrected. Together they are the aspects of time cycles in the universe. They are especially important to the Analysis of the Keyword ritual of the Golden Dawn. IAO is also a Greek form of YHWH. HRU is an angel from the Enochian magical system of John Dee and Edward Kelley. The Golden Dawn associated him with secret wisdom, especially the Tarot. Some magicians associate HRU with Horus.

8. If this story is not quite accurate, do not be discouraged. Perhaps the querent does not know everything. But the main lines ought to be laid down firmly, with correctness, or the divination should be abandoned.

Second operation: development of the question

1. Shuffle, invoke suitably, and let querent cut as before.
2. Deal cards into twelve stacks, for the twelve astrological houses. These are
   1. **House of persona,** ruled by Aries and the planet Mars
   2. **House of value and possessions,** ruled by Taurus and the planet Venus
   3. **House of communication,** ruled by Gemini and the planet Mercury
   4. **House of family and home,** ruled by Cancer and the Moon
   5. **House of pleasure and creativity,** ruled by Leo and the Sun
   6. **House of health and work,** ruled by Virgo and Mercury
   7. **House of partnerships and marriage,** ruled by Libra and Venus
   8. **House of shared resources, investments, debts, secrets and the occult,** ruled by Scorpio and Mars (and/or Pluto)
   9. **House of purpose, philosophy, and the big picture,** ruled by Sagittarius and Jupiter
   10. **House of social status and career,** ruled by Capricorn and Saturn
   11. **House of friendships and social standing,** ruled by Aquarius and Saturn (and/or Uranus)
   12. **House of subconscious, spirituality, and the shadow,** ruled by Pisces and Jupiter (and/or Neptune)
3. Make up your mind in which stack you ought to find the Significator, e.g. in the seventh house if the question concerns marriage, and so on.
4. Examine this chosen stack. If the Significator is not there, try some cognate house. On a second failure, abandon the divination.
5. Read the stack counting and pairing as before.

Third operation: further development of the question

1. Shuffle, etc., as before.
2. Deal cards into twelve stacks for the twelve signs of the zodiac.
3. Divine the proper stack and proceed as before.

Fourth operation: penultimate aspects of the question

1. Shuffle, etc., as before.
2. Find the Significator. Set it upon the table; let the thirty-six cards following form a ring round it. These are the astrological decans.
3. Count and read as before.

Fifth operation: final result

1. Shuffle, etc., as before.
2. Deal into ten packs in the form of the Tree of Life.
3. Make up your mind where the Significator should be, as before; but failure does not here necessarily imply that the divination has gone astray.
4. Count and pair as before.

A full example reading of the Mathers spread

Question: The querent is a man in his late fifties, whose wife died a year ago. He's very lonely but he keeps getting signs that she is communicating from beyond the grave. He wants to know if something spiritual is going on, or if his mind is playing tricks upon him.

The Significator card: I chose the King of Cups to reflect the age and gender of the querent, and the fact that he is asking a question of love, emotion and reminiscing (cups/water).

First operation

The cards were arranged according to the instructions, steps one to four.

Step five: The King of Cups, was found in the first 'H' pile pertaining to love and marriage. As this fits perfectly to the querent's situation, so the reading is continued.

Step six: The cards of the first 'H' pile were spread out face upwards. The King of Cups (the Significator) is facing right so I counted the cards from the right. The cards were:

- The Significator: King of Cups
- Five of Pentacles

- Eight of Pentacles
- King of Swords
- Four of Pentacles

Step seven: Make a 'story' of these cards. This story is that of the beginning of the affair.

- The Five of Pentacles. A financial hardship that the marriage faced. This is most likely to be due to the wife's illness, which, as I was told, eventually resulted in her death. Pentacles can be thought of as the body. Also, there is an injured person depicted amongst the pair of figures in the card. The husband took it upon himself to weather the burden of this financial hardship. It is also likely that he had to put in many hours of physical care for his wife. As a practical man, this became his concern more than the romantic connection or mental health within the marriage. My intuition is that the wife was suffering from cancer.
- The next card is the Eight of Pentacles, so the husband was driven into a period of very hard work. He took on extra hours at his job on top of the household chores and physical care of his wife.
- The next card is the King of Swords. Despite their hardship the husband was promoted at his work, which took on a more intellectual role. I believe he took a management role, because the card is a King. If the wife had not been ill, they would have used some of their money to celebrate, perhaps by traveling or upgrading their house. However, the success was overshadowed by their hardship at home and so the husband continued to save, with the idea of staying ahead of mounting medical costs.

Really Advanced Tarot Reading   133

Second Operation

1. Cards shuffled.
2. Cards dealt into twelve stacks, for the twelve astrological houses of heaven.
3. I found the significator in the ninth house which has to do with the sense of purpose, faith, philosophy, travel, and the big picture.
4. The querent asked me to continue so I did so.
5. Read the stack as before.

The King of Cups is facing right, and there are two cards after him. This gives us the cards

- King of Cups
- Queen of Cups
- Two of Wands

As the wife has now appeared in the reading as the Queen of Cups, the same suit as our querent, it is clear that they were in accord about their marriage in her final years. The Two of Wands shows two plans, one which was acted upon and one which got left behind. One plan was to be followed if the wife returned to health, the other if she passed away, which is unfortunately what came to pass.

As these cards are in the 'big picture' house, and the man in the image of the Two of Wands is holding a world in his hand, the husband and wife planned to travel if she got better.

As the husband asked me if she is contacting him from beyond the grave, this is a reminder that he should make good on the promise to travel and enjoy the left-over money that was put away for her medical costs. She would have liked him to enjoy it. Also implied, is that she would have liked him to rededicate his life to something that he finds meaningful now that she has passed.

Third Operation

1. The cards were shuffled.
2. Cards dealt into twelve stacks for the twelve signs of the Zodiac. The King of Cups was found in stack six, which corresponds to Virgo.
3. Divine the proper stack and proceed as before. The cards drawn were:
   - King of Cups
   - Three of Pentacles
   - The Chariot.

Since the death of his wife, the husband has been occupying his mind by focusing on details (Virgo), especially to do with tidying and fixing up the house. He has been carefully giving away and selling items that he inherited from his wife that are no longer of use to him (Three of

Pentacles), especially noting the things that have been wanted by family members, such as her jewellery, clothes, kitchen appliances, sewing machine, books and some tools she used for hobbies; for some reason I think of leatherwork and embroidery. There were also many family pictures. At first this was enough to help with his grief, but as these small jobs come to a close, he finds his grief harder to balance, and his mind pulled in two directions (the Chariot). It is required that he take the reins of his life again and decide on what he would like to do with his future.

Fourth operation

1. The cards were shuffled.
2. The Significator was found and the following thirty-six cards arranged into the decans in a ring around it.

3. Reading:

Card 1. Aries first decan ruled by Mars: Seven of Cups.
Mars is a planet of action, movement, and divisions. To let go, he must move on, even though it may hurt. It would do him well to move house, and to find a way to redefine himself in relation to other people. He is now a widower. Finding a personal drive that moves him into a new emotional territory is vital. Aries is a sign for people getting things started for themselves. As this is a card of indulgences, he must be careful not to rely on luxuries, perhaps drinking to dull his emotions.

Card 2. Aries second decan ruled by the Sun: Ace of Cups.
The Sun symbolises optimism, the self in relation to others, and personal charm. Seeking new relationships is vital for the future. His wife would be happy for him to remarry one day. In any case, the rest of his life will find fulfilment by being defined in a new relationship. As we are in the sign of Aries, he must take the lead to make this happen.

Card 3. Aries third decan ruled by Venus: The Empress.
Venus is a planet of nurturing. His wife would have wanted him to take stock of the younger members of their family. Especially any pregnancies that come along (The Empress). There may be a family member who is pregnant at the moment, who he can be of service to. Otherwise, finding time to keep a garden or animals would help him.

 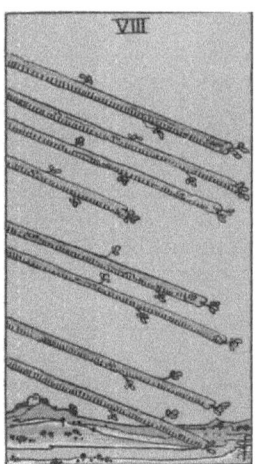 

Card 4. Taurus first decan ruled by Mercury: Six of Wands.
Taurus often has to do with the home. Mercury is communication. This is a card of celebrations. Making efforts to celebrate birthdays and achievements with family and friends will also help him in his grief, by maintaining his connection to others. Offering his home as a centre for some celebrations would be appreciated. Sending out birthday messages and other communications that previously his wife would have done is a good way to remember her.

Card 5. Taurus second decan ruled by the Moon: Eight of Wands.
The moon is a symbol of hidden things come to light. There are some hidden things on his wife's computer (Wands as electricity and Eight of

Wands as the internet, where messages are sent quickly) and especially her social media account that she would like him to know about. If he has access to her emails, there is something there of importance.

Card 6. Taurus third decan ruled by Saturn: King of Swords.
He should seek a connection with one or more other widowers in his circle of friends or family. This card suggests he knows an older man (Saturn and King) who has been through the death of his spouse. Though this person is not very emotional they have advice on how to process the death intellectually (Swords). As this is the sign of Taurus, some of the advice may be on how to make his home (Taurus) easier to live in and more his own now that his wife is gone.

Card 7. Gemini first decan ruled by Jupiter: The Lovers (also Gemini).
Jupiter is the expansion of boundaries and good fortune. Though she is gone in body, his late wife will always have a connection to him, through his ability to remember how she would have acted. She will be ever present for him in his memory. In answer to his question of whether or not she is contacting him beyond the grave: he can 'create' her as a spectral memory from his own mind and shared memories, and this is a powerful enough form of 'afterlife'. She wishes him good fortune in this.

Card 8. Gemini second decan ruled by Mars: Nine of Swords.
Mars in this situation is a malefic or difficult planet. There are, and will continue to be, unpleasant dreams. When someone passes, we often

dream that they are still alive, only to wake up and find them gone. This is very distressing. It is normal though, and after a time it will eventually pass.

Card 9. Gemini first decan ruled by the Sun: Temperance.
The Sun in relation to this card is 'good health'. She would like him to stay healthy for as long as possible. She hopes he will not drink heavily during his grief. It would be good for him to engage in fitness.

Card 10. Cancer first decan ruled by Venus: Five of Wands.
Cancer is a guarded but emotional sign who considers the way they appear to others. Despite his age, if he were to ever date again, there are possibilities in his age group. It will be hard at first, and may feel like a contest against many competitors. This suggests that he may be trying out some dating services at some point. If so, he must not get discouraged too early on, and should take it in a light-hearted way at first. He would gain some confidence by buying some new, more fashionable clothes.

Card 11. Cancer second decan ruled by Mercury: Four of Pentacles.
The husband had pulled out of a lot of community and social events, and had become very private (another trait of Cancer) during the wife's illness in order to conserve his energy (Pentacles). According to his wife, this habit is no longer serving him.

Card 12. Cancer third decan ruled by the Moon: Page of Wands.
The sign Cancer is ruled by the Moon, so here the message is positive. When the husband and wife met, they were very young. The wife felt during the last years that the youthful spirit that the husband had throughout the marriage had begun to fade. She would like him to remember the artistic, impulsive and spontaneous youth he once was and if he is now able to draw upon that part of his personality she hopes it would help him find a new lease of life.

Card 13. Leo first decan ruled by Saturn: Seven of Pentacles.
The wife wonders if the husband shouldn't take some leave from work and spend a little bit of their money in order to help his grief. He should be proud (Leo) of his efforts. It's now okay to take some time off. It looks like he has continued to work hard instead of facing his emotions. In this card Saturn suggests depression in relation to work.

Card 14. Leo second decan ruled by Jupiter: Judgement.
Despite his diligence in caring for his wife during the last years, the husband has unresolved guilt as to whether he did enough and in the right way. The wife would like him to rest his conscience knowing that he was a good and loving husband. Here the relation to the planet Jupiter (expansion) shows his reluctance, or his self-judgement getting in the way of moving on. He has lost some confidence about how others see him (Leo). He is judging himself.

Card 15. Leo third decan ruled by Mars: Nine of Pentacles.
Because the wife's illness took a turn for the worse, she didn't live as long as they expected, and because of his hard work, the husband is now in a secure financial position. He can be proud (Leo) of his past personal drive (Mars).

Card 16. Virgo first decan ruled by the Sun: Nine of Wands.
Feeling scuffed and tired from his efforts, the husband may feel that he himself 'lost the battle' he was fighting in response to the wife's illness. However, as the wife's diagnoses was terminal, the battle was one of caring for a dying person, not saving her life. He must therefore understand that, framed this way, the battle was won. In this case the Sun is his sense of self and Virgo is a concern over details or obsession. In relation to the Nine of Wands he has had a lot of nagging thoughts affecting his self-esteem. He went through an ordeal.

Card 17. Virgo second decan ruled by Venus: Six of Pentacles.
The wife suggests he might feel better if he were to make a small charitable donation to a cancer foundation. This way his efforts could help another in the same situation. Venus is a sign of aesthetics and Virgo is an intellectual sign concerned with detailed learning, so perhaps a donation to a music school, or a children's art programme would also suit him. Music and art are governed by Venus.

Card 18. Virgo third decan ruled by Mercury: Seven of Swords

In his grief there are obsessive thoughts over loss and what was taken from him. This is normal, and not exactly controllable, but it is also reinforced by habit. If he can start to refocus on things he still has, it will help recondition his mind towards finding the meaning he needs in order to keep living. Mercury is the planet of communication. He may benefit from a counselling session, or a talk with a close friend.

Card 19. Libra first decan ruled by Moon: Three of Swords.

He has been having difficulty socially (Libra) as a lot of his relationships have become framed by his loss. As a proud man, this is difficult for him. If he can find social activities that serve another purpose it might help. Perhaps something like a poker game. This would allow him to socialise without feeling like he is 'bringing everyone down'.

Card 20. Libra second decan ruled by Saturn: The Hermit.

There is a very understandable feeling of solitude and perhaps a loss of confidence in relating to the people around him. Saturn here is depression, and the Hermit is solitude.

Card 21. Libra third decan ruled by Jupiter: Five of Pentacles.

His wife would like him to know that he should not be too proud to accept the help of others. He doesn't want to be a burden, but accepting help would actually allow him closer connections to others (Libra). By reaching out, he will broaden his horizons (Jupiter).

 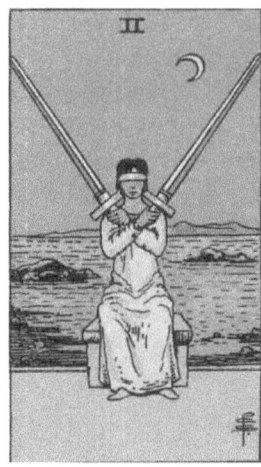 

Card 22. Scorpio first decan ruled by Mars: Justice.
In Tarot, the Justice card is not idealised. It usually means accepting a pragmatic victory over a perfect one. The husband might feel angry or resentful for his lot, but he can rest assured that he met his responsibilities, and that all people must deal with death at some point. The people around him judge him admirably. Scorpio is the probing of deep, often emotional, subjects and also death. Mars is personal drive, but also anger and aggressive emotions. He has some anger or difficult emotions about what has happened to him.

Card 23. Scorpio second decan ruled by the Sun: Two of Swords.
The husband has, for some time now, been hedging his bets. This allowed a kind of stability that was serving him and his wife. Now however this approach is preventing him from moving into the next stage of his life. He will need to make a move, and take a risk in order to get out of his 'holding pattern'. It might feel like he is turning over soil and bringing deep problems to the surface. This is the nature of Scorpio in relation to the Sun. A reassessment of his sense of self.

Card 24. Scorpio third decan ruled by Venus: Five of Swords.
Here is another card suggesting that he should accept his losses and gains for what they are rather than worrying about the past.

Venus suggests that he should go easier on himself. This card can often be an upset about what is 'unfair'. In this case this is not practical.

Card 25. Sagittarius first decan ruled by Mercury: Four of Swords.
Though he was once idealistic, he has at the moment lost touch with his higher order beliefs (Sagittarius). It would benefit him to meditate on what he now finds important. He might find it useful to read some books about spirituality, or philosophy (Mercury).

Card 26. Sagittarius second decan ruled by the Moon: The Hierophant.
This suggests a secret club (the Moon) based on higher order ideals (Sagittarius). Was his father or grandfather a freemason or something similar? Such a group may benefit him greatly at this point in his life. Otherwise getting back in touch with his spirituality, especially through group experiences.

Card 27. Sagittarius third decan ruled by Saturn: The Tower.
Around him, amongst people he grew up with (Saturn), there is a general mourning for the past and a feeling of instability around world events (the Tower). Though deeply unpleasant, his grief (Saturn) might actually allow him a more pragmatic view. The world is changing, not ending. There is as much to be excited about as there is to be afraid of.

Card 28. Capricorn first decan ruled by Jupiter: Page of Cups.
To change his fortune (Jupiter), he must allow himself a new relationship with his own emotions (Cups). Despite his life experience, at first he might feel like a clueless adolescent (a Page) for a time, especially when faced with the prospect of future fortune and future relationships. This is nevertheless the right way forward. Capricorn suggest he ought to take a pragmatic approach to life as a 'new beginner' for a while.

Card 29. Capricorn second decan ruled by Mars: The Star.
Mars is a great motivator, and the Star is a lofty goal. Capricorn is a sign of logistics and self-discipline. He would do well to chose one ongoing thing to improve in his life through daily practice. This will probably be some active activity (Mars). Some kind of exercise combined with some kind of meditation (the Star) done daily will have positive effects on the rest of his life.

Card 30. Capricorn third decan ruled by the Sun: Queen of Wands.
Though it might be a long time since he has felt attractive, he still has this power (the Sun). As discussed earlier, new smart clothes would go a long way towards improving his image. He is often attracted to feminine, glamorous women (Queen of Wands). If he can spice himself up, and keep this habit, he has more of a chance with this type of woman than he thinks, and that would in turn help his self-esteem. As Capricorn is concerned with logistics, he might organise a new

wardrobe so that he has an outfit for each day of the week. The discipline will help him.

Card 31. Aquarius first decan ruled by Venus: Queen of Swords.
If there is an authoritative woman in his town who runs things for the community (Aquarius), he would do well to befriend her and volunteer to help out with her plans. These types of people, I call 'hubs'. Befriending one person of this type will win one many friends by association. There may be an opportunity to flirt here also (Venus).

Card 32. Aquarius second decan ruled by Mercury: Wheel of Fortune.
Times are changing. A focus on the future, and an excitement about what is to come will help. He might look into new technology, and learn new ways to use the internet. He should keep an eye on the news regarding new trends.

Card 33. Aquarius third decan ruled by the Moon: The High Priestess.
Similarly, it is time to redress his spirituality, and try something he hasn't before. Perhaps Tarot is a way in. Other spiritual systems that fit the 'Aquarius' mode for Westerners are Buddhism, Yoga, Wicca, Magick, Spiritualism, meditation and mindfulness, etc. Trying a couple of these out in a group setting would certainly shake him up in the right direction. Even if he ultimately decides it's BS, he will learn to admire the energy that these people bring to their spiritual beliefs.

Card 34. Pisces first decan ruled by Saturn: Death.
Pisces is a sign of liminality, the blurry fringe between two spaces. Saturn is old age, and the Death card is big changes. After death comes new life, if one is able to let go of what went before. The querent is in a liminal period between his old life and his new life.

Card 35. Pisces second decan ruled by Jupiter: Queen of Cups.
To bring the reading back to his question, 'Is my wife communicating with me from beyond the grave?', Pisces is here the spiritual realm, Queen of Cups is his wife, and Jupiter is his fortune to come. The truth is, he will probably never have definitive proof that his wife is speaking to him from beyond the grave. The better question is, does accepting this belief, or just making space for the possibility, serve him and his future? The cards suggest that it is healthy, in this case, for him to 'talk' to his dead wife. Even if he only brings the wife back via his imagination, pondering what she may think about things can be helpful. She lives on in this way through him. The experience of talking to the dead is much more common than he may think, but our culture does not openly talk about it.

Card 36. Pisces third decan ruled by Mars: Nine of Cups.
As the last part of the zodiac, I am treating this as a conclusion card for this part of the reading. The husband will find a way through. The spirit of his wife is serving him well, motivating him towards a new brighter chapter of his life. With effort and a change in habits, he will become

a host, like the figure in the card, for a plethora of new relationships. This will give him a new lease on life and give him a sense of drive and control (Mars) over the future. Here Pisces is family connections, and identification with groups.

Fifth operation: final result

1. Shuffle, etc., as before.

2. **The Significator, King of Cups**, was found in the Yesod pile and was followed only by the **Nine of Pentacles**. This is how the wife will mostly be remembered by him. Just out of reach. In her own domain. Out in the garden by herself enjoying what she has grown and what is around her. Though she has passed away, many of the things she set in motion during her life continue on. There is a part of him that she will continue to dwell in.

My thoughts on this method

This type of reading, especially the thirty-six card spread of the fourth operation, is too long to keep the interest of all but the most dedicated of readers and querents. However, any single one of these operations is quite interesting as a stand-alone reading in its own right, and I recommend using one of these operations at a time.

This use of a Significator card has a very interesting effect on the reading by keeping it grounded to a central narrative. Every card is then a series of relationships back to the Significator. In past methods of Tarot reading, Significator cards were very common, but they have, since the second half of the twentieth century, fallen out of popular use.

Readings without Significators allow for a wider variety of narratives. Cards can go off and have 'subplots' and relationships away from the querent. In this way you might find that not using a Significator may be more interesting. This may be part of why the trend shifted over time.

Multiple decks

Another technique for a high information spread is to use two decks at once. An interesting result of this is that it allows for repeating cards, which significantly opens up the amount of interactions that the cards may have with each other. In a sense one has made the spread 'three dimensional'. That is to say, if for example there were two Emperor cards drawn, one may treat these as if they are the same card, living out two contexts, and with twice as many links to the other cards in the spread.

I propose a 'double Celtic Cross' spread, with two cards from two decks in each position:

REALLY ADVANCED TAROT READING 149

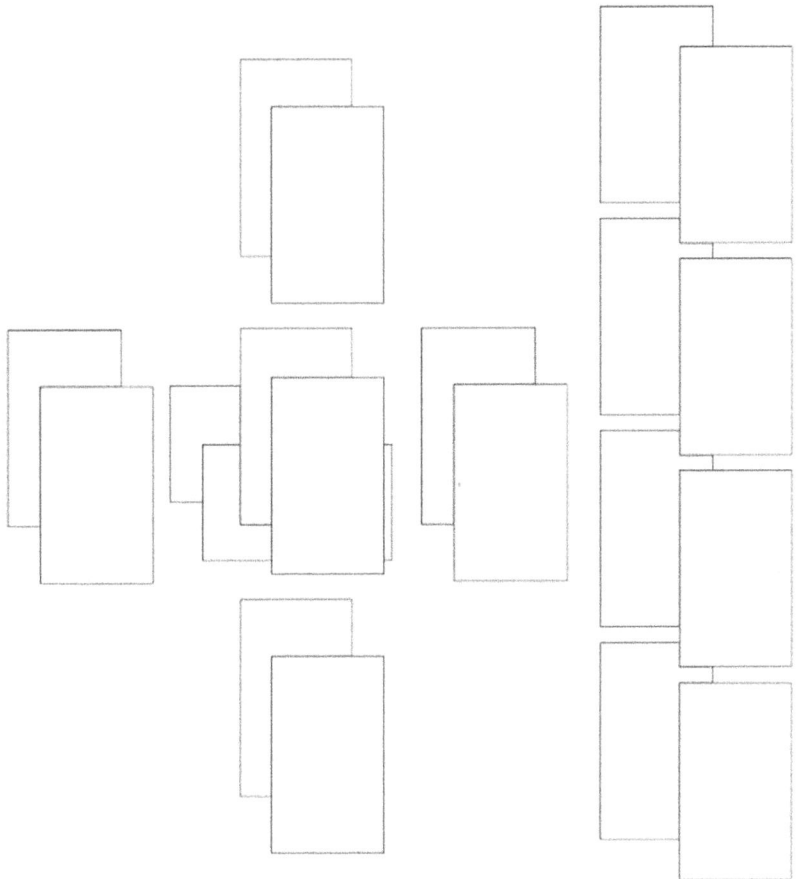

Two deck reading example

Question: Dear Tarot, give me a philosophical framework for analysing complex systems. (From the point of view of a philosophical global model, for instance Marxism, Postmodernism etc.)

Example. I have used the Rider Waite Smith deck for the first cards in each position and a Thoth deck for the second cards.

150 TAROT MAGIC FOR THE REALITY HACKER

The Cross

The middle top position, what you think is going on

Card one: The Tower
Card two: Ten of Cups (Satiety)

Many, if not most, important historical systems of philosophical thought have arisen as a result of rebellions against previous 'status quo' models. The Tower card suggests a deconstruction, or a reaction, to calamities, or corrupt modes of government, politics and education. Put simply, it is a mass 'loss of faith' in the establishment.

Since Postmodernism and its predecessors, especially Nieztsche and existentialism, we have been in a period of distrust of 'meta-narratives'. That is, the idea that any idealised story or framework will ever be complete enough to explain the world in all its complexity. In response, we have had a fracturing of philosophical systems, especially in academia. For instance, Jacques Derrida's idea of 'deconstructionism'. Here the meaning of any text exists only in relation to its reader. Therefore, the meaning of a text is affected by our changes in culture and language. In this way the text will change meaning over time, and any idea that the text has a core 'true' meaning is de-emphasised or abandoned: one has never finished analysing a text (Satiety).

With philosophical ideas like this, there was a loss of faith (the Tower) in any 'truest meaning' or 'capital T Truth'. The problem is that we have now lived in this rebellious philosophical space for so long, that we have reached a kind of reactionary saturation (Ten of Cups). A 'watery formlessness', devoid of any clarity.

If what you are rebelling against is a deconstruction of a deconstruction or a rebellion against a rebellion, then you end up with a crisis of loss of faith. If one is always tearing down structures without building new ones, then one is left with nowhere to live.

Nobody has enough time to deconstruct everything and instead consider every moving part of a system, in order to fully understand it. The only way out is a return to some kind of order. A 'big picture' philosophy.

The middle underneath position (which is crossing it) is an underlying reality

Card one: Strength
Card two: Knight of Swords

The next important philosophical systems will be led by philosophers who have a strength of will, a self-belief and a scholarly self-reliance in the face of a philosophical academy that has been trained to always play the critic, and not to make serious predictions, or come up with new ideas for how things could be.

The new philosopher will have to take risks and put skin in the game (Knight of Swords). They need to have a force of personality to withstand all the naysayers. There will need to be a return to faith. In response, the 'critical mob' will dig in their heels without providing a proper alternative.

The left position is the past

Card one: Five of Cups
Card two: Prince of Wands

The new philosophical system will have to use a 'glass half full' approach (Five of Cups), in light of the failure of past systems such as Age of Enlightenment values and scientism (the idea that scientific knowledge is the only worthy knowledge). The place to start is to concentrate on those of our values which have survived. Especially those belief systems and values that were never served by the Enlightenment, Marxism, Deconstructionism, Postmodernism etc.

A great place to start looking is with those indigenous cultures who have resisted colonisation with their faith intact and are getting things done that the dominant cultures have been unable to, such as reforming environmental law through a sacred relationship to land, or through animism, which is the attribution of personhood and personified relationships to things which other cultures consider 'lifeless'. For instance, considering a tree, hill or river to be an ancestor or a member of one's family. The Prince of Wands card suggests that there is an underlying creativity that has been overshadowed by cynicism and that this creativity, especially the marriage of the traditional with modern politics and technology, will be the basis for the new philosophical wave.

The top position is what is helping the situation

Card one: Page of Swords
Care two: Fortune (Wheel of Fortune).

Young thinkers (Pages of Swords), who are finding value in nearly forgotten traditional knowledge, will be the custodians of the new system. There are now young adults who were born after the year 2000. These people have grown up without twentieth-century values such as a belief that the future will either bring a utopia or a dystopia. This twentieth-century obsession came from biblical eschatology;

that we are either headed to the end of the world, or else a perfect world; Armageddon, followed by 'God's kingdom on Earth'.

Put simply, these youth have a different relationship to time (Wheel of Fortune) than their elders who were taught to walk through life facing a projected (and imaginary) future. In the face of the crisis of meaning and their relationship to time, these young people will be looking to the distant past to bring about a new philosophical age. At first these young philosophers will be criticised for their 'naivety', but in time they will produce real results and the cynical voices of their elders will fade.

The bottom position is what is not helping the situation

Card one: Ten of Pentacles
Card two: Nine of Wands (Strength)

To bring about the next philosophical age, we must let go of nineteenth- and twentieth-century economic theories, such as capitalism and Marxism (Pentacles). Ten is the number of completion, and therefore a new story must be started, even if it ultimately hearkens to something more ancient. Marxism for instance and its enemy, Neoliberalism, have both become tired. As reductionist systems that put economics before all, they have failed to fully consider human value systems and faith-driven behaviours, as they actually play out in the world.

Nine of Wands suggests a battle well fought, but because it is in the position 'not helping' this presents instead a 'sunken cost fallacy'. That is, the battle should have been abandoned long ago for something more useful regardless of how 'well fought' it was. Likewise, theories of political power have missed where most of the power is actually happening. This is obvious from the fact that they are failing to make accurate predictions. The new theories will come from places outside of the academy, places which were not valued in the past for their authority. Many of the twentieth-century philosophers will be online rather than in the academy.

The right position is the future

Card one: Two of Swords
Card two: Six of Swords (Science)

The new framework will value the unseen (Twos are Chokhmah, the ethereal realm of inspiration). There will be an acceptance of the fact that our drives for science and technology have not only been led by rationality but also by faith-based ideologies: specifically the idea that, given enough time, humans will unlock the secrets of the universe.

The new philosophy will first incorporate the intuitive and the irrational, and then apply science and logic as a filter, showing new things that can be done. It will be more pragmatic and less dogmatic. More playful and more beautiful (Tiferet), and less self-righteous.

This will involve a distrust of old models and a focus on fascinating, outlying information: a compromise between rationality, science, and intuition, belief and emotion. A kind of 'science of the heart' (Tiferet). A 'peace treaty' (Two of Swords) of sorts between the scientific method, the occult and the spiritual.

The Column

The bottom position of the column is what is motivating the querent

Card one: Nine of Pentacles
Card two: Three of Swords (Sorrow)

The new system needs to incorporate nature as a full complex system, full of entities with their own agency, valued along with the human. (The imagery of Nine of Pentacles has a feminine human figure in harmony with animals and plants.) It will be motivated by the sense of loss (Three of Swords), both at the collapsing faith in twentieth-century values and also environmental concerns.

For studying complex systems, look to 'cognitive systems' such as the human brain, the internet and biological systems in nature. It is especially important to consider situations where we have disrupted those systems. Ask 'how does a forest think' and 'what does a river want?'

The next position represents the behaviour of people around the querent in regard to the situation

Card one: The World
Card two: Four of Swords (Truce)

Politically, on the global scale, we must broaden our horizons (The World). The new philosophical framework must allow for more cultures than just those of 'the West'. Otherwise the only alternative is an existential battle the likes of which we have seen in both the Russo-Ukrainian war and the ongoing conflicts between Israel and Palestine.

With the looming loss of faith, in, for instance, the American dream, the European Union, NATO, and the United Nations, trying to incorporate all other cultures into 'the West' will result in failure and further wars. Globally, the new system must have an attitude of 'live and let live', therefore a truce (Four of Swords).

The second position from the top represents the hopes and/or fears of the querent

Card one: Two of Cups
Card two: Five of Swords (Defeat)

The hope lies in truce and union, a marriage of the traditional with the new, of science and faith (Two of Cups). Behind this hope is much emotion. The fear lies in discordance (the tense number five disrupts its predecessor, the stable number four). If no truce between systems is achieved between tradition and the new, and between cultures, then the 'winner' will win only a 'pyrrhic victory'.[67] That is a win which comes at such a cost that it leads to their own collapse.

The top position the column is the finality, or conclusion cards

Card one: King of Wands
Card two: Prince of Swords

For the new philosophy, look to the charmers, the leaders of the zeitgeist, the ideological daredevils, the performers, and those brave enough to brazenly stand behind their beliefs, even if these beliefs are in faith rather than rationality (King of Wands). In time, these 'performers of concepts' will achieve things that once seemed impossible. Out of this renewed faith will come a new intellectual system (Prince of Swords). These leaders and rebellious souls define the energy that will bring the next philosophical wave.

---

[67] Named after the general Pyrrhus of Epirus (319/318–272 BCE) and the pyrrhic victory that he suffered against the Romans during the Battle of Asculum in 279 BC.

Notes on this system

Though perhaps beyond the interests of many Tarot readers, hopefully I have shown that my double Celtic Cross method is capable of dealing with a very dense and difficult topic. I especially recommend it for political, philosophical and social questions. For the ordinary counselling of querents, it is almost certainly too much. This type of spread may also be especially useful for script writers or novelists, especially if they are writing intriguing stories with many characters.

The ultimate spread

After these enormous spreads, the logical endpoint seems to be to try a full seventy-eight card reading. This may take days to complete and is probably best performed by more than one reader as a team effort, or at least, by one reader and one scribe. I considered recording a seventy-eight card example reading here, but I feel that you already get the idea after the thirty-six card 'Fourth Operation' of the five-part MacGregor Mathers spread, and my twenty card 'double Celtic Cross' operation. It would have unnecessarily extended this section of the book by about twenty pages, making it laborious to read.

On the other hand, such a spread forces one to engage with every card, and will definitely flex your muscles! Think about the bragging rights and head-swelling powers of such an operation! You'd be the greatest Tarot reader of your generation![68]

---

[68] The world of the occult is full of these enormous spells and the braggadocios who claim to have completed them. I for one have included in this book the Shem HaMephorash, which took me about six weeks, and which I wasn't able to find a full detailed description of anywhere else. However, the most famous example of a really long spell is the Abramelin ritual, originally six months long, which only a few people in history claimed to have completed. Not even Crowley got all the way through it before deciding insead, to go on holiday! Later the ix- month version was found to be a mistranslation, as the ritual was originally intended to be **eighteen months long**. I guess all of those super-magicians will have to start over?

LEVEL 5

Bending the fabric of the universe with Tarot

Tarot spells

Until now, we have explored Tarot's use for divination or fortune telling. Another use for the cards discussed by some magicians is manifestation. This involves the manipulation of our perception of reality itself, in order to get you the things you want: a new car, a new place to live, a boyfriend, enormous biceps, etc.

In the narrative game of fortune telling, we try and score 'hits', determined by the querent's connection to our story. With spells, we are turning this game in on ourselves. This time, we score 'hits' via meaningful coincidences or 'synchronicities' that happen after the spell is cast.[69] Just as before, I am not asking you to believe in paranormal

---

[69] Synchronicity is a term coined by the psychologist Carl Jung to refer to the uncanny 'acausal' yet meaningful chance events that make a big impact on our sense of meaning. Some have found this term a little weaselly, preferring that Jung would have professed a belief in magic, something which he aways avoided. Despite this, and perhaps ironically, the term has become common amongst the New Age crowd who often use it precisely to mean magical events. These tend to be the same people who say things like 'everything happens for a reason'. I have found that if one treats this as if it is true then the results come, but equally that if one remains sceptical, the results disappear. Is that just a cognitive bias? Perhaps, but if so, it's a usable one.

effects, only to abide by the rules of the game for the duration of the experiment.

Allow a few days for the spell to have an effect, and keep a record, where all meaningful coincidences are counted. As we tend to revert to our habitual modes of thought, and because outlying information is often not easily remembered, the diary is important. A couple of times I have forgotten about the past effects of spells and have lapsed back into scepticism, because this is my habit. In reviewing my magic diary, I have been quite surprised by how much I forgot, and that there did appear to be some powerful results. In this way, a sceptical attitude can also produce a kind of cognitive blind spot, via misremembering and dismissal. So, record your results.

As with nearly everything in life, not everything works all the time. Some things turned out differently than my intentions, and in retrospect, though it was clear that I had achieved results, I sometimes ended up with a 'pancake' when I thought I was baking a 'scone'. The most outrageous of these events was when I was looking for a new flat to rent and having a very hard time of it.

I cast the hexagram rituals (from the Golden Dawn) to invoke Jupiter, for expansion of territory, and Venus for the home (in retrospect, Venus wasn't a good fit, and perhaps not Jupiter either). Instead of a new flat, a few hours later I was stunned by the loudest lightning strike I had ever heard. It sounded like it had hit the road just outside of my house.[70] There were multiple other thunderclaps also. Jupiter is of course the flinger of thunderbolts. About an hour later, an old school friend contacted me out of the blue to say that he was now becoming a woman (Venus) and that s/he now believed in magic, after previously being a sceptic. I certainly got results, but I didn't find a flat until later when I tried again, this time casting the Pentagram ritual for Earth (which governs the home), at the advice of another magician. This time it worked.

This type of occurrence is a common complaint amongst magicians. It is often suggested that one ask very carefully for what one wants. In any case, in this section I will explain how to do a manifesting operation. As always, I urge you to first play the game by its own rules and then only later apply scepticism to your results.

---

[70] That evening in the news, 12th December 2023, it was stated that my city had been struck by several lightning strikes.

Manifesting an intention

Clearing your headspace

This is all important, as one doesn't want perverse or involuntary thoughts acting as accidental ingredients in your spell. A huge part of the efficacy of magic is in the psychology. The best ways to clear a space of unintentional influences is to act out a ritual with your body. Remember the 'actions' done to songs when you were in kindergarten? Or those that fans of the Village People do along to the song YMCA? It's just like that.

These rituals can be complex actions and recitations of words, such as the common Lesser Ritual of the Pentagram, or simpler exercises such as imagining yourself covered in a sphere of white light that pushes away outside influences. It is common to then turn to each of the four cardinal directions and mime pushing away the unwanted 'energy'.

Many people meditate first. The easiest way I've found to do this is 'fourfold breath'. This is a beginner exercise influenced by Pranayama, also known as 'Breath Yoga':

- Breath in for four counts: 1,2,3,4
- Hold your breath for four counts: 1,2,3,4
- Breath out for four counts: 1,2,3,4
- Hold your breath for four counts: 1,2,3,4.

Continue for several minutes. I sometimes do this to a metronome set to sixty beats per minute. Some meditators practice longer and longer counts. In the past I have got up to fifteen counts for each stage at sixty BPM for each cycle. This was however very taxing, and I no longer find it necessary.

Another good thing to do is to tidy and vacuum your area before starting. Most people find this makes them feel better, and they can sit with a clearer head. As far as I am concerned, if nagging thoughts are equivalent to mini 'demons' then tidying up is equivalent to a mini exorcism. Don't knock it till you try it.

In my current personal practice I use both the Lesser Rituals of the Pentagram and the Lesser Rituals of the Hexagram, as prescribed by the Golden Dawn. Generally, I will use the banishing versions first to clear the space (and more importantly the head), and then the invoking versions to bring down fresh influencing 'energy',[71] uncorrupted by the worries of my day. I consider the effects of these to be purely psychological, and yet they work very well for me.

I also do the banishing rituals every night, and my sleep has improved a lot since doing this. My general anxiety levels have also gone down as a result. I have pretty severe lifelong insomnia, and very few other things have worked as well.[72]

Deciding on an intention

Write down what you would like to happen. As this is an exercise in intentionality, try and be precise. Remember that more unlikely things will be harder to produce via magic (or any other method). However, things that are too likely to happen will be too indistinguishable from pure chance to be considered 'hits'.

Instead of writing down your desire, such as 'I would like to drive a Ferrari', which may end up increasing your desire rather than making it happen, it is better to imagine what it would feel like when you already have the thing. Put it in present tense: 'I am speeding down the road in a Ferrari, and I can feel the acceleration pushing me back into the driver's seat.'[73] This helps to make the exercise more than a rational exercise, and generally magic (reality tunnel manipulation) works better when both the right side of the brain and the full attention are engaged. Similarly, 'I have paid my power bill and I feel relieved' is better than saying or writing 'I would like money to pay my power bill.'

It is also worth considering what type of intention is better for you. For instance if you are lonely, it is probably better for you (and the rest of us) to say something like, 'I am on a date with a person I like', than to try and force a particular person to date you against their will.[74]

---

[71] 'Energy' is one of those bothersome words, that means many different things. This confusion is often exploited by new age writers, practitioners and magicians. In this sense I pretty much mean the emotion that goes along with setting an intention.
[72] If this sounds good to you, and you want to jump in as quickly as possible (taking your own responsibility for what happens), you can find these rituals at the following links: https://hermeticorderoftheroundtable.angelfire.com/files/pentagram-rituals.html. https://hermeticorderoftheroundtable.angelfire.com/hexagram-rituals.html.
[73] This method is suggested by the writer Gordon White.
[74] The curse of magical coercion is in-built. Not only does it suck for the person charmed, but it's hardly an achievement to force someone to 'like' you, if that is possible at all. The desire will simply shift to 'it would be better if they liked me of their own volition'.

For one thing, the former is more likely to happen, and is therefore not such a hard ask. Try not to feed selfish power dynamics, which probably aren't going to be great for you or that person if you actually get what you asked for.

Some suggestions for intention:

> 'I have a new job, and I feel proud.'
> 'I have a clear head and am in good health.'
> 'My daughter is home safe.'
> 'Thousands of people are reading my book.'
> 'My grandfather's watch is returned, and I have it in my hand.'
> 'I have won the karate competition, and I can rest.'

Choose cards to help with your mission

Here are some suggestions:

- For a date: Two of Cups
- For reunion: Four of Wands
- For perseverance in a difficult time: Nine of Wands
- For courage to leave a difficult relationship: Eight of Cups
- To hold your own in a debate: Seven of Wands
- For perseverance in work or study: Eight of Pentacles together with the Star
- For artistic inspiration: Ace of Wands
- For travel: Two of Wands or The World
- For romance: The Lovers, and/or Two of Cups
- To overcome depression: Strength
- To overcome addiction, or to stick to a diet: Temperance
- For financial security: King or Queen of Pentacles
- To win a competition: Five of Swords
- For friendship: Three of Cups
- To win at gambling: Wheel of Fortune with King of Pentacles
- For safe and successful delivery: Eight of Wands
- For good weather: The Sun
- For the safety of family: Ten of Cups

Human desire is complex and perverse. Black magic of this type is an 'own goal' situation rather than a true win.

- To pass a test: Six of Wands
- To help with car troubles: The Chariot with Eight of Wands

Focusing your attention

After relaxing, imagine your intention in your head, or stare at what you have written down in meditation. Have the card or cards you have chosen out in front of you and focus on them. Continue this for several minutes. Give your full attention to the spell.

Close the spell

While some people repeat the banishing rituals, I generally just rouse myself from the meditation, clear my head, and then go on with my day. Many magicians will visualise the intention spreading out into the world. Some will wash their hands or try to fully empty their head so that the spell enacts on their subconscious rather than their intellect. I'll leave the specifics up to you. Magic is a very individual exercise.

Casting a net for opportunity, and being ready to dodge misfortune

Contrary to fictional depictions of magic, you will still need to try to act out your intention in the world in a way that your intention may happen. If for instance you are trying to win the lottery (which almost never works, as every ticket is already a spell of intention that someone else has cast in order to win), one still needs to buy a lottery ticket. If you are asking for a date, you need to ask some people out or at least make yourself available, for instance by joining a dating app. If you have asked for a new job, you will still need to apply for that job.

Magic can wake you up to notice opportunities as they happen, and to notice problems before they arise, but you still need to seize the opportunity and dodge the misfortune by your own efforts. Like Tarot divination, the most common way that magic works is by simply changing what you pay attention to, in order that you can act to get what you want.

This might seem mundane to those of you raised on Dungeons and Dragons, or Harry Potter novels, where magic is treated a bit like a 'cheat code' for reality; however, despite the lack of fireworks, this is still a useful result. As magic is a skillset, expect small results first. The fireballs can wait. While sometimes outrageously unlikely things will happen, you are more likely to notice that your magic plays out at first in quite ordinary ways. This is okay. Try and be happy with what you get.

'Flashing' magic

This method was given to me by my friend Ciaran MacCoinneach:

- Decide on an intention.
- Pull a card that matches to that intention.
- Stare at it until you can see it in your mind's eye.
- Then look at whatever you are trying to impact and imagine it 'superimposed' on the target. Think of it as like a 'prayer'.
- Hold the image in your head until you can't hold it anymore.
- Afterwards, clear your head and you wash yourself of it (some magicians will literally wash their hands).

Engaging cards in conversation

This is an exercise in animism: granting 'personhood' to things as a heuristic[75] towards understanding them or getting things done. In this case we will be using one or more cards to 'summon' that concept into our life towards meeting an aim or receiving guidance or understanding. One does this by engaging the card in conversation as if it were a person. This is really a creative exercise which is similar to those which are used to train actors who are learning roles.

For example, if the issue was the following:

'My five-year-old son is always getting in accidents, how do I help him achieve body awareness?'

- The Fool card is chosen in order to understand the causes of the son's clumsiness.
- The Page of Pentacles is chosen to understand how to train the son to be aware of his body.

---

[75] Heuristic: A mental shortcut or a 'good enough' solution that allows you to get a thing done.

Ask the Fool to explain to you how your son is perceiving or not perceiving his environment. Take note of all the ideas that come into your head. Try to see it from the Fool's perspective.

Ask the Page of Pentacles how he feels to be a learner who is learning to be aware of his own body and the things around him. Which parts are working, and which parts are challenging?

Other possible questions to ask the cards:

- 'What are "you" trying to get done in my life?'
- 'Who are "you" affecting in my life at the moment?'
- 'If I was this card how would I act?'
- 'If I were to act like this card, what would happen?'
- 'If the forces of these two cards were to come into contact with each other, how would they interact?'

Apply your imagination (or psychic sixth sense!) and take note of the answers, images and ideas that 'flash' or drift into your mind. Write them down, and revisit them in a week to see what has happened. Record any synchronicities.

Irreverent tarot experiments

While it is clear to you by now that I have spent a lot of time studying Tarot and other forms of magic according to their tradition, I often find it a shame that most magicians and diviners are so conservative in how they practise their arts. Some of the most interesting results can be had by altering the rules of the game, or applying Tarot or other practices in new ways. The following are some of my ideas to get you thinking outside of the box. My hope is however that you will also come up with some of your own.

Tarot soup

- Get a hat or large box.
- Throw as many decks as possible in there.
- Stir or shake them.
- Pull out 10–20 cards at random, regardless of which deck they came from, making sure to pull out some small and large ones (if they are different sizes).
- Read them. Any repeating cards or themes symbolise amplified story elements.

Television show readings
One thing I have enjoyed doing with Tarot is watching a TV series and pulling out cards to help explain what is about to happen in the plot, and what the different characters' motivations are. This can turn even the silliest drama into a stimulating narrative exercise that flexes your creative 'magical' mind 'muscles'. Games like this are excellent ways to practise the cards.

Try pulling out cards while:

- Reading a novel.
- Watching a political debate or interview.
- Before going to a party, and seeing if the people and events at the party match the cards.
- While sitting at a bar, in order to understand other people in the room and what they are experiencing.

Reduced decks

In this section I will explain Alejandro Jodorowsky's method for reading using two sets of only Major Arcana cards, and how to read using playing cards, which is effectively the same as reading with the Minor Arcana, only with one fewer court card per suit.[76]

Other reduced deck methods can be derived by separating the cards into piles by their type. These can then be shuffled and pulled from in order to ask specific questions such as 'What kind of people will I meet on my trip? or 'What can I expect from the earth and nature if I go camping?'

For instance, one may plan a holiday by separating one's deck into five piles:

- All the Wands cards representing inspiring activities.
- All the Cups cards representing emotional activities.
- All the Swords cards representing intellectual and learning activities.
- All the Pentacles cards representing natural activities, rest, food and drink.
- All the Major Arcana representing people and events to watch out for.

Another way to play is to separate the entire deck into cards you find positive and cards you find negative, and to then do a reading where

---

[76] I personally treat the Jack as a combination of the Knight and Page cards.

you pull an even number of each in order to ascertain the pros and cons of an undertaking or a situation. Alternatively, during a bad situation for which you want to see the positives, remove all the 'negative' cards from the deck to read for the 'bright side' of the situation. Or if you want to know what might go wrong, you might do the opposite. Other options are to read only with Court Cards, only with 'character' cards, only with 'event' cards, or only with cards of a certain suit.

The options are endless. Be inventive with your readings. It has been my experience that these types of games are where I've learned some of the most interesting things about Tarot and the meanings of the cards.

Reading with only the major arcana: The jodorowsky method

The controversial esoteric filmmaker and Tarot expert Alejandro Jodorowsky (b. 1929) has a method for Tarot reading that uses two sets of Major Arcana only. He insists on using only the Marseilles Tarot, but similar results can be achieved with whichever deck you have handy.

Preparation
You will need two decks, each with the twenty-two cards of the Major Arcana only.

- One deck is in order from zero, the Fool, to card twenty-one, the World.
- The other deck is shuffled.

The ordered deck shows you what you understand about yourself. From this, cards will be deliberately chosen. The shuffled deck tells you what you need to know that hasn't occurred to you. (Jodorowsky doesn't use reversals.)

Step 1
The querent asks a question. Then they directly choose three cards, knowing which ones they are choosing. Note down the numbers of each of these three cards. These three cards are the 'face value' of the story, representing the querent's understanding of a situation. These are in narrative order, so card one is the beginning of the story, and the last card is the conclusion. They aren't however in any exact timing and your reading can be flexible in this regard. If your querent is unfamiliar with the Tarot, then you may help them select the three cards. Be careful not

to impose your own idea of what is going on for the querent. Instead, let them form their own description.

Step 2
Shuffle the second deck of twenty-two cards. Pull out the cards that correspond to the chosen numbers in their order from the top. For example, if the original trumps were four (the Emperor), eleven (Force/Strength) and fifteen (Diable/the Devil), then one would pull out, face-down, the fourth, eleventh and fifteenth cards from the top. These will be the underlying reality of the story. Leave these face-down for now.

Step 3
Look through the remaining cards to see if the original three were left out. If so, put these to the side in the order they were chosen.

Step 4
Uncover each of the secondary cards in turn, and consider how they relate to the original three.

One interesting thing about this method is that it may run differently when reading for someone who is new to the Tarot, and is therefore choosing the cards without a good understanding of their meaning, compared with someone who has memorised the numbers of the Major Arcana and is consciously choosing their cards. I think this is a very good way to keep Tarot fresh for jaded experts.

Jodorowsky insists that the Marseilles Tarot is the 'correct' Tarot for divination. I have included one example with Marseilles, but as I don't hold Jodorowsky's bias, I will also include one example with the Rider Waite Smith deck.

Examples:

Marseilles deck

Question: A single woman in her late twenties has always fought hard for a career, but has a strong emotion that she wants to have kids and wants to know whether to go for kids now or put it off for later.

Card one, top left: VII The Chariot, chosen to represent her career and the things she can control. In the image is a royal driver, representing her agency. The two horses pulling the card are the two different things she wants. One is her career and the other motherhood. The questions is,

will they pull her life in the same direction or in two different directions and can she keep control over them both?

Card two, top middle: III The Empress, chosen to represent motherhood and fertility. The Empress, as consort of the Emperor, is responsible for the continuation of the family line.

Card three, top right: X The Wheel of Fortune, chosen to representing time cycles, birth and death, fortune, chance, fate and unknown things. The three figures represent order, disorder and mystery.

After pulling out the seventh, third and tenth cards from the top of the shuffled deck, I looked through to see if our first three cards were left over. In this case no repeating cards were chosen. We may therefore deduce that her fate has something else in store for her.

Card four, bottom left: XXI The World. This is a broadening of horizons. In the past the querent has been focused on small details and events, and has not taken the time to look at the bigger picture. Her work is involving, and requires a lot of thinking. While she finds it fulfilling, it makes her world look very small. Having a child (or even considering having one) will open up her viewpoint to a much wider perspective. She will have to start thinking in longer time scales. Having a child will not only alter her schedule, but also her family relationships, her friendships, her spiritual outlook, her concept of self in relation to others, and her relationship to time. In relation to the Chariot card, the World is an easing of control and an acceptance and exploration of a bigger picture on its own terms.

Card five, bottom middle: II The Popess (equivalent to the High Priestess). There are two ways of looking at this card that are both relevant to the situation. In one, the legend of Pope Joan, a woman disguises herself as a man and rises to the top role in the Vatican. This is possibly the way she has been feeling about her career in relation to motherhood. In comparison to her own mother, who probably had children at her age or younger, she has put her career first. While the querent is proud of her achievements, she feels a little bit like she has been wearing a costume, or 'drag' to get ahead. She has been feeling this more than the other women at her work, who have not been promoted as quickly, yet from her outside point of view it looks like they have retained more of their femininity.

The other meaning of the Popess or High Priestess is personal and spiritual knowledge gained through direct experience (in contrast with the more dogmatic Pope, or Hierophant, who tells us what to think as a group). Our querent is becoming aware that there is no true way to experience motherhood other than by becoming a mother. As she is used to controlling outcomes at her job and elsewhere in her life, this is an exciting but uneasy and 'risky' proposition. In relation to the Empress who has a role facing the outside world, perhaps that of the family, the Popess has an inward-facing perspective and spiritual experience. Our querent must factor in her spiritual and emotional world and not just how she appears to and in relation to others.

Card six, bottom right: XIX The Sun. In the whole deck, this is the card most directly referencing childhood, and is largely considered to be the most positive card. The querent will make a loving mother and will feel a lot of fulfilment in this role. Depicted in the card are two infants, traditionally considered to be a boy and a girl. While it is perhaps too 'on the nose' to say that she will have two children, even the raising of one child ends up putting one in the company of other children and parents. There is a wider 'World'-sized relationship to parenthood and children that is to be gained by becoming a parent, which cannot be experienced any other way.

The cards say to push for motherhood.

Example with the Rider Waite Smith deck

Question: A middle-aged man has let his romantic relationship and his career take over and doesn't have friends or people to talk to anymore. He doesn't feel 'rooted'. He wants to know how to make new connections with people outside of his job and relationship.

Card one, top left: IX The Hermit most reflects the solitude of the querent, so I have chosen it as the first card. In this position it reflects his past up to this moment. In this situation the meaning of the card is not complex, but it is worth mentioning that the querent has had his reasons until now for being isolated. Perhaps in the past his marriage provided more social engagement, but his partner has entered into a new quieter life stage, and he can no longer expect her to organise or motivate him to meet other people. This is a healthy decision, as we ought not to expect our romantic partners to solve all our problems, and we should expect that they will change over time.

Card two, top middle: VIII Strength. This was chosen to reflect his resolve. He has been a creature of habit, and has suffered from shyness or even social anxiety in the past. He has a certain trepidation in actively meeting people. He is not usually the type of person to walk up to and engage in conversation with a stranger.

Card three, top right: VI The Lovers. Though many people treat it as such, this card is not always romantic. In the deck we also have the Two of Cups which is more explicitly about romantic relationships, especially new ones. So here I am using the Lovers card to represent love in general and close friendships in particular. The Hermit card represents introspection. The Lovers card is union and deep connection to other people. The things the querent has learned in solitude will be amongst the things he will bring to a friendship and there will be an affirmation of his qualities in relation to any new close friend. This card was also chosen from an intuition that it is not so much acquaintances that our querent is seeking, but closer relationships.

In this case no cards were repeated.

Card four, bottom left: IV The Emperor. The querent is more capable that he may currently feel. This card, associated with Aries the ram, shows that he should exercise leadership in response to the solitude of the Hermit. Rather than joining a group, he might want to organise one, especially around a common interest. Sports, a poker game, a philosophy or book club, Dungeons and Dragons… Some kind of social activity. As the Emperor is only the Emperor in relation to his own territory, he ought to play the host at his own house. This will be appreciated and earn the respect of the group. Four is the number of stability, so he must be dependable.

Card five, bottom middle: XVII The Star. In relation to the card Strength, the Star says that personal resolve will come in the form of living up to an ideal. If the querent is religious, he should start a church or temple group. Perhaps he could join a society such as the Freemasons or the Lion's Club. If he is political, he should start a meet for his cause. This will help keep him on course. In Kabbalah, the Star is the path from Netzach to Yesod, denoting leadership and resolve, moving to communication and creation. The Star is also Aquarius, which has a humanitarian character.

Card six, bottom right: XI Justice. This furthers the idea of responsibility, especially in relation to the Lovers card. The querent should aim more for a responsible position in his community and amongst a group rather than worrying too much about one-to-one friendships in particular. In time this approach will be more sustainable and just as fulfilling. The Justice card is attributed to Libra, the scales. Libra is the sign of diplomacy. He would make a great mediator, referee, judge, coach, games coordinator or a role of this type.

Reading with playing cards

The history of fortune telling with playing cards is at least as old as Tarot reading (though the playing cards have changed over time), with fifty-two card decks or 'stripped' thirty-two card decks (with all the twos through to sixes removed) being common. There are numerous traditions and methods for reading with playing cards, but the easiest for Tarot readers is to treat the cards as a minors-only Tarot deck as follows:

- Clubs replace Wands
- Hearts replace Cups
- Spades replace Swords
- Diamonds replace Pentacles/Coins

Kings and Queens remain as they are, Jacks replace Knights, and are either combined with Pages or Pages are left out. Then the reading can be done just as a Tarot reading is done.

Playing card example reading

I will use six cards for this example. As playing cards are a 'low information' deck in comparison to Tarot, especially the Rider Waite Smith and Thoth decks, this reading will be simpler and less esoteric.

BENDING THE FABRIC OF THE UNIVERSE WITH TAROT

Question: A middle-aged woman has, through an acquaintance, found a job overseas. She is comfortable where she is and feels rooted. Should she take a risk and move overseas for her career?

Top left, the past, what is known: Jack of Hearts (equivalent to Knight of Cups). As it can be inferred from her question that the woman is either single or not in a committed relationship, the Jack, as an active 'doing' card, here refers to her desire to travel. The suit of hearts is emotions. So the card represents the cliche 'follow your heart'. As there is more movement in going overseas than there is in staying put, the card is suggesting a will to move.

Bottom left, an underlying reality: Queen of Diamonds (equivalent to Queen of Pentacles). Diamonds, as a place holder for Pentacles, represents time, money and resources. The Queen is a woman in an established role and home. While she has mentioned it in her question, she may be underestimating just how much she has become used to living where she does. A move will be more difficult than she may realise.

Top middle, the present, what is known: Three of Clubs (equivalent to Three of Wands). As with the Rider Waite Smith card, this denotes that a clear decision must be made and that this will come with a sacrifice. She should factor in what she is giving up as much as what she stands to gain if she doesn't want to regret the decision later.

Bottom middle, an underlying reality: Ace of Spades (equivalent to Ace of Swords). A new intellectual pursuit starting from scratch. Moving overseas will feel like a clean slate. It will, at first, be a 'fish out of water' situation. There is much excitement in this, but she must understand that it is not just like moving to a new town in her own country. It will be demanding on her mind. There will be many new problems to solve.

Top right, what is known: Jack of Clubs (equivalent to Knight of Wands). This shows a desire to have a role where she can express herself more fully. She would like a job that gives her more opportunities to be creative. It is very important to her to be in charge and able to act under her own power. There may be opportunities for this in the new country.

Bottom right, an underlying reality: Two of Hearts (equivalent to Two of Cups). As another Hearts card, this refers back to her first card. Part of her motivation, perhaps unconscious, for wanting to shift has been a long period of being single. She had become resigned to this for a long time. Moving to the new country will allow her to meet a new partner, her 'Jack of Hearts', and this may become more important to her in time than the job, which she was focusing on while single.

All in all, the move will be very challenging but if she wants a big change, a lot of excitement, a new life and an opportunity for new romance she should go for it. If she does, she ought to make a clean break from the things she is leaving behind, so that she doesn't feel tied down, or anxious about far-off things that she cannot control.

Choosing cards rather than shuffling

Peter J Carroll, the seminal chaos magic writer, has an interesting take on divination and magic in his classic occult book, *Liber Null & Psychonaut* (1987). To Carroll, the point of sortition (for instance the shuffling of cards), is not for the universe to line itself up in order to send you a message, but rather to allow the magician to 'get out of their own way' in order to speak to their own intuition, which he suggests is 'tapped in' to a creative property of the universe he calls 'Kia'.

Kia is a term invented by the magician and artist Austin Osman Spare to describe the proto-patterns of reality that slightly precede manifestation. In this model of reality, it is proposed that before each event, there is a moment where the universe has not yet decided to go one way or the other. Spare and Carroll's theory of magic is that all effective magical acts intent on manifestation are interventions at these 'decision points'. The magician's will then tries to nudge or persuade the universe into going one way instead of the other.

Carroll writes that therefore, the best type of sortition for divination is not true randomness, but instead, a partial deliberateness, where the goal is to 'wake up' the intuition. In his model the intuition, which interfaces more with the subconscious than the conscious, can be made aware of these 'Kia' or 'decision' moments.

He suggests first looking through the cards, then only slightly shuffling them, rather than fully randomising them. If he is right, then the predictive power of the Tarot reading ought to be increased. The idea being that a magician already has a latent power to predict the future with a certain degree of accuracy, and that the reason we normally can't do this is that our left brain or rational faculties get in the way.

In his classic book *The Occult* (1971), Colin Wilson put forward almost the same theory, calling it 'Faculty X'. This is his name for a person's latent ability to produce paranormal or psychic results. Wilson's study of reports of psychic phenomena suggested that these events happen more frequently when a person can relax into a receptive 'right-brained' type of flow state. By now I'm fairly sure that almost every experienced Tarot reader can relate to this idea, even if we cannot explain it.

Low information decks

By now, if you have tried out my suggestions you ought to be getting a feel for the differences between decks. As we have explored the concept of high information decks, it seems sensible to explore the opposite.

Oblique Strategies

This is a set of cards created by the music producer Brian Eno (b. 1948), the inventor of 'ambient music', and the German multimedia artist Peter Schmidt (1931–1980). Oblique Strategies is a deck of cards designed to act as creative prompts for musicians or artists, and especially to overcome writers' block and other similar creative ruts. It was first published in 1975 and has since undergone many revisions with decks ranging from 100 to 213 cards. The cards themselves each contain only a single phrase and are intended to promote lateral thinking. Since then, these decks and the concept have achieved a cult following.

Functionally, Oblique Strategies feels a bit like a minimalist, Westernised version of the I Ching,[77] and is an interesting example of what a minimalist or 'low information' divination deck can look like. While it was primarily intended to prompt the creation of art, especially music, I have found it also works perfectly well for divination.[78]

Some examples of the advice given by the cards are as follows:

- *Discover the recipes you are using and abandon them.*
- *Go outside. Shut the door.*
- *Honor thy error as a hidden intention.*
- *Remove ambiguities and convert to specifics.*
- *Define an area as 'safe' and use it as an anchor.*
- *What mistakes did you make last time?*
- *Imagine the piece as a set of disconnected events.*
- *Make an exhaustive list of everything you might do and do the last thing on the list.*
- *Take away the elements in order of apparent non-importance.*

Example reading

Question: A woman in her late twenties is finally a successful musician. She is finding it a grind since going professional. How should she make her music career fun again?

Card one: Be less critical more often.
Card two: Don't break the silence.
Card three: Question the heroic approach.

Answer: By this I can advise her to take a more playful approach to her music. She must take time to put away the inner critic and not expect perfection every time she makes a piece of music. The ultimate

---

[77] The three-thousand-year-old Chinese divinatory book, and an early form of both binary code and hypertext.
[78] An online, self-shuffling, version can be found here: http://stoney.sb.org/eno/oblique.html.

purpose of music is to entertain and move people, rather than to play perfectly. It is likely that her heroes are people who took risks with their art, for the sake of saying something new. What she might not be reminding herself often enough is that they were willing to fail, and probably did fail more often than we realise, looking back only at their successes.

The second piece of advice is that the flow of inspiration can often become jammed by trying to fill a space with too many ideas. As an exercise for the next while, she should try playing less, and see if this, by omission, creates a space whereby a simple idea can start to make sense, rather than one idea being interrupted by the next.

The final advice is similar to the first. She ought to serve the piece of art rather than chasing accolades. The latter will break the focus that can make each piece as good as it can be. An alternative to being 'heroic' is to be playful. Young children in their purest moments don't play in order to receive awards, accolades and paycheques. Instead, they explore and then share their exploration: for instance, the mashing of crayons onto paper for the pure sensation and glut of colour. Only after the act of creation (which always also involves some kind of destruction) do they judge whether they like the effect. Implicit in this is the idea that the process is worthy in itself, as much as the destination or finished product. Stop worrying about what the art is 'for', or whether it is 'good', until the art is deemed finished.

My minimalist deck

Inspired by Oblique Strategies and Tarot, and in the spirit of fun, I have created my own minimalist 'deck' for divination. The idea is to reduce the information on the cards to the absolute minimum required for divination.

In order to achieve a balance, I have opted for seventy cards, each with a dichotomy, amounting to a total of one hundred and forty terms. One can print these out with one term on the top half of the card and its opposite on the bottom half, and then shuffle them like one shuffles a Tarot deck when using reversals. Alternatively, one can use a random number generator for one to seventy, and then flip a coin, with heads being the positive attribute and tails being the negative. My deck is designed specifically to understand the motivations of people around you, and has a bit of a black humour flavour.

The Reality Hacker's Deck:

1. Rose-coloured spectacles/Waiting for the world to end
2. The imp of the perverse/The master of restraint
3. Ennui/Lust for life
4. Frisson/Visceral disgust
5. Faithful/unfaithful
6. Femme Fatale/Ingenue
7. The individual/the group
8. Pervert/Prude
9. Gambler/Miser
10. Comedian/Sourpuss
11. Know-it-all/Dunce
12. Catharsis/repression
13. Scoundrel/Goody-two-shoes
14. The romantic/The friend-zoner
15. Addict/Teetotaller
16. Head in the clouds/Head in the sand
17. False certainty/Over-caution
18. Pregnancy/Barren
19. Children/Elderly
20. Ambition/Procrastination
21. Thrill-seeker/ Homebody
22. Misanthrope/People person
23. Co-dependency/Free spirit
24. Nuance/Black and White
25. Heaven/Hell
26. The John/The whore
27. Minimalist/Maximalist
28. The scholar/The numbskull
29. The zealot/The faithless
30. The conspiracy theorist/The mainstreamer
31. Escapist fantasy/The sceptic
32. Rich/Poor
33. Butthurt/Water off a duck's back
34. The status-seeker/Nonchalant
35. The prophet/The false prophet
36. Burnout/Hyperactivity
37. Familiar territory/Exploration
38. Lost cause/Diamond in the rough

39. Hiding in plain sight/The man behind the curtain
40. Sacred/Profane
41. Godfather/Henchman
42. Altruism/Self-interest
43. The Idealist/The Pragmatist
44. Order/Chaos
45. Neurotic/Down to earth
46. Tabula rasa/Hereditary
47. The student/The master
48. Nerd/Popular
49. Right place, right time/Wrong place, wrong time
50. Right place, wrong time/Wrong place, right time
51. The conservative/The radical
52. Good in theory/Good in practice
53. Smart person trap/Pool of wisdom
54. Faux pas/Social grace
55. Contrarian/People-pleaser
56. Responsibility/Excuses
57. Learned helplessness/Daredevil
58. Sunken cost fallacy/Throwing the baby out with the bathwater
59. In-crowd/Black sheep
60. Onto a good thing/Barking up the wrong tree
61. Things you know you know/Things you don't know that you don't know
62. Things you know you don't know/Things you don't know you know
63. Mary Sue/Milquetoast
64. Plain Jane/Belle of the ball
65. White knight/Beast
66. The gossip/The confidante
67. Prowess/Fluke
68. Windfall/Bad luck
69. Good goes bad/Bad goes good
70. Frenemy/Friendly competition

Example reading with five cards:

Question: A twelve-year-old boy has written a play. He thinks it is brilliant, and he can't understand why he can't get the other kids to agree to do his play with him.

Card One: The student

The boy needs to understand that, despite his ambition, he is not an expert or a teacher, but merely a student. The other kids at school have been conditioned to value the authority of teachers, and will generally ignore or undermine the authority of a fellow student. However, if he was able to convince a drama teacher to put on his play, he might stand a chance. He will have to be willing to rewrite parts of the play in order that the teacher can make it work for the school. This is a remote chance, as teachers are busy people. However, it is worth a try, and better than going to the other students directly.

Card Two: Barking up the wrong tree

Writing a play is an admirable ambition. His fellow students are not mature however, and not as forgiving as his parents. They will often take a success and invert it as a failure. This is an unfortunate fact of being a twelve-year-old amongst peers the same age. If he were a university student, the reception might be very different.

Card Three: Nerd

Rightly or wrongly, the other students have taken his approach to the play as a slight to their own egos. To convince someone of anything, it is important to first present to them what is in it for them. One gets the impression that he instead blew his own trumpet, causing the other students to react by making fun of him, to 'take him down a few pegs'. Unfortunately, one sometimes only gets one chance to make an impression which each person.

Card Four: Black sheep

Writing a play at twelve is unusual, and I admire his gumption. It might take a while before he finds 'his people'. For the time being, he is going to have to stick it out at school amongst kids who think very differently to him. It is important that he accepts this, rather than becoming overly resentful. It is better to adapt his attitude to get by, until he finds a more convincing way to get what he wants. In the meantime, I recommend he takes as role models, successful people who started as outcasts. Each of these people found their power of charm. When he finds his charm, doors will start to open for him.

Card Five: Right place, wrong time
Putting a play on at school is not completely out of the question, but he has jumped the gun. If he is willing to continue to refine his play, and his manners, in a few years' time, he may find a way to get it put on.

Have a go with my deck or try making your own. How do you find it works in comparison to Tarot? The fact that divination seems to work with nearly any system that has had a bit of thought put into it, suggests to me that by far the most important part of the equation is the human ability to 'join the dots' into a story; the specifics of the system, while still important, are secondary. Though complex systems within divination and magic bring detail to the results, many magicians and Tarot readers get overly bogged down by what they think is or isn't 'the right way'. My explorations and tests suggest to me that making it work is the most important part. There is no fixed right or wrong way to do magic or fortune telling. There are only better or worse results.

Tarot reading without cards

Just as one can apply a Tarot reading to a situation, one can analyse a situation back to a selection of Tarot cards. This can be an interesting practice exercise, that can improve one's understanding of the cards. For the dedicated Tarot readers who have memorised all the card meanings, the symbols will almost certainly start to have their effect on the way you perceive the world. This is akin to learning how to read and write, and being able to understand the meanings of the words on signs in a city around you. The symbols become a way to orient yourself. Likewise, the cards will start to jump out at you in the way events unfold, in the way people behave, and in the way stories are told.

When something noteworthy or unusual happens to you ask, 'Which card does this most align with?' When you are listening to a noteworthy news broadcast, consider how it would look in the form of a spread of cards.

For example, here I have taken the famous 'Spanish Armada' speech given by Queen Elizabeth I to her British troops at Tilbury in 1588:

> *I am come amongst you, as you see, at this time, not for my recreation and disport, but being resolved, in the midst and heat of the battle, to live and die amongst you all; to lay down for my God, and for my kingdom, and my people, my honour and my blood, even in the dust. I know I have the body but of*

a weak and feeble woman; but I have the heart and stomach of a king, and of a king of England too, and think foul scorn that Parma or Spain, or any prince of Europe, should dare to invade the borders of my realm: To which rather than any dishonour shall grow by me, I myself will take up arms, I myself will be your general, judge, and rewarder of every one of your virtues in the field.

As a significator, I attribute to Elizabeth I the card **Queen of Wands**. This is a person who finds power in a feminine role, and who finds a way to use this power in a way which isn't available to a person playing a masculine role. In Elizabeth's case, this was an act of inversion; turning the role of woman from a subservient or passive power into an active 'masculine' one.

The first line, *'I am come amongst you…'*, invokes the **Judgement** card. She appeals to the soldiers to find her worthy as a leader, thus seeking their trust. Before she issues orders to them, she first humbles herself. In the Judgement card there is an appeal to the past. In this case the men have traditionally served a king, and they are called upon to fight for their ancestral land. In the coming war is the threat of **Death**. The 'Judgement card' is about to be handed from the Queen to the soldiers to be tested on the field and on the seas.

'[T]o lay down for my God, and for my kingdom, and my people, my honour and my blood, even in the dust': this is an appeal to religion and the Bible passage 'Ashes to ashes, dust to dust', thus invoking the **Hierophant** card. As the first Queen of the Church of England, Elizabeth was head of the state religion as well as the state.

As an undercurrent, she is also invoking the **High Priestess** card as she, the 'Virgin Queen', was often compared to the Virgin Mary. This is a very **Queen of Wands** power move, one that could not be undertaken by a man. This was a powerful part of Elizabeth's propaganda, and her mystique.

'I know I have the body but of a weak and feeble woman; but I have the heart and stomach of a king, and of a king of England too, and think foul scorn that Parma or Spain, or any prince of Europe, should dare to invade the borders of my realm.' In an about turn, she transforms herself immediately with her words, and dons the role of **King of Swords**: powerful masculine military power with a sword ready to smite.

'I myself will take up arms, I myself will be your general, judge, and rewarder of every one of your virtues in the field.' The soldiers themselves, who she is speaking to, are now **Knights of Swords.**

Now the judgement card which was originally projected onto her is turned on each and every soldier and she 'wears' instead the card **Justice**. She has declared herself worthy and she becomes the judge of her men. The Spanish have also been judged, and the verdict is **Death**. If successful (and she was), she will perhaps rise to become the **Emperor**. It is under the reign of Elizabeth I that the British Empire was founded, and over time it grew to become the largest Empire in all of human history.

Using Artificial Intelligence for divination

Interpretation into cards

During the writing of this book (2023 and 2024), we entered into the age of mainstream Artificial Intelligence, with AI technology going from a tool behind the scenes, to a tool available to everyone with a computer. This caused me to ask the question, 'How good is AI at generating a Tarot reading?'

Using ChatGPT (Chat Generative Pre-trained Transformer), a popular chatbot developed by OpenAI and launched on 30 November 2022, I generated the following reading. As ChatGPT refuses to do 'real' predictions, probably for legal reasons, I had to frame the question in terms of fiction. I guess this raises the ethical dilemma, 'is it okay to lie to robots?'[79]

Question: 'I'm writing a novel which is an alternative history. Please give me an imaginary Tarot card reading based on the question: What will be the outcome of the 2023 New Zealand General Election?'

ChatGPT answer:

'Of course! Here's an imaginary Tarot card reading for your alternative history novel:

Question: What will be the outcome of the 2023 New Zealand General Election in this alternative history?

Card 1: The Tower (Reversed)

In this alternative reality, The Tower card appears reversed, signifying a departure from the usual chaos and upheaval associated with this card.

---

[79] The answer is yes.

It suggests that the election in 2023 will not bring about a sudden and dramatic change or upheaval, but rather a sense of stability and continuity. The people of New Zealand may have chosen a path of gradual reform and evolution instead of a radical transformation.

Card 2: The Hierophant

The Hierophant represents tradition, institutions, and established systems. In this context, it suggests that the outcome of the 2023 election may result in a government that prioritizes the preservation of New Zealand's cultural and political traditions. There could be a focus on unity, education, and adherence to existing norms and values.

Card 3: The Wheel of Fortune

The Wheel of Fortune symbolises cycles and change. In this scenario, it suggests that the outcome of the election will bring about a new phase in New Zealand's political landscape. While the previous government may have focused on stability, the Wheel of Fortune implies that change is inevitable. The people have decided to steer the course of the nation in a new direction, embracing a sense of optimism and adaptability.

Overall Interpretation

In this alternative history, the 2023 New Zealand General Election appears to be a turning point without the dramatic upheaval usually associated with such events. The reversed Tower card indicates stability, the Hierophant suggests respect for tradition, and the Wheel of Fortune hints at a new phase in the nation's journey. Perhaps the election results in a government that seeks to balance tradition with progress, offering the people a sense of hope for the future.'

What do you think? Can robots tell fortunes? If I may play the harsh critic, I think the AI has given us a reading that is so general that it could be true of nearly every election and I would therefore rate this reading as somewhat of a 'miss'.

I'll give it a second chance with a bit of a prod:

Question: 'This reading is too general. Please give the same reading again and be more specific.'

ChatGPT answer:

'Card 1: The Chariot

In this alternative reality, The Chariot card emerges, symbolizing determination, control, and a clear path forward. It suggests that the 2023 election will result in a decisive victory for a party or coalition that exhibits strong leadership and a clear vision for the country. The people have rallied behind a charismatic and goal-oriented leader.

Card 2: The High Priestess (Reversed)

The High Priestess reversed signifies an openness to unconventional ideas and a departure from traditional wisdom. In this context, it suggests that the election outcome will challenge established norms and institutions. The winning party may implement innovative policies and embrace a more open and transparent approach to governance.

Card 3: The Ten of Pentacles

The Ten of Pentacles represents wealth, stability, and prosperity. In this scenario, it indicates that the 2023 election outcome will lead to economic growth and financial stability for New Zealand. The government elected during this period is likely to prioritize economic development, job creation, and the well-being of its citizens.

Overall Interpretation:

In this alternative history, the 2023 New Zealand General Election is predicted to bring about a resolute leader with a clear agenda for the nation. This leader will challenge traditional beliefs and practices, promoting innovation and transparency. The Ten of Pentacles suggests that under this government, New Zealand will experience economic prosperity and stability, benefiting its citizens in various ways.'

This is perhaps a little better, but notice how it fails to mention any parties or make a firm prediction. I'd still class this as a bad reading. I therefore asked one final question.

Question: 'Based on this last reading, which New Zealand political party will win?'

ChatGPT answer:

'I'm sorry for any confusion, but Tarot card readings are not a reliable or accurate means of predicting specific real-world political outcomes or determining which political party will win an election. The reading I provided is entirely fictional and based on a fictional scenario for your alternative history novel.

In reality, election outcomes are influenced by a complex interplay of factors such as political campaigns, voter sentiment, candidate performance, and many other variables. To know which political party will win the 2023 New Zealand

General Election, you would need to follow real-world political developments, polls, and election results.'

Oh well, it was worth a try. For the time being, human Tarot readers reign supreme.

In the end the National Party, our mainstream, centre-right, mildly conservative party won the election with 38.06% of the vote, against our centre-left party Labour, who received 26.91%. Christopher Luxon of the National Party was elected to become our new Prime Minister. National formed a coalition with two other minor right-wing parties, the ACT[80] party and New Zealand First.

The government's early statements and decisions have be plagued by criticism and protests. I think the ChatGPT reading was a miss.

Divination by radio surfing

Another method for a cardless reading is as follows. Come up with a question. Then flip channels on a radio or TV. Treat the images, words or song lyrics that come up as the reading. I did this reading using my car radio.

Question: What is in store for Ari's life in 2024 (the year after the writing of this book)?

As I flipped the stations on the radio of my car, using the programmed buttons, I heard the following snippets of interviews, announcements and song lyrics.

Channel One: Radio New Zealand: *'So it became your dream, perhaps it was your father's dream as well?'*

Channel Two: Concert FM: *'Definitely brought up memories of my playing it.'*

Channel Three: The Edge FM: *'It's 10:35 and I can feel your arms around me'.* (The song '10:35' by Tiësto feat. Tate McRae.)[81]

Channel Four: RDU FM: *'A riddle'*, *'Our favourite study spots'*

---

[80] ACT stands for the Association of Consumers and Taxpayers.
[81] Despite being unaware of this song before the reading, it has often been stuck in my head ever since. Consider this a potential side-effect to this method of reading.

Channel Five: Magic FM: *'Monday Monday, so good to me... Monday morning gave me no warning of what was to be'*. (The song Monday Monday by the Mamas and the Papas.)

Interpretation

One: I associate the concept of life-goal type dreams with **The Star**. So I would expect a year filled with goal-orientated effort, and perhaps one which brings me closer to my father as mentioned.

Two: I'm professional musician so it's inevitable that I'll be playing music in 2024. The card most associated with memories and nostalgia is the **Six of Cups**. I often organise and play tribute shows of music such as the Beatles, David Bowie, Black Sabbath, Tom Waits and others, so I would expect that I'll be performing one of these nostalgia shows in 2024.

Three: A love song implying new love. As I am single during the writing of this book, I interpret this as **Two of Cups**. Some dating with a strong connection made, probably leading to a new relationship seems likely.

Four: *'A riddle'*. Riddles are represented in Tarot by the Sphinx. The Sphinx appears on the **Wheel of Fortune** and **the Chariot** cards. One would expect then, a change in fortune and a concerted and controlled effort to take control of it. The second phrase, *'Our favourite study spots'*, suggests much more writing, which I have been doing primarily at cafes this year and it has become one of my favourite things to do with my time.

Five: Monday is the day of **the Moon**. So I interpret the Moon card. The song is by the Mamas and the Papas, so I would take that as uncovering knowledge and mystery with, and in relation to, my parents. This points to the first bit of information, 'perhaps it was your father's dream as well?' The Moon would suggest spiritual searching and the Star would suggest personal growth. My Mother had a particularly rough time in 2023, and this suggests to me that 2024 will be a time of introspection and healing for her, which will have a personal effect on me also.

What do you think? A worthy alternative to a Tarot reading or an exercise in temporary madness? I'll leave it up to you to decide.

CONCLUSION

The twenty-first century occult revival

A survey of the myriad subjects and practices contained within the umbrella term 'the occult' leads us to many contradictions. On the one hand, especially in America, the term is often wielded as an antagonist to dogma, and especially organised religion. Alchemical symbols, reinterpreted as atheistic or 'satanic' emblems are paraded on T-shirts or tattooed on visible body-parts like talismans to ward off perceived, or actual, intolerance and bigotry. While the inversion of values can be a practical stepping-stone from which to leap out of restrictive or abusive parts of society, it doesn't ultimately set one free. For one thing, in many cases, these symbols and images were originally created by pious Christians, Jews and Muslims. A case in point is the inverted cross, a Catholic symbol for St Peter.

Another battle of our age lies between scientific materialism and spirituality. Both the occult and the New Age sections of the bookstore are rife with terms such as 'etheric energy'[82] and 'the astral plane'.[83] It seems to be almost entirely forgotten that these terms were once coined for 'scientific' models of the past.[84] Despite this history, spiritual believers now use these terms for their own idealist cosmologies in opposition to materialism.[85]

The common thread amongst occultists and new-agers is an attempt to create something new, by using something old. I admire this approach, if only the old was better understood on its own terms and the new was actually new.

This has been the purpose of these two books, *Tarot for Sceptics* and *Tarot: Magical Results for the Reality Hacker*. These are my attempts to teach Tarot with reference to its history, while also modifying it into a tool that has use in the future.

Tarot as a magical framework

Despite its sometimes cobbled-together nature, I have hopefully shown how useful Tarot has been as a scaffold for magical principles and techniques to the magicians of the past. Implicit in my writing of these books is the question, 'Is Tarot the right scaffold for the magical systems of the future?' Despite the dedication of years of my life to the study of Tarot and the writing of these books, I'm equally excited by the idea of a new system of magic for the twenty-first century, built on something else. It is therefore my wish that magicians take the lessons of my books and use them to create something new, hopefully as profound and useful as traditional Tarot. This may look like a modified

---

[82] Ether or aether was a substance and medium which was proposed by natural philosophers of the early scientific revolution to explain how light travelled from one place to another. It has been superseded in science by field theory. The word comes from the mythical substance that the Greek gods were said to breathe, and Aether was likewise a deity in his own right. Plato used the term as a proposed fifth element or 'quintessence'. Isaac Newton later popularised the idea by introducing it into his optical theories.

[83] The astral plane was part of the astrological model of reality. Put simply, it was the realm of the heavens through which the planets and constellations worked their effects on human beings. It also overlaps with the realm of dream and the sensory, especially visual, imagination. These were later called the 'imaginal' by the philosopher Henry Corbin (93–1978).

[84] Perhaps the term 'proto-scientific' is better. In any case they were part of an older model of the universe, and were deemed (scientifically) defunct as we developed later models.

[85] Idealism is the idea that the world of concepts, spirit or 'mind' are more real than matter and that matter derives from this rather than everything deriving from matter.

version of Tarot, or it may look like something completely new to all but the most studied magicians.

Where will Tarot head in the future?

I believe that world society is at the beginning of a major shift in thinking, the likes of which was last seen in the scientific revolution of the late sixteenth century and the Enlightenment of the seventeenth and eighteenth centuries. Though the systems of the past will be wielded as tools to inform what is coming next, a post materialist, post-reductionist age that reevaluates right-brain thinking and creativity in science and society, I don't think that Tarot and occultism will survive unchanged. I therefore urge my readers to first learn from the past, to strive for results, and then to start hacking in the spirit of progress. This is the difficult challenge for the future: how to address the novel problems of our age, while also reconnecting with a past that many of us feel cut off from, due to numerous factors such as the Enlightenment, organised religion, economics and secularisation.

In this future, I can imagine post-Tarot divination both in the form of decks and in the utilisation of computers and AI. These new divination systems ought to repurpose and reconfigure the symbol set and associations that have been used by the occult and Tarot for centuries. These adaptions will undoubtably split the already fragmented occult community into occult conservatives and occult progressives. May those who achieve the best and most interesting results win!

Slaughtering the sacred cow

While I have offered new ways to divine with cards in this book, I also want to provoke readers towards their own reading styles, so that they go further than I have. (Even failures are interesting to me!)

What would a divination system look like built on a totally different system than the four classical elements? Perhaps instead of Fire, Water, Air and Earth, we might have Intention, Emotion, Concept and Matter. Perhaps instead of 'masculine' and 'feminine', we might also add the third and fourth qualities, 'hermaphrodite' and 'androgyne'.[86]

---

[86] Where masculine is active, and feminine is receptive or passive, hermaphrodite is both working as a system (or in tension) and androgyne is the absence of either.

Instead of Kings, Queens, Knights and Pages we might have Instigators, Recipients, Theoreticians and Materialisers? Perhaps we may alter the numerology, with six or seven suits rather than four?[87]

What would an astrological system look like that reflected the cosmic astronomy of modern science rather than the solar astronomy of the Renaissance? These ideas are not nearly as difficult to have as people make out, if only people would be more playful.

Consider this a rallying call.[88]

> *'Every profession has their own bullshit, but Wizards have the best bullshit.'*
>
> —The Wizard of New Zealand.[89]

---

[87] There are rare Tarot decks and playing cards with six suits rather than four.
[88] Let me know how you go: arifreeman@gmail.com.
[89] 25 March 2024, retrieved from the Wizard himself by phone call.

APPENDICES

Mythology

This section serves as a reference for the card meanings given in the first book, *Tarot for Sceptics*. As I have given associations to gods and other spirits for each card, in this appendix I give a description of the relevant deities. While this information is extra, I have found it valuable in understanding the symbolism of the cards, and also in understanding their use as an oracle.

Greco-Roman gods

Aeon

Originally meaning 'life', 'vital force' or 'generation', an aeon eventually came to mean a period of time. In Greek it literally means 'one hundred years'. Plato used the word aeon to mean the eternal world of ideas, which he thought lay 'behind' the perceived world, as demonstrated in his allegory of the cave.

In Gnosticism, an aeon is a type of deity, with the highest concept being Aion Teleos (αἰών τέλεος). This is the broadest aeon, also known as the Monad, a concept similar to Brahman in Hinduism and Buddhism, and Ein Sof in Kabbalah. From this come a succession of other aeons arranged in a hierarchy. Within Teleos is Ennoea (ἔννοια) meaning 'thought/intent', inside that is Nous (Νοῦς) meaning 'Mind' and so on, culminating in the realm of human experience. These aeons are simultaneously deities and environments, in which other entities can exist. This idea of personifying concepts as gods is core to mythology, though we sometimes forget that they also remain concepts. In this way an aeon may be both a god and a period of time.

Aleister Crowley drew from the aeon idea, in order to prophesise a coming 'aeon of Horus'. This is a transgressive, libertine and creative age, led by the archetype of the child, who will upend the previous paternal 'aeon of Osiris'—which took place from the classical period through the middle ages and into the present—as well as the earlier, original 'aeon of Isis', a pagan, maternal age of Mother Earth.

Crowley's Thoth Tarot deck is designed around this idea of the coming age of Horus. This then became a rallying concept during the counterculture movement of the 1960s and 70s and its revival in the 1990s. In this way (at least for a limited time) Crowley's prediction came true.

Related to an aeon, is the Greek god Aion who is depicted holding the zodiac, similar to the later god Chronos. Aion represents cyclical time, whereas Chronos is considered by some to be an early conception of linear time, which is the dominant conception in modern 'Westernised' cultures, and almost nowhere else.

Aphrodite/Venus

Aphrodite is the goddess of love, beauty, art, desire, procreation, sex, prostitution, prosperity, fertility, and the youthful aspect of the divine feminine. Her cult in ancient Greece drew heavily from the worship of the earlier Phoenician (Canaanite)[90] goddess Astarte, as well as the goddess Ishtar of the Akkadians, Babylonians and Assyrians, and the Sumerian goddess Inanna. By around 300 BCE, the Romans had syncretised Aphrodite with Venus, who as well as being a goddess of love and beauty was also a deity of springtime agriculture and of the harvest.

In Greek mythology, Aphrodite was the mother of the Trojan hero Aeneas, which one Roman tradition claimed as the founder of Rome.

---

[90] 'Phoenician' is simply a Greek name for those Canaanites who lived along the coast of the Mediterranean, and who were seafarers. These people are originators of all alphabets and are the ancestors of the Jews, Palestinians, Syrians, Jordanians, and Lebanese.

So Venus became venerated as Venus Genetrix, the mother of the Roman nation. Julius Caesar claimed to be directly descended from Aeneas' son Iulus and became a proponent of the cult of Venus. This trend was continued by his nephew Augustus and the later emperors.

According to Hesiod (approximately 750 to 650 BC) in his *Theogony*, Aphrodite was conceived when Cronus severed Uranus' genitals and threw them into the sea. The foam from his genitals gave rise to the goddess. Her name is interpreted by Hesiod as 'foam-arisen'.

Aphroditus/Hermaphroditus

Aphroditus is a male version of Aphrodite who originated on Cyprus but was also worshipped in Athens. He is depicted as more or less feminine, and wearing women's clothes, but lifting his dress to show an erect penis, hence his male name.

Statues with this gesture are thought to have been used to ward off bad luck. He is thought to be the same as Hermaphroditus, who is the offspring of Hermes and Aphrodite and whose name gives us the term 'hermaphrodite' meaning both male and female. His cult is thought to have worshipped the intersection of male and female divine aspects in nature. It is also thought that he presided over weddings, as the symbolic union of husband and wife. The historian Philochorus of Athens (340–c. 261 BCE) described a ritual where men and women exchanged clothes under the moon, in worship of Aphroditus.

Later on, the symbol of the hermaphrodite was adopted by Christianity in the negative, as a sign of the transgression of the 'natural order', hence the Devil is sometime depicted with both breasts and male genitals (for instance, Éliphas Lévi's Baphomet). This attitude persists to some degree in the present, though most have forgotten that Aphroditus/Hermaphrodite was once worshipped as a positive deity.

Apollo

Apollo is a complex god who is associated with the sun, male beauty, poetry, music, truth, archery, philosophy, civic order, and prophecy (through the oracle of Delphi). He is also the god of shepherds, herds and crops (farming).

He is the inventor of the music of stringed instruments after Hermes gifted him a lyre he had made of one of Apollo's tortoises. The lyre was a popular portable instrument used by singers to accompany themselves, in the same way that the guitar is today. In this way, Hermes created the first musical stringed instrument, and perhaps a kind of disordered music, whereas Apollo made the first ordered, harmonious music. Hermes can thus be thought of as 'right brain creativity', and Apollo as 'left brain creativity'.[91]

Apollo was also the god of both healing and disease, though later this role was taken by his son Asclepius. In the Greek tradition, Apollo and Helios, the personifications of the sun, were often conflated as a single deity. The Romans however, considered them separate as Apollo and Sol until the first century CE.

The nineteenth century philosopher Friedrich Nietzsche popularised the idea of a dichotomy between two states, the Apollonian which is rationality, order, logic and reason, and the Dionysian, which is wild creativity, passion, emotionality, chaos, irrationality and instinct. These concepts are a very useful way to conceptualise how a deity can manifest in the world, through creativity and in conceptual form.

Ares/Mars

Ares is the god of war and battle, both just and unjust. Unlike many of the other gods in Greek mythology, his role seems to be rather straightforward as a soldier and instigator of violence and temper. He is sometimes outsmarted by Athena, a goddess of military tactics.

In this sense I think of Ares/Mars as the god for foot soldiers and Athena as the god for generals, though this not a hard distinction.

As the Roman Mars, he was given a more dignified role as the father of Romulus, Rome's mythological founder. Mars was therefore the guardian deity of Rome, being a military state, though Mars was originally an agricultural god. Ares is the son of Zeus and Hera, and Mars is son of their equivalents Jupiter and Juno.

Artemis/Diana

The goddess of the hunt, she is the twin sister of Apollo, and the daughter of Zeus and Leto. In her myth Artemis refused to marry and instead remained an eternal virgin, spending her time as a huntress in

---

[91] This is my own interpretation of the myth, and one I have found extremely useful as both a musician and a teacher of music.

the wild, accompanied by dogs, nymphs and sometimes hunters and mortals. She is also symbolised by her game, the stag.

In her myths, Artemis was usually the first twin to be born, under moonlight. She then proceeded to assist her mother, Leto, in the birth of her brother, Apollo, who was of the sun. She is therefore a goddess of midwifery and associated with the moon. As the eternal virgin who swore never to marry, she is the patron and protector of young children, especially young girls, and of women, and was believed to both bring disease upon women and children and relieve them of it. This idea of a god or goddess being the harbinger of both good and negative aspects of fortune is common in Greek mythology. Artemis is also associated with another moon goddess, Selene, and the goddess of boundaries and magic, Hecate.

Widely worshipped, Artemis was considered a wrathful deity who would punish any who crossed her, and was therefore invoked as both a protector and a bringer of vengeance. It was considered a good omen when Artemis appeared in the dreams of hunters, or of pregnant women.

As well as being associated with the hunt and the wilderness, Artemis was also a goddess of dancing and singing. Many of her lunar associations were assigned to her as Diana by the Romans, who combined her with ideas about Selene, just as they conflated Apollo with Helios.

Athena/Minerva

The Greeks also knew her as Pallas (meaning both to 'brandish a weapon' and a 'youth' or 'young woman'). As one of the most widely worshipped of all the Greek deities, she probably derived her name from the city of Athens, of which she was the tutelary spirit,[92] though some have questioned if the city is named after her.

She is usually depicted wearing a helmet and often holding a spear. She is the goddess of war, especially of battle tactics, wisdom, and handcrafts such as weaving. As a warrior goddess, she was believed to guide soldiers into battle. She was widely revered in the Panathenaia festival which occurred every four years. This was a combined religious and cultural festival as well as a sports competition. It was held in a stadium and was one of the inspirations for the modern Olympic Games.

---

[92] Tutelary: pertaining to a guardian or patron.

Athena was said to have been born from the forehead of Zeus and was (sometimes) without a mother. In another version of the tale, she was born after Zeus swallowed Metis, a Titaness of wisdom and deep thought, who was pregnant with Athena, his child. Despite this traumatic birthing experience, Athena became the favourite child of Zeus and he gave her great power. In a sense Zeus was both father and mother to Athena.

In other stories she acted as the guide and aide to the heroes Perseus, Heracles, Bellerophon, Jason and Odysseus. In this sense she functioned as an advisory oracle spirit in times when wisdom was needed, especially pertaining to adventures and tactics.

Though they are both gods of war, in contrast to the hot-blooded Ares, who represents violence, vengeance and temper, Athena represents level-headed strategy and discipline, and was thought to only support the righteous. Ares also represented violent wrath, and was neutral, sometimes committing evil.

After the Greek and Roman ages, Athena has become a symbol of the West, especially representing Liberty and Democracy.

Castor and Pollux

These are twin half-brothers, known together as the Dioscuri. Their mother was Leda (an Aetolian princess who became a Spartan queen), but they had two different fathers; Castor was of Tyndareus, the king of Sparta, and a mortal, while Pollux was the immortal son of Zeus, who raped Leda in the form of a swan. Her children were sometimes said to have been born from eggs. In Latin the twins are also known as the Gemini, the Castores, or the Tyndarids. Pollux asked Zeus to let him share his own immortality with his twin, in order that they could stay together forever and they were transformed into the constellation Gemini.

Together they were the patrons of sailors, and their omen was St Elmo's fire, a weather phenomenon in which a luminous plasma is created from a mast in an atmospheric electric field. They were also associated with horsemanship and are almost certainly a retelling of the Indo-European 'horse twins', who serve as rescuers and healers, and who guide travellers, especially sailors, who invoked them for favourable winds. In their role as horsemen and also as boxers, they were patrons of athletes and athletic contests.

From the fifth century BCE onwards, Castor and Pollux were revered by the Romans, who believed that the twins aided them on the battlefield. They were especially revered by cavalry.

Chronos

The personification of time in pre-Socratic philosophy and in later literature, Chronos was originally a different deity to Cronus, the Titan father of Zeus and the Olympians. The two were however later conflated, giving rise to 'Father Time', an old man with a scythe who harvests the dead, an earlier version of the Grim Reaper.

In Greco-Roman artworks, especially mosaics, Chronos is depicted turning the zodiacal wheel, and served a similar function to Aion (Aeon), as a god of time cycles. In astrology this connotation is given to Saturn who is the Roman version of Cronus.

Chronos was important in the Orphic mysteries, where he used the elements Earth and Water to create Aether, a personified god of the starry sky, as well as Chaos, the primordial state (sometimes a goddess) out of which creation springs forth, and an egg which hatched into the hermaphrodite god Phanes, who is the parent of all the other gods and of the cosmos.

By the time of the Romans, Chronos and Cronus were both considered to be Saturn.

Cronus/Saturn

The Titan father of the first Olympians: Hestia, Demeter, Hera, Hades, Poseidon, and Zeus. Cronus became the king of the Titans by killing and castrating his own father, Uranus, with a stone sickle. Fearing a prophecy that one of his own children would overthrow him in turn, Cronus swallowed each of them as they were born. Appalled by these acts, Cronus' wife Rhea swapped the sixth child, Zeus, for a rock, which the foolish Cronus then swallowed.

Zeus was then spirited away to a safe place where he was raised by a surrogate; depending on the story, this was the goat Amalthea, the nymph Adamanthea, or his grandmother Gaia.

Once Zeus had grown up, he and Rhea used an emetic potion to make Cronus regurgitate his sibling gods. Then, with the aid of the Hecatoncheires and Cyclopes, they fought a great war against the Titans called the Titanomachy. The Olympian triumphed, whereupon Cronus was imprisoned and, in some retellings, castrated in turn by Zeus.

Cronus therefore represents old kingdoms and stifling institutions that have outlived their usefulness, especially those which have become tyrannical. The implication is that the new 'Olympian' kingdom is fairer, more just and less corrupt. However, the Olympian myths should also hold a warning that the new kingdom is not necessarily better just because it is new, and history often reflects this. Zeus is hardly more moral than his father and his tyranny over humans is the cause of a later rebellion by the titan Prometheus.

In Roman times, Cronus merged with Saturn, a god of time, generation, dissolution, abundance, wealth, and agriculture. He was venerated during the festival of Saturnalia each December, a time of feasting, role-reversals, free speech, gift-giving and revelry. This later influenced the development of Christmas, and also Carnival. Saturn represented an element of societal chaos to the Romans, and especially also in astrology. To some this 'chaos' was an idyllic state of freedom, libertinism and play, whereas to others Saturn represented debauchery, primitivity, disorder and brutality. This dichotomy is still played out in many European Carnival festivals today.

In Greco-Roman Egypt, Cronus/Saturn was equated with Geb, 'father earth', in relation to Nut who is 'mother sky'.

In astrology Saturn represents the properties of restriction, blocked movement, old age, conservatism, depression and sorrow, tyranny, tradition, enduring institutions, long time-cycles and lifelong pursuits.

Demeter/Ceres

This is the goddess of agriculture and harvests, especially crops and grain, and also of marriage, health and birth. Demeter is most well-known through the myth of Persephone, her daughter by her brother Zeus.

In this story, Persephone is kidnapped to be the lover of Hades and taken to the underworld. In her grief, Demeter allows the Earth to grow cold and infertile. Zeus orders Hades to return Persephone, to remedy this perpetual winter, and Hades agrees on the condition that no food should pass the mouth of Persephone during her stay. However, Persephone in her hunger is tempted by the morsel of six pomegranate 'arils',[93] representing six months of the year. As a compromise, it is

---

[93] Aril: a seed inside a fleshy pulp.

decided that Persephone will spend six months above ground in the fields with Demeter, and six months below in the underworld with Hades, as his wife. Thus, the seasons are born of Demeter's cyclical longing for her daughter. Demeter and Persephone therefore are the dual goddesses of the seasons, and of cycles of death and rebirth.

Demeter is usually equated with the Phrygian (present-day Turkey) goddess Cybele and the Roman goddess Ceres. She is also often identified with the zodiacal sign Virgo.

Dike/Justitia

The goddess of justice and moral order. Her parents are Zeus and Themis (also a goddess of justice), and she is depicted holding scales and wearing a laurel wreath, sometimes with a sword by her side. She is associated with the zodiacal sign Libra, and is often depicted to this day outside institutions of law, especially courthouses and government buildings. As such, she is similar to, or the same as, the later 'Lady Justice' and the Roman Justitia who was introduced to the pantheon by Emperor Augustus.

Though she had a temple established by the Emperor Tiberius, Justitia is generally considered more of a symbol than a goddess who was directly prayed to. Since the sixteenth century she has been depicted wearing a blindfold; this was possibly originally a satirical addition suggesting a blindness to injustice, but came in time to mean the positive attribute of 'impartiality', especially in regard to social class.

As a goddess wielding scales of balance, she is similar to the Egyptian goddess Ma'at (goddess of cosmic morality) and some of the later depictions of Isis, where she also takes the role of balancer of societal and cosmic order.

Dike is sometimes known as Astraea.

Dionysus/Bacchus

One of the most mysterious and complex of all the Greek gods, most know of Dionysus as the Greek god of wine, orchards, fruit, theatre and excited states of spiritual consciousness (or of frenzies, if negatively expressed). He became a symbol, in the second half of the twentieth century, of 'sex, drugs and rock'n'roll', especially invoked by male rock stars like Little Richard, Elvis Presley, Jimi Hendrix, Jim Morrison, Robert Plant and David Bowie.

For a long time mythologists believed Dionysus to be a foreign god who was later accepted into the Greek pantheon, but we now have written records referencing Dionysus from Mycenaean Greece dated approximately 1300 BCE, making him in truth one of the oldest attested of all the Greek gods.[94]

There are several stories of Dionysus' conception and birth. One has it that he was conceived from Zeus' romance with Semele, the daughter of the Phoenician king Cadmus and the goddess Harmonia. This romance angered Zeus' wife Hera, and she tricked Semele into asking a favour of Zeus, which he promised to deliver. Semele asked to see Zeus in his true form, the same in which he would appear to Hera. Zeus, compelled to comply, did so, and the intensity of his star-like form burned Semele to death. Zeus then took the foetus of Dionysus from her body and implanted it into his 'thigh' (a euphemism for his scrotum), in order to bring the pregnancy to term. Dionysus was then born of this gender inversion, where Zeus was both his father and, in a sense, his mother. The young Dionysus was moved to an island that was only inhabited by women, and raised in disguise as a girl in order to fool Hera, who was looking for a male child. For this reason, he was often depicted in female clothing; along with his unusual birth, this meant he took on the quality of androgyny, subverting a taboo in Greek culture that men should never present as women. In the Dionysian cult, members were said to partake in a ritual whereby men and women would exchange clothes and act out roles of the opposite gender.

Another origin story has Dionysus as the son of Zeus and Persephone, his daughter by Demeter. In her jealousy Hera had the Titans destroy the child, ripping him apart. Both these stories comply with the idea that Dionysius is 'twice-born', later allowing him to be associated with the also twice-born Egyptian god Osiris, with whom he was syncretised into a single god during the Greek rule of Egypt.

One of Dionysus' many names is Acratophorus (Ἀκρατοφόρος), 'the giver of unmixed wine'. In this role, he was the god of a ritual whereby cultists would drink to achieve a state of fervour, like wild beasts, which was considered a communion with his spirit. This has led some to speculate as to whether the wine was adulterated with entheogenic drugs that induced visions, such as psilocybin or amanita mushrooms,

---

[94] Carl Kerényi, *Dionysos: Archetypal Image of Indestructible Life*, tr. Ralph Manheim (Princeton: Princeton University Press, [1976] 1996).

or opium. In this state, Dionysus was said to be accompanied by wild Maenads. These were dangerous frenzied women who would sometimes tear mortals apart. Also accompanying him where the satyrs, half goat-men who symbolised male sexuality, especially that observed in nature. The cult of Dionysus therefore took on a reputation for subversion of societal norms and debauchery that has seen Dionysus reborn as a symbol of moral inversion, drug use, and open sexuality throughout history.

Somewhat in opposition to the idea of Dionysus as a subversive and immoral god in mainstream Greek and Roman society, Dionysus was the central and most revered deity in the Orphic mystery cult often known as the Dionysian mysteries. The origin of this religion, of which Orpheus was the prophet, is unknown but it has been highly influential on theology and occult societies ever since. In this tradition Dionysus represented rebirth and reincarnation, and because of this and other qualities he was syncretised with the Egyptian god Osiris, especially during the Greek reign of Egypt, Osiris himself being a god who was dismembered and then reborn.

The Romans identified Dionysus with 'Liber Pater', the 'free father' of the festival Liberalia, a coming-of-age rite for Roman boys, and an influence for later festivals such as the European 'Carnival', where dressing up allowed one to subvert social class and societal norms for a day.

Eros (Cupid) and Psyche

This is a story we know from the Roman Lucius Apuleius Madaurensis, from the second century CE, but which is also depicted in Greek art back as far as 400 BCE. Psyche was the youngest daughter of an unnamed king and queen. She was so beautiful that people started worshipping her instead of the goddess of beauty Venus (Aphrodite). Venus was offended and asked her son Cupid (Eros) to shoot Psyche with an arrow so that she may fall in love with a hideous person or thing (in some versions a dragon or monster). Eros accidentally scratched himself with the arrow and fell for Psyche himself, causing him to disobey his mother's plan. When psyche remained unmarried, her father consulted an oracle of Apollo. Here he found out that Psyche was destined to marry a dragon-like beast who was prophesied to torment the kingdom. To avoid this fate, Psyche was dressed as for a funeral and led to a cliff (in a combination of marriage and death symbolism). Instead of falling to her death, the spirit of the west-wind, Zephyrus, carried her safely to a field where she slept. She awoke to find herself at an ornate house in the middle of a grove of trees. She entered and a disembodied spirit told her to be comfortable. She was then fed a feast and entertained by an invisible lyre. Afterwards she entered a bedroom in the dark, and the spirit seduced her. The same thing happened every night, with the lover always gone by the morning and remaining unseen. She longed to see him, and she soon became pregnant.

After hearing her sisters pine for her, Cupid partially relented and the Zephyrus took the sisters to the house for a visit. They become envious at the riches of the house and cajoled Psyche to reveal the identity of her new husband. They were especially concerned that her husband might be the dragon-like beast as foretold by the oracle.

The sisters talked her into a plan whereby she hid a lamp and a dagger in the bedroom to reveal and kill the beast while he was asleep. When she flashed the light at her lover, she found him instead to be the beautiful youth Cupid, and she accidentally scratched herself on one of his arrows, becoming herself enamoured. The lamp spilled some oil, which burned him, causing him to wake. He fled, and she followed him, becoming lost by a river. Lovesick, Psyche began to walk the world looking for her lost lover.

Her sisters, jealous that her husband was Cupid, each threw themselves off the cliff hoping to also be carried by the west wind in order to become Psyche's replacement. Instead, they fell to their deaths.

In her travels, Psyche appealed first to Ceres (Demeter) and then to Juno (Hera). As Psyche was cursed under the power of Venus, they refused to help her. Finally, Psyche appealed to Venus herself. To prove her worthiness, Venus put Psyche through a series of ordeals. First, Psyche was handed over to Venus' handmaidens 'Worry' and 'Sadness', who tortured and mocked her. Venus then presented Psyche with a pile of wheat, barley, poppyseed, chickpeas, lentils, and beans, and demanded that she sort them out by morning. Venus then left to attend a wedding and in her absence an ant took pity on Psyche and together with a team of insects, sorted the food into piles for her. Venus was furious when the she came back to find the trial completed, and set Psyche a new task, to collect wool from the fleeces of Helios' dangerous sheep who lived on the other side of a river. In despair, Psyche attempted to drown herself but a spirit of a reed growing by the river took pity on her and gave her the wool that was rubbed off the sheep into the reeds. Venus was again thwarted and set Psyche a third task, to collect black water from the rivers Styx and Cocytus which bordered the underworld and were protected by dragons. Jupiter intervened and sent a great Eagle to battle the dragons and collect the water for her.

For the fourth and final task, Venus sent Psyche to the underworld to obtain a dose of the beauty of the queen of the underworld Proserpina (Persephone), and bring it back in a pyxis box (which is used to contain cosmetics and jewellery for women). Psyche despaired, climbing a tower in order to throw herself off, but the Tower itself talked to her and offered its aide. With the instructions of the Tower, Psyche passed a series of convoluted traps, and achieved audience with Proserpina. The wish was granted as long as Psyche didn't peer into the box. Psyche however was tempted by the idea of enhancing her own beauty, and the box, which contained only sleep, put her into a coma.

Cupid, now healed from his burn, escaped Venus' mansion and found the sleeping Psyche. He returned the sleep to the box, took it himself to Venus, then went to Zeus. Here he made a pact with Zeus, that he would aide him in obtaining the love of maidens of his choice in return for granting Psyche immortality, via ambrosia, the food of the gods, so that Psyche may become Cupid's eternal bride. Zeus accepted and Venus was reprimanded and forced to back off. A 'happy ending'.

The symbolism of the story explores the relationship between sex and death, love and sorrow, as well as the fatefulness of romantic passion. Psyche became the goddess of the soul, which in Latin is Anima, the feminine part of the human spirit.

Fortuna/Tyche

This is the goddess of Fortune, who was a popular deity to pray to for good luck, from ancient times through to the Renaissance. She is still prominent in Italian folk traditions today. Her symbols are a ship's rudder, representing the fickle nature of fair winds, a cornucopia, the symbol of plentiful harvest, and the Rota Fortunae, or Wheel of Fortune, which gives the Tarot card its name.

Ganymede

A divine hero from Troy, who was abducted by the gods for his perfect beauty to serve as Zeus' cup-bearer. The implication is one of pederasty, that Ganymede became Zeus' lover. Ganymede became immortal, never aging, thus becoming a symbol for an impossible ideal of beauty.

Hades/Pluto/Dīs Pater

The lord of the underworld, he was the oldest son of Cronus and Rhea. After the battle with the Titans, the Olympians were allocated domains: Zeus took the sky, Poseidon the sea, and Hades the underworld of the dead. His symbols were the bident (a spear with two forks) and Cerberus the three-headed dog, as his guard.

Perhaps fearing his name as an omen of bad luck, the Greeks began to refer to Hades as Pluto, meaning the 'wealthy one'. There is perhaps an implication here that Hades also ruled the wealth of the Earth: minerals and metals that can be accessed by mining, and also the richness of the soil which can produce harvest, especially in Hades' association with his wife Persephone, a fertility goddess.

Pluto was also sometimes called Ploutodótēs (Πλουτοδότης) the 'giver of wealth'. Hades comes into stories such as the origins of the Olympians, and the abduction of Persephone, which brings about the seasons, especially winter.

Hades, while neutral in temperament, was extremely protective over the souls of the dead and while there are tales such as that of Orpheus, where heroes and gods attempt to retrieve the dead, usually they are offered terms in exchange for their loved ones that are impossible to comply with, resulting in the dead being returned to Hades.

As well as being a god, Hades is simultaneously the name for the realm of the underworld, and the word is also used in the New Testament of the Bible in its original Greek as the realm of the dead. This is a common theme in Eurasian mythology, where gods can be environments as well as persons. In some cases, gods can exist within other gods as layers.

While Hades was the ruler of the realm, he was not himself the personification of death, only its guardian and its locale. The god of death itself is Thanatos, son of Nyx (night) or Erebus ('darkness', sometimes taken to be a name for Hades himself). Hades was rarely depicted in art, due to a taboo held by the ancient Greeks.

The realm of Hades was said to have five rivers: Acheron (sorrow), Cocytus (lamentation), Phlegethon (fire), Lethe (oblivion), and Styx (hate). The river Styx was special in that it was the river upon which the gods swore oaths and in which Achilles was dipped to give him invincibility. The Styx was also believed to be the boundary between the upper and lower worlds, and it was this river that was crossed by the dead in the ferry of Charon, to reach their resting place in Hades.

The custom of leaving coins on the eyes of corpses was symbolically to offer payment to Charon for safe passage. Unlike Zeus and Poseidon, Hades was monogamous and faithful to his wife Persephone.

The Romans had a less fearful conception of Hades, who they called either Pluto or Dis Pater, 'Rich Father'.

Hebe/Juventas

The goddess of youth and rejuvenation. In Greek mythology, Hebe is the female cupbearer to the gods, serving them nectar and ambrosia, which was said to allow them eternal life.

In some stories she was said to be the wife of Hercules. After her marriage she was replaced as cup bearer by the boy Ganymede.

As Juventas, in Roman society she was a guardian of young men who had just come of age.

Hecate

A goddess of the crossroads, entrance ways, light and dark, the moon, herbal medicines and poisons, magic and magical protections, graves, ghosts and necromancy. All these represented liminal places or states between conceptual worlds or states of consciousness. Though less often talked about today, Hecate is ancient, being mentioned in Hesiod's *Theogony* from the eighth century BCE, which is the earliest book of Greek and the earliest still existing text discussing the origins of the Greek gods. Hecate was associated with the witches of Thessaly. She was also often invoked to protect households, especially in ancient Athens.

Although her earliest depictions are singular, she was later frequently depicted as having three bodies, joined back-to-back and pointing in three directions. Sometimes she is depicted as having a single body and three faces. This triplet form is not well understood, but may be associated with the three feminine life stages, maiden, mother and crone, and with the three human spiritual parts, the body, the soul (consciousness) and the spirit (concept). She was also the governess of the three parts of the Earth: sky, ground and sea. Three-way crossroads were symbolic of Hecate.

As the goddess of entranceways, she was not only a guard but also had the power to unlock any door. In this role she was also a psychopomp who was said to be able to grant entrance to the underworld and communication with other spirits including the dead.

While Hecate's origins are unknown, she is considered by some mythologists to be a foreign goddess, albeit one who joined the Greek pantheon early. While there are many guesses as to her origins, the one I find the most magically compelling (regardless of the truth of it) is to associate her with the Egyptian god Heka, a masculine personification, not only of all magic, but also of all formation, and a precursor to the Greek concept of 'logos', that which grants form. This inversion of male/female is not uncommon when comparing Egyptian mythology with others, especially Greek. For instance, the Egyptians considered the earth, Geb, to be masculine, and the sky, Nut, to be feminine. This is inverted in most Eurasian cultures to our more familiar dichotomy of mother-earth/father-sky. In this way Hecate may be, in part, a gender inversion, or feminine sub-aspect of the more abstract Heka.

Hecate later took on a central role in the 'Chaldean Oracles'[95] of the second and third century CE, where she was said to have rulership over the earth, sea and sky, to be the mother of angels, and the guardian of the world-soul. Despite being a very important goddess, her mysterious nature and association with 'in-betweens' have meant that she is not discussed often in relation to the rest of the Greek pantheon. This has begun to change in modern times as magical practices that centre on the divine feminine have become more popular, in particular Wicca. Hecate is perfect for this role as a feminine power-symbol who grants protection, knowledge of herbs, communication with spirits, and knowledge of magical secrets.

Her familiars are the dog and the polecat. In Roman times she was often conflated with Diana.

Helios/Sol

The personification of the sun, Helios is depicted with a radiant crown and as the driver of the sun chariot. Helios is sometimes considered the same as Apollo, and sometimes as a separate deity, often his son. In one

---

[95] Chaldea was an ancient region located in the southern part of Babylonia. This region is now southern Iraq. The Chaldeans spoke Akkadian, a semitic language. They were renowned for their astrology, and their culture dates back to roughly 1000 BCE.

myth he is said to be the son of the Titans, Hyperion and Theia, and the brother of the goddesses Selene (the moon) and Eos (the dawn).

The most well-known myth of Helios recounts how he begrudgingly allowed his own mortal son Phaethon (meaning 'shiner') to drive the sun chariot for a day. Phaethon swerved the chariot out of control, alternating between burning the Earth by getting too close to it and freezing it by driving too far from it. A concerned Zeus struck Phaethon down with a thunderbolt to prevent everyone from being killed, and his body fell in the Eridanus river.

In the Odyssey, Helios was enraged when Odysseus' crew killed and ate his sacred cattle. In retaliation, he asked Zeus to attack their ship, and they were all killed except for Odysseus, the only one who did not eat the cattle.

As the sun was the symbol of sight, overt knowledge, and an all-seeing witness, Helios was considered the guardian of oaths. This theme is also present in Egyptian mythology. As the sun, he was often worshipped as a life-giving creative force.

Helios bears a relationship to the Egyptian sun-god Ra.[96] Where Helios was said to drive through the sky in a chariot, Ra was said to sail through the sky in a ship. They were both considered to be 'all-seeing'.

Helios was usually considered to be the same as the Roman god Sol, but different to the later 'Sol-Invictus' (of the cult of Mithras). Like the Egyptian god Ra, Sol was conflated with the Empire and the Emperor was usually his incarnation or representative.

Hephaestus/Vulcan

The lame smith-god of the ancient Greeks and Romans, he is either the son of Zeus and Hera, or otherwise the fatherless child of Hera alone. He was born with a deformed leg and was cast off Mount Olympus by his mother. Or in another legend, he was cast off by Zeus for getting in between him and Hera, and thus, in this version, his lameness was caused by the fall.

In different accounts, he fell in the ocean and was cared for by Thetis and the other sea nymphs, or he fell on the island of Lemnos and was raised and taught to be a master craftsman by the native Sintians

---

[96] There are numerous Egyptian sun-gods, depending on the location and the time they were worshipped and the nature of their worship.

(the Thracians).[97] Hephaestus was also a god of volcanos, and it is implied that the volcano is his forge.

The exiled Hephaestus made a magic golden throne for Hera, and in sitting on it she found herself stuck, unable to stand up again. Ares was sent to get Hephaestus to release her, but was repelled by Hephaestus' fiery torches. Eventually Dionysus was sent, who befriended Hephaestus and got him drunk, then bringing him to Olympus on the back of a mule.

Zeus offered a deal with Hephaestus to release Hera. Hephaestus was allowed to choose a wife from the goddesses. Urged by Poseidon, who had a feud with the goddess, Hephaestus chose Athena (or in another version of the tale, Aphrodite) as a bride. Hera fulfilled the request. (I like the version with Athena, as she is a goddess of the military and Hephaestus is the forger of weapons.)

As an Olympian, Hephaestus created many of the gods' magical objects: Hermes' winged helmet and sandals which allow him fast travel, the Aegis breastplate which protected Athena, Aphrodite's girdle which granted her the power of charm, Agamemnon's staff of office, Achilles' impenetrable armour, Diomedes' golden cuirass, Heracles' bronze clappers (Krotala) which allowed him to make a noise as loud as thunder, Helios' sun chariot, Pelops' prosthetic ivory shoulder, and Eros' bow and arrows.

To the Romans he was known as Vulcan.

Hera/Juno

The queen of the gods and the sister and wife of Zeus. She was the goddess of marriage, women, childbirth and family.

In many myths she was portrayed as a jealous and vengeful wife, reacting to Zeus' many infidelities, and she was usually an enemy to Zeus' lovers and sometimes also to their children. In this way she can be considered the female 'shadow' or the dark side of the feminine nature, especially in relation to marriage to men (Zeus on the other hand can be said to portray many of the worst properties of masculinity, especially in his philandering and raping).

---

[97] The Thracians lived in the lands which have become present day Bulgaria, Romania and northern Greece. Though they were Indo-Europeans, we know little else about their origins. They were described as 'barbarians' by the Greeks and Romans.

As a very ancient goddess it's possible that Hera's role diminished over time, as two of the most ancient Greek temples ever constructed were dedicated to her, the Heraion of Samos and the Heraion of Argos in the eighth century BCE.

As the daughter of Cronus and Rhea, Hera was one of the original twelve Olympians. She was the mother of many gods and creatures including Ares, god of war, Eris, goddess of discord (although said by Hesiod to be the daughter of Nyx), Hephaestus the smith god, Hebe the goddess of youth, and in some stories Prometheus and Typhon.

As the Roman goddess Juno, she had a place as the guardian of female lineage in every household. Juno is the female counterpart to the masculine Genius, which started as the male spirit of the household or clan, and over time developed into a concept for all the aspects of the person and their sphere of influence which extend far beyond their body. Eventually the Genius became attributed to entire nations, especially of Rome from Augustus onwards, who was the first Emperor to have the nation drink a toast to his own Genius spirit. There is a precursor to this in the god-emperors of Egypt.

Hermanubis

A syncretism of Hermes and Anubis. See Egyptian gods.

Hermes/Mercury

The messenger of the gods, who governed communication, language, travel, divination, initiation, commerce and merchants, orators and thieves. Via his winged sandals he was able to travel between the world of mortals and the divine realm of gods. In this way he was a psychopomp: one who can allow magicians or mediums access to the world of spirits, be they other gods or the dead.

Hermes was the son of Zeus, and Maia, one of the 'seven sisters' of the constellation Pleiades. A child prodigy, Hermes was able to walk, talk and charm people as soon as he was born. He was a trickster god who was able to pull new concepts out of chaos (much like Loki and Óðinn). For this reason, he is sometime depicted as an infant god.

Along with his winged hat and sandals, made by Hephaestus, he carried the Caduceus, a winged staff depicting two snakes copulating.

This symbol is much older than the Greek pantheon, dating back to the dawn of civilisation around 4000–3000 BCE, and having its roots in Mesopotamia with the god Ningishzida (another psychopomp god, like Hermes). While ahistorical, as a symbol of information and the procreation of information the caduceus shares its form with the double helix of DNA. This can be a useful way to understand its symbolism even though the ancients were unaware of DNA as a concept. This symbol, along with other clues, suggests that Hermes is actually older than most of the Greek gods, though the particulars of this are beyond my scope here.

In America and beyond, the Caduceus is used as a symbol for medicine and hospitals. This is almost certainly a mistake, as the correct ancient Greek symbol is the rod of Asclepius the healer god, which has a single snake rather than two.

Interestingly, both symbols suggest a connection to the Biblical Egyptian trick of turning a snake into a stick. When a cobra is wrapped around a stick it becomes completely immobile, causing the unaware onlooker to think it is dead, or even an inanimate carving (it helps if one covers the snake in paint). With a flourish, one can uncurl the snake, at which point it will usually stand bolt upright and hiss, thus making this one of the oldest stage-magic tricks, and one that is still performed in Egypt today. In the Bible, Aaron and Moses take this trick to the next level, by having their magic snake attack and eat those of the Egyptian magicians.

Hermes is a god of boundaries, and he was invoked in markers used to help travellers get around. These could be a pile of stones, where each traveller would add a stone to the pile as they went past. Later these could be Herma, rectangular stone statues with a bust of Hermes at the top and an erect phallus at the midpoint.

Hermes was sometimes depicted as a shepherd god, a youth carrying a lamb on his shoulders. In combination with Hermes' roles as guide of souls, this may have in turn influenced the symbol of Jesus Christ as the 'Good Shepherd', which was also a title of Hermes. One who 'shepherds' souls.

My favourite story of Hermes concerns the creation of music:

Shortly after his birth, the infant Hermes, already able to walk, talk and get himself in trouble, roamed around until he found a tortoise, an animal sacred to his brother Apollo. Fascinated by its shell, he killed the animal and butchered it. Finding its shell resonant, he stretched gut strings across it making the first lyre.

After an afternoon of noisy twanging, he eventually became bored. He put the noisemaking instrument in his cradle and continued on to other mischief. Finding beautiful cattle belonging to Apollo, he stole fifty of their number. Hiding them in a cave, he sacrificed one of them to himself, and one to the other gods in a magical ritual. He then carefully covered his tracks.

However, Apollo (here conflated with Helios), as the eye of the sun, was 'all-seeing'. He went to Maia, Hermes' mother, and demanded justice. Hermes, however, was found back in his cradle 'asleep', pretending to be an innocent babe. Apollo couldn't be so easily fooled, and snatched up the baby and took him to be judged before Zeus. Though his cover was blown, Hermes still tried at first to cover up the lie, and acting as his own attorney, he proclaimed that a cattle-stealing baby is an absurdity (despite acting as a lawyer baby!). Zeus, amused, made Hermes take them to the cave. About to be punished by an enraged Apollo, Hermes relented and produced the tortoise-shell lyre, and as an undisciplined musician twanged it noisily. Apollo was suddenly curious, as he had never seen a musical instrument before. As a god of order, he was suddenly inspired by all the ways he could turn the noisy sounds of the strings into harmonious music. Hermes gifted him the lyre in reconciliation and was forgiven.

I have my own spin on the story: as Hermes is a chaotic god, perhaps of the right side of the brain, and Apollo is a harmonious and ordered god, associated by philosophers with logic, and what we now consider the left side of the brain, here we have two aspects of creativity, both of which are vital to music. Hermes is the experimenter, the improviser and the 'fire' of musical performance. Apollo is the theory, the order, the rhythm and the harmony of music. All worthy music (and by extension, all art) is some balance of these two aspects.

The Romans knew Hermes as Mercury. Mercury is of central importance in astrology, as the planet that governs (amongst other things) communication styles, magic, messages and business. In the twenty-first century, often defined as the 'information age', Mercury/Hermes has taken on a role for many magicians as a custodian of the internet.

Hestia/Vesta

The goddess of the hearth, and by extension the family, the home, and family lineages. Hestia is the daughter of Cronus and Rhea, and one of the twelve Olympians (though some lists omit her and list

Dionysus instead). She is not well attested in Greek literature. It is said that she opted never to marry, remaining instead (like Artemis) an eternal virgin, and was tasked with tending the hearth at Olympus.

Despite a dearth of stories, Hestia was a very important goddess to the ancient Greeks. She was prayed to wherever fires were lit, especially in the family home and at temples, and a small offering was to be made to her before any other burnt sacrifice. At family feasts she was offered the first and last libations of wine.

As the first to be devoured by her father Cronus, and the last to be disgorged, she is both the oldest and the youngest of the Olympians, a dichotomy which reflects her role as the guardian of family progeny. The responsibility of Hestia's worship would normally befall the matriarch of the family, though sometimes a man would also take this role.

Her Roman equivalent is Vesta. Her temple at the Forum Romanum was guarded and tended to by the Vestal Virgins, who embodied her eternal virginity.

Janus

The Roman god of beginnings, endings, dualities, time, gateways and doorways. He is normally depicted as having two faces pointing away from each other. The month of January is named after Janus, and it is the beginning, or 'entrance' of the year. There is no direct equivalent for Janus amongst the Greek pantheon, though Janus is similar to Culśanś, of the Etruscan pantheon, and may have been imported from there. The Etruscans were pre-Roman inhabitants of Italy, who first fought and were then incorporated into the Roman Empire.[98] It is uncertain whether they were truly native to Italy or if they emigrated from Anatolia. It is also uncertain to what degree Romans were descendants of the Etruscans. They are usually considered to be a neighbouring tribe that was annexed. In any case Etruscan mythology had an influence on Roman religion.

Janus may appear to be similar to Hecate as they both act as guardians of doorways, however Hecate is Greek and by the time of the Romans she had been conflated with Selene and Artemis. Janus,

---

[98] The Etruscan language was a language isolate. It is not part of the Indo-European family of languages and may therefore, like modern day Basque, be a remnant from before the Indo-European migration.

originally Etruscan, represented dualities, perhaps a more Roman concept, whereas Hecate represented triplicities, offering a much more mysterious quality.

Justitia

See Dike.

Juventas

See Hebe.

Orpheus

A tragic hero of Greek myth on one hand and the central prophet of the cult of Orphism on the other, Orpheus holds a complex position in Greek culture. To most Greeks he was a legendary Thracian bard. The Thracians were an Indo-European culture with their own language who lived in the region now known as the Balkans and Anatolia.

Orpheus was said to have the ability to charm all with his music, even stones. He was said to have composed the Orphic Hymns, a set of eighty-seven poems claiming to be ancient, but thought to have been composed around the third century CE. These have been very influential in Western magic; for example, they are recommended as invocations of the seven astrological planets and their associated gods by Cornelius Agrippa in the *Three Books of Occult Philosophy* (1533 CE).[99]

Orpheus is also said to be the composer of the Orphic Argonautica (from the fifth to sixth century CE). This is the story of Jason and the Argonauts, which is written in Orpheus' voice in the first person, and in which he is a character. This in turn is based on the older Argonautica from the third century BCE, in which Orpheus is also a character.

Aristotle thought that Orpheus never existed, but all other ancient writers present him as an actual historical person, who lived before Homer around the eighth century BCE.

Orphism was an important mystery cult, dating back to the sixth century BCE. It has been very influential on esoteric secret societies up

---

[99] Agrippa (1533), ed. Tyson (1993), Book I, chapter 71.

to the present day. Its adherents were initiated, taught spiritual secrets, and practised rites that look similar to Pythagoreanism.[100] Vegetarianism and abstinence from sex were practised, and beans and eggs were forbidden. Orphism is thought to be a reformation of an earlier Dionysian cult, and Dionysus was the central deity with Orpheus his prophet. Far from being merely the ecstatic drunken god of wine as described in much of Greek literature, Dionysus was, to the Orphic cult, a much more dignified god, and his powers of rebirth were emphasised, associated by some with the Egyptian god Osiris.

The goal of Orphism was remarkably similar to both Buddhism and Gnosticism. Certain rites, initiations and purifications were practised in order to transcend eternal reincarnation of the imperfect human body and instead return to spirit, in this case an afterlife amongst the heroes such as Orpheus. Orpheus was thus emphasised because of his return from the underworld, which we will discuss in the next section, Orpheus and Eurydice.

Instead of the drunkenness and a return to a carnal animal nature presented by most depictions of Dionysus, for the Orphics the wine and ecstatic state were symbolic of and part of the rite of 'enthusiasm',[101] an altered state of consciousness where one becomes possessed by the gods and divine energies.

Though they are beyond the scope of this book, the Orphic religion has many unique teachings and a separate cosmogony from mainstream Greek belief, that is fascinating in its own right.

Orpheus and Eurydice

The best-known story of Orpheus is that of him and his wife Eurydice. As the most famous musician in the Greek world, Orpheus was beloved by all. He fell in love with Eurydice, an Auloniad, or nymph of the pasture. These were nature deities who were often in the company of the god Pan. Eurydice and Orpheus were married, and all were affected by the lifting of his heart, which was reflected in his music.

---

[100] Some scholars consider Pythagoras to have been trained in Orphism, and to be a reformer of that school, though this is not without controversy.

[101] Enthousiasmós (ἐνθουσιασμός): 'in-god-essence'. To take in the essence of a god.

One day, while out in the long grass, Eurydice was beset by a satyr (or in some tellings the demigod Aristaeus[102]), and she fled. She stepped upon and was bitten by a viper and died of its poison.

Upon discovering her death, Orpheus was grief-stricken and his music turned mournful. The sadness of his singing moved the nymphs and other deities. They beseeched him to travel to Hades to retrieve Eurydice and he undertook the journey. There he played so compellingly that he swayed even the heart of Hades and his wife Persephone, and they allowed Eurydice to follow Orpheus back to the realm of the living, on the one condition that he not look upon her until they arrive.

Orpheus began the journey back, but with each footstep he was filled with ever more doubt that the light-footed Eurydice was following him at all. Just as he crossed the threshold of the world of the living he looked back in doubt, and there he saw Eurydice, who had not yet touched the boundary, being dragged back to Hades without him. She was doomed to remain there forever.

Orpheus remained ever saddened until he was killed by the Maenads of Dionysus, allowing him to be reunited with Eurydice, in Hades. In some versions of the story, this was because he had disdained the worship of Dionysus. In others the Maenads had grown weary of Orpheus' sad singing. Implied is the idea that Orpheus had become life-weary and nihilistic.

This story has many parallels in other mythological stories throughout Eurasia and even the Americas; for instance, the Japanese myth of Izanagi and Izanami, the Mayan myth of Itzamna and Ixchel, the Indian myth of Savitri and Satyavan, and the Biblical story of Lot and his wife. These similarities suggest either that the core story may be archetypical, or that it could be ten thousand to seventeen thousand years old.

Ouranos/Uranus

The son and husband of the Earth-mother Gaia, Uranus is the first Greek personification of the sky. Together he and Gaia begat the Titans who were eventually replaced by the Olympians.

Uranus and Gaia are more abstract beings than the later gods. Like many of the Egyptian deities, and also the deities of animistic religions,

---

[102] A bee-keeper god whose name means 'the best'.

they are considered fundamental forces and environments as much as they are considered persons.

Uranus was castrated and usurped by his son, the head Titan Cronus. In some tellings this act goes together with the separation of the Earth (Gaia) and the Sky (Uranus) which as a myth element is seen in many cultures around the world.[103] In Hesiod's version of the story, Gaia is complicit. After Uranus hides her children the Cyclopes under the Earth, she compels Cronus to attack Uranus with the help of a sickle which she provides. From the blood of Cronus she becomes pregnant and gives birth to the Furies (female deities of vengeance), the giants, and the Melian nymphs, associated with the ash tree.

Pan

The goat-legged god of the pastures, the wild, shepherds, pastural music and musical improvisation, Pan is associated with spiring and fertility.

He appears to be an extremely ancient god, sharing etymology with the reconstructed Proto-Indo-European god '*Péh₂usōn' and the god Pushan from the Rigveda, the oldest part of Sanskrit literature. In Sanskrit this name means 'nourisher'. The true Greek meaning of his name is lost, though some suggest the meanings 'to guard or watch over' and 'companion', and his name is the same as the word πᾶν (Pan) meaning 'all'.

Pan was worshipped more in the Greek countryside than in the cities, especially in Arcadia, a district of mountain people. He was also worshipped in caves on the north slope of the Acropolis of Athens.

Pan's parentage is disagreed upon, with stories having him be variously a child of Apollo, Hermes, Cronus or Zeus, and his mother is often Penelope, the wife of Odysseus (via Hermes), or a daughter of Dryops. Other sources say he is more ancient than all the other gods, as it is Pan who gifts Artemis her hunting dogs and the gift of prophecy to Apollo.

---

[103] It is present in some form in Europe, Asia, Polynesia and the Americas, suggesting that this mytheme of the separation of the world parents of Earth and Sky may be up to 40,000 years old, the approximate age of the common ancestor of both European and Asian populations.

Pan was said to be able to produce a horrible screech which would cause all to flee in terror, giving rise to the term 'panic'.[104] He later became a central figure in the folklore of the European Romantic Movement of the eighteenth and nineteenth centuries and a central deity in some twentieth-century neo-pagan movements.

Where Hermes and Apollo are together responsible for the invention of stringed instruments, Pan is associated with the panpipes, and therefore wind instruments.

Persephone

The daughter of Demeter and the wife of Hades. See Demeter.

Poseidon/Neptune

The Olympian god of the sea, storms, earthquakes, floods and horses, and the brother of Zeus and Hades. At the beginning of their reign after defeating the Titans the three brother gods divided up the kingdoms of the world by lot. The sky was won by Zeus, who considered it the most prestigious, the underworld (including the realm of the dead) was taken by Hades, and the seas and oceans taken by Poseidon.

Poseidon was both the protector and antagonist of sailors, and he plays a role in the misfortunes of Odysseus in Homer's *Odyssey*, written in the eighth century BCE. This tale describes how the roughly 750km journey (which ought to have taken perhaps four days) from Troy back to Ithaca, that Odysseus must take to get home, becomes an ordeal lasting roughly ten years at sea after Odysseus blinds Poseidon's son, the cyclops Polyphemus.

In Plato's *Dialogues*, the legendary island of Atlantis was said to be Poseidon's realm. The story was an allegory, like the Biblical Tower of Babel, for the hubris of nations and the corresponding fall which follows the angering of gods.[105]

---

[104] Does this make Pan the first heavy metal singer?

[105] Plato said that Atlantis was to be found outside the Pillars of Hercules, which is the narrowest part of the Strait of Gibraltar; the mouth of the mediterranean. Suffice to say there is no sunken continent to be found in the Atlantic. This has not stopped people looking for the Atlantis. In my opinion this is missing the point. In a general sense, all sunken pieces of landscape that once held towns or cities are Atlantises.

As the ancient Greeks were a sea-faring empire that conquered coastlines, Poseidon was an extremely important god. In Athens he was second only to Athena in terms of importance. The stories of Poseidon are numerous, and beyond the scope of this book, but the general themes are that he brings great misfortune and calamity to those who cross him and that his sexual voracity rivals that of Zeus.

He is usually portrayed as the father of Atlas and Theseus, as well as a plethora of other gods and demigods. Poseidon's symbols are the trident, the horse, the dolphin, and the fish-tailed horse 'hippocampus' which is often depicted pulling his ocean chariot.

There are many myths as to how Poseidon is responsible for the creation of horses, sometimes as a result of him spilling his seed on a rock, or fathering the horse after copulating with a goddess (sometimes Demeter) or another creature. My favourite story is that Poseidon had fallen in love with Demeter, and to impress her he showed her his kingdom of the sea and all the monsters in it. Not impressed by hideous things, Demeter asked him to create something beautiful. Poseidon spent so long producing the horse, and was so impressed at his own work, that by the time he had finished he had forgotten all about pursuing Demeter.

To the Romans he was Neptune. In comparison with Poseidon, Neptune is also a god of freshwater, especially springs and rivers, perhaps because the Roman Empire advanced much farther inland. Neptune was honoured by the festival Neptunalia on 23 July, the height of summer and droughts, showing that he had an important role in providing water for drinking and for the watering of crops.

In Tarot symbolism, water is closely identified with the subconscious, dreams and the emotions. In astrology, the formlessness of water in emphasised, and Neptune is therefore associated with the blurring of boundaries, hypnotic and drugged states, grey areas and 'watery' people who cannot be pinned down to black and white opinions.

Satyr/Faun

These were masculine nature spirits who were the companions of Dionysus. They are often depicted as men having the ears and tail of a horse, sometimes with horse legs, long hair and erect penises.

In theatre they were celebrated as comical characters with crass, sexual, and irreverent humour, leading to the term 'satire'. In stories they are wild-men with voracious sexual appetites, often chasing nymphs or copulating with beasts. In later depictions they became associated instead with Pan, and their appearance became more goat-like, with goat legs instead of those of a horse.

The Romans syncretised the Greek satyr with their own native nature deity, the faun, and these eventually became indistinguishable. In mythology the satyrs represented uncivilised behaviour, and this was later used by Christians to represent those who are controlled by sinful desires, leading to the depiction of the Devil as a goat-legged and sometimes goat-headed man-beast.

Selene/Luna

Selene is the Greek feminine personification of the moon and one of many lunar deities along with Artemis and Hecate. She is the daughter of the Titans, Hyperion and Theia, and the counterpart and sister of the sun-god Helios. Like Helios she drives a chariot across the heavens.

Over time, just as Helios became associated with Apollo, Selene became associated with his twin Artemis. Although there were several lunar goddesses, it is generally accepted that only Selene was the personification of the moon itself. She was sometimes called 'Mene' which is cognate with the word 'moon'. Going back to a Proto-Indo-European origin this word 'Mene' appears to be a feminisation of an original male lunar deity, making Mene/Selene a very ancient goddess. Despite this, she is not a primary figure in Greek mythology, though she is mentioned in passing many times. The Romans called her Luna and often depicted her with a crown bearing a moon crescent.

In astrology the cycles of the moon are of upmost importance, not only in determining one's Moon sign, but also for short cycles of times, the moon being the fastest observable natural object in the Earth's sky (with the exception of comets).[106] As the moon gave us the lunar calendar and the concept of months, she is very important as a time-keeper.

In neo-paganism, since the Romantic movement of the early nineteenth century and especially later in Wicca, Luna became associated with a central universal goddess who is personified by priestesses wearing the crescent crown in rituals. For this reason, Luna has become a major symbol in spiritual and New Age feminism.

---

[106] Apparent speed from Earth's surface.

Sirius

The canine companion of the hunter Orion. Both were transformed into constellations by Zeus. See also the goddess Sopdet/Sothis in Egyptian mythology.

The Fates/Moirai/Parcae

These are three goddesses who appear in a very similar fashion in many European cultures, usually as a maiden, a mother, and a crone. Together they weave the fate of mortals and gods alike. They may represent an ancient Proto-Indo-European myth, or a later cross-cultural transmission. (See also the Norns in Norse Mythology.)

To the Greeks they were known as the Moirai, three sisters: Clotho (the spinner), Lachesis (the allotter) and Atropos (the 'unturnable', implying death). Their role was to make sure that all people live out their allotted destiny. They are usually considered above even the power of the gods. They have served as an important motif throughout European literature wherever fated characters are to be found, such as the 'Weird Sisters' in Shakespeare's Macbeth.

To the Romans they were known as the Parcae: Nona (the goddess called upon in the ninth month of pregnancy), Decima (the tenth) who measures each person's lifespan, and Morta (the dead one) who cuts the life-threads determining the time of death for each individual.

Themis

Another Greek personification of justice, similar to Dike and the Roman Justitia. Rather than the lot of individuals, she represents the law of groups and divine justice. She is the governess of the affairs of committees and institutions. With Zeus, she is the parent of Dike, the goddess of individual justice.

Typhon

The ancient Greek serpent god, similar to the Egyptian Apep (Apophis) and the Norse Jörmungandr. (See also Apophis/Apep under Egyptian gods).

Typhon was a chaos deity who fought with Zeus for supremacy of the cosmos. Typhon was defeated and thrown into the underworld abyss,

Tartarus, a place within Hades where wicked souls and the Titans are imprisoned. Tartarus is also sometimes a deity and in some versions of the myth, the father of Typhon by Gaia. In other versions, Typhon is the fatherless son of Hera or the motherless son of Cronus.

Vesta

See Hestia.

Zeus/Jupiter

The king of the Olympian gods. The word Zeus was pronounced variously as 'Tsee-oos' or 'Thee-oos' in Ancient Greek.[107] His name is therefore the same word as the Latin 'Deus', and goes back to the Proto-Indo-European root, 'Di̯ēus'. The name Jupiter is from the same root plus the term 'Pater' (father) also from PIE: 'Dyeus ph2tēr' meaning 'sky father'. This is cognate with the Vedic Sanskrit terms 'Dyaus' and 'Dyaus-Pita'. The name of the Norse god Týr, is also thought by many Etymologists to come from the same root. This makes Zeus/Jupiter, in one form or another, one of the oldest gods of Eurasia.

To the Greeks, Zeus was the king of the Olympians who overthrew his father, the Titan Cronus. Cronus, fearing the prophecy that he would be overthrown by one of his own children, just as he had castrated and slaughtered (or imprisoned) his own father Uranus, swallowed each of the Olympians upon their birth. Their mother Rhea hid the youngest, Zeus, replacing him with a rock wrapped in swaddling clothes. Zeus was spirited away and raised in secret by the Nymphs Adrasteia and Ida, who nursed him with the milk of the goat Amalthea.

As he reached the age of manhood, Zeus conspired with his mother, and they tricked Cronus into drinking a potion which made him regurgitate the other Olympians. A great war, the 'Titanomachy', was fought between the Titans, the Olympians, and hordes of monsters that sided with one or the other.

After the victory, Zeus won the sky as his kingdom in a game of lots with his brothers Hades, god of the underworld, and Poseidon god of the sea.

---

[107] Though different words in Greek, 'Zeus' (Ζεύς) and 'theos' (θεός), meaning 'god' more generally, both have the same etymology.

Zeus married his sister Hera, and fathered many gods, goddesses and heroes either with Hera or one of his many sexual conquests, who always attracted the jealous wrath of Hera. She usually ended up punishing either Zeus' lover, or the offspring of the liaison.

In astrology, Zeus, as Jupiter, is a central figure in promoting fortune, the expansion of kingdoms, good luck, career expansion, extroversion, optimism, confidence and power.

Egyptian gods

Egyptian mythology represents thousands of years of religious belief and practice, and therefore there is no 'Egyptian mythology' as a singular entity. Any perfect or complete summary of Egyptian gods is therefore nigh-impossible. It is however still enlightening and fruitful to try. As such, my list of gods may seem sometimes contradictory and certainly incomplete, but if one is to use Tarot as a window into mythology or even as a contact with gods, then such a list is a good place to start.

In truth all mythologies represent this same complexity in their pantheons, and if it appears at first that some, such as the Greek or Norse mythologies, are more consistent, this is only an illusion caused by the fact that very few, very limited literary sources survive. In contrast, Egyptian religious documents are diverse, more accurately reflecting the complexity of human relationships to deities.

Amun

Over its 4000-year history as a civilisation, ancient Egypt went through many gods, but sun gods were especially revered and associated with the pharaoh. As we will see, there were many sun gods separated by either time or location. The sun god Amun began as the patron god of Thebes, but rose to the level of the head god of the state after the rebellion of Thebes against the ruling Hyksos by Ahmose I.[108] His success cemented him as the new pharoah, beginning the Eighteenth Dynasty, which ruled from approximately 1550 to 1292 BCE. Amun became the national deity and was fused with the earlier sun god, Ra, as Amun-Ra. Thebes then became the new capital of the empire.

---

[108] Many historians consider the Hyksos to be a tribe of Canaanites.

This dynasty under the god Amun-Ra lasted approximately 250 years, with only a short punctuation from the 'heretic' pharaoh Akhenaten, who tried to start a 'monotheism' under a new sun god Aten from roughly 1353–1336 BCE.[109] After this ill-fated rule, Amun-Ra returned with the rulership of Tutankhamun, the son of Akhenaten, who rejected his father's religion.

Amun-Ra, along with Osiris, was the most widely depicted of all the Egyptian gods and his influence spread to many other cultures, especially Libya, Nubia, and—as Zeus-Ammon and Jupiter-Ammon—also amongst the Greeks and Romans.

Amun-Ra was a pragmatic deity for Egypt to choose in order to build a new nationalism. He was considered the champion of the less fortunate, upholding rights for the poor and justice for all: the concept of divine order, Ma'at.

Those who prayed to Amun were required to purify themselves first by confessing their sins, a tradition also held by the Christian Catholic Church, Judaism, Islam, and reflected in baptism and ghusl.[110]

When Egypt conquered the kingdom of Kush, in Nubia (the region of modern-day Sudan), they identified the state deity of the Kushites as Amun. As this Kushite deity was depicted as having the head of a woolly ram, with curved horns, Amun became associated with the ram. Later depictions of Amun sometimes had ram's horns on a human head, known as the Horns of Ammon. For this reason Amun has come

---

[109] It may be beyond the purposes of this book, but I find the separation between 'polytheism' and 'monotheism' to be mostly a misunderstanding. Almost all Eurasian religions have a concept of 'the all'. This is Brahman, Chaos, the Monad, Te Kore, Ein Soph. All these concepts are remarkably similar. They also always have a collection of sub-deities, be they gods, angels, saints, jinn or otherwise. Therefore, the only difference between 'monotheisms' and 'polytheisms' is whether one focuses one's worship on the abstract 'higher' deity, or the more specific and understandable 'lower' deities. In this sense even the Catholics, Jews and Muslims are 'polytheists' in a sense, because they interact with or pray to saints, martyrs, jinn, and angels. The distinction between polytheism and monotheism is therefore, in my opinion, not very useful when comparing mythology and religion. Though many will disagree with me, I find this disagreement comes down to the difficulty that the word 'god' in English (and many languages) is used for many categories of spirits. In this I am arguing from the more general use of the word, and also from the practical concerns that religions cannot get much done with only an abstract Godhead which is defined as 'unknowable'. It is simply necessary to divide God up into relatable concepts, and these concepts invariably become sub-deities, or avatars.
[110] Islamic ritual bathing or washing.

to be associated with the zodiacal sign of Aries, as symbolised in the Emperor card of the Rider Waite Smith and Thoth Tarot decks.

Although associated with the sun in the Eighteenth Dynasty and after, Amun was originally the god of air and wind. As Amun-Ra he became a solar, creator and fertility god.

In the Leiden hymns, a group of Egyptian poems written in 1238 BCE during the reign of Ramses II, the gods Amun, Ptah, and Re (Ra) are treated as a trinity: three aspects of a unified divinity. This sets a precedent for the later Christian trinity, which proved to be a theologically pragmatic concept.

Starting in the tenth century BCE, the worship of Amun in Egypt gradually began to decline, with the exception of the city Thebes. Outside of Egypt he remained a relevant god in some places, especially in Nubia, where he was a national deity, known as Amani. Here he was consulted by seers whenever they chose a leader or during military campaigns. Elsewhere, in areas outside Egypt where the Egyptians had brought the cult of Amun, his worship continued into classical times.

In Greece he remained worshipped, as Ammon, at temples at Thebes (not to be confused with the Egyptian Thebes), and Sparta, dating to the fifth century CE. When Alexander the Great occupied Egypt in late 332 BC, He was pronounced the son of Amun by the oracle at Siwa. Amun was re-identified as a form of Zeus, and Alexander began referring to Zeus-Ammon as his real father. After Alexander's death, currency depicted him with the Horns of Ammon, a tradition that continued for centuries, including in the Quran where he is called 'Dhu al-Qarnayn' (the Two-Horned One).

As an Egyptian god, Amun is depicted with blue skin and often paired with a female deity called Amunet. Their names are the masculine and feminine forms of a word meaning 'the hidden one'. They were believed to be primordial, preceding creation. Later, Amunet was replaced as Amun's consort by Mut, whose name means 'mother'. Amun-Ra was by now considered the creator of the world and Mut the mother of everything in it. In other versions of the myth, she gave birth to the world herself through parthenogenesis. Their son is Khonsu, a male moon deity, whose name means traveller, perhaps because of the moon's nightly journey through the sky.

Several English words derive from Amun via the Greek form, Ammon, such as ammonia and ammonite.

Anubis

Anubis is a Greek version of the Egyptian name Anpu or Inpu. Anubis is the god of funerary rites, protector of graves, and guide to the underworld, usually depicted as a dog or a man with a dog's head.

An extremely ancient deity, Anubis was a protector of graves from the First Dynasty (approximately 3100–2890 BCE). He was also an embalmer of corpses, holding an important place in Egyptian religion which was particularly centred around the concept of death and the rites that allowed one a successful afterlife.

Anubis was said to perform the rite of the 'weighing of the heart', which was said to take part after the death of humans. One's heart was weighed on a scale against the 'feather of Ma'at' (the concept and deity of cosmic justice and order). If the heart was light, the soul was allowed to enter the realm of the dead. If the heart was heavy, the soul would be consumed by the monster Ammit, a chimera who had the head of crocodile, the forequarters of a lion and the hind quarters of a hippopotamus. While he was one of the oldest, the most depicted and most mentioned of the Egyptian gods, there is no still existing myth involving him outside of the weighing of the heart.

Anubis was usually depicted in black, a colour that symbolised regeneration, because of the black soil of the Nile which was relied upon to flood and fertilise crops, and also the discoloration of the corpse after embalming. Anubis is sometimes associated with his brother Wepwawet, another dog-headed or canine god who had grey or white fur. It is thought that these two deities were eventually syncretised. Anubis' female counterpart is Anput and their daughter is the serpent goddess Kebechet, who was associated with embalming fluid.

In the Middle Kingdom (approximately 2055–1650 BCE), Anubis was replaced by Osiris as lord of the underworld.

Apophis/Apep

Apophis is the Greek name for Apep, a serpent god who embodied and enacted chaos and darkness, a concept called in Egyptian 'Isfet', which was the counterpart of Ma'at, the concept of divine order and justice. Together these formed a dichotomy.

In Egyptian mythology there is often no clear distinction between a deity and a divine concept, so Ma'at was both a concept and a goddess. Isfet was similar, with Apep being the deity that enacted Isfet.

As the god of darkness, Apep was generally considered a negative deity and the opponent of Ra, the solar deity and bringer of light. He was said to have been born from Ra's umbilical cord, though in other myths he was around since the beginning of the universe. The symbolism of the serpent or snake as an antagonistic, doubt-bringing, or evil force is prehistoric, so it no surprise that it is almost a human universal. It is supposed by some that it even dates back to our lemur-like proto-primate animal ancestors who were preyed upon by snakes. While there is no real way to prove or disprove this, it is a magically useful idea, albeit not a scholarly one.

In different versions of the myth, Apep was said to dwell before the dawn or in the underworld, but in one version he is the 'world-encircler', just like the Germanic Jörmungandr. Again, this is evidence, though not proof, of the age of such an idea. Apep is also said in some myths to possess a dangerous gaze with which he tried to overwhelm and subdue Ra. One thinks of the Greek Gorgon, her snake hair, and petrifying gaze.

In one myth Ra, as the sun, is said to battle Apep every night before his victory with the dawn. In religious rituals, similarly to the Christian Satan, Apep was treated with irreverence in order to expel him. A detailed guide to expelling Apep was written, called *The Books of Overthrowing Apep*, where his wax effigy, or depiction as a drawing, was to be desecrated in various ways, including 'spitting upon Apep, 'defiling Apep with the left foot', 'taking a lance to smite Apep', 'chaining Apep', 'taking a knife to smite Apep', and 'putting fire upon Apep'. Suffice to say they weren't keen on the serpent-god.

As Apophis, he is invoked in Golden Dawn and Thelemic magical rituals as a necessary death-bringer who follows the life-bringer, the goddess Isis, who was able to overcome death by resurrecting her husband Osiris. There is an obvious comparison to be made here to the revived Jesus Christ (and the Greek Dionysus). Apophis is depicted as one of the three figures present on the Wheel of Fortune card in both the Rider Waite Smith and the Crowley Thoth decks. He is associated by the ancient Greeks, the Golden Dawn and by Crowley with Typhon.

Aten

Meaning 'disc' in the Egyptian language, Aten was originally an aspect of Ra. Though worshiped under the reign of Amenhotep III of the Eighteenth Dynasty, Aten is now mostly associated with the reign of

Akhenaten (approximately 1353–1336 BCE), who created a monotheistic state religion around Aten. Akhenaten had changed his name from Amenhotep IV in order to align himself with his chosen god Aten, and he prohibited the open worship of any other gods. This proved so unpopular that after Akhenaten's death there were attempts made to destroy all records of his existence.

Despite this, we have evidence of his reign from archaeology. He constructed a city, also called Akhenaten, as a the spiritual centre of his religion. He also constructed temples without roofs so that worshipers could pray directly to the sun overhead. This was a direct inversion of the classical temples which were enclosed, secretive and almost certainly required initiations in order to enter the deepest and most holy sections. Now everyone had equal access to the god of the sun disc. No statues of Aten were allowed, so statues of Akhenaten and his family were constructed instead as a worship by proxy, and Akhenaten himself was considered a human incarnation of Aten. This must have massively undermined the power of the Egyptian priesthood. Aten himself was not personified to the same degree as other deities, remaining abstract, and as sunlight itself he was considered to be everywhere, without a body. Akhenaten positioned himself has the only human who could directly commune with or decipher the true will of Aten.

Following Akhenaten's death and the very short reign of Smenkhkare, likely either the son or brother of Akhenaten (some even speculate that he was Akhenaten's lover), Egypt had a female pharoah called Neferneferuaten, thought to be either Akhenaten's daughter Meritaten (the wife of Smenkhkare), or Akhenaten's wife Nefertiti, who was also called Neferneferuaten during Akhenaten's reign.[111] Her reign also seems to have been extremely short, perhaps only a couple of years from 1334–1332 BCE.

After that was Tutankhaten, who quickly changed his name to Tutankhamun, famous for his golden funerary mask. Tutankhamun reverted the state religion back to the worship of Amun, and in opposition to Akhenaten brought a period of religious tolerance where people were able to revert to the worship of their chosen deities. This brought an end to one of the strangest eras in religious history.

---

[111] The practice of name-changing, and both symbolic and actual incest, amongst the royal families of Egypt complicate the identification of these individuals.

The misfortunes of the previous reign were blamed upon the displeasing of the gods which had occurred as a result of Akhenaten's iconoclasm. Tutankhamun rebuilt many of the state temples that were destroyed during Akhenaten's reign and reinstated the traditional pantheon of gods.

Atum

Atum was a primordial deity who was said to have created himself out of nothing (like the Vedic Brahman), and who was the creator of the gods Shu and Tefnut, who were the parents of all the other gods. He was variously said to have spat these two out of his mouth, or to have formed them by his hand. Atum's name means roughly 'to complete' or 'to finish'. In other versions of the myth, Atum was born of a cosmic egg (similar to that described in Orphism) which existed in the primordial formless waters (a concept also put forth in Genesis of the Bible), and was hatched in a flood which became the source of all things along with Atum.

In yet another version, Atum was preceded by Ptah, who spoke himself and the world of concepts into existence (as YHWH is said to have done in Kabbalah), and so Atum was then created and began his own creation of the physical world.

In worship, Atum was associated with the evening sun, in contrast to Ra who was the morning sun. In the Coffin Texts (2100 BCE), Atum has a conversation with Osiris, a god of afterlife, death and rebirth, where he says that one day he will uncreate the world, and it will revert to the primordial waters of Nu.

As a self-created deity, Atum bears relation to similar concepts in other cultures such as the Vedic Brahman, the Orphic Night, the Polynesian Te Po (or Te Kore), the Gnostic Monad and the Catholic 'Father' from the Trinity.

Bastet

A cat-shaped or cat-headed goddess who was worshiped at least as early as the second dynasty (2890 BCE). She has similar qualities to the goddess Sekhmet and the two were later regarded as aspects of a single goddess, with Sekhmet the lioness-headed being the active warrior aspect, and Bastet, now a domestic cat-headed deity, representing the more gentle aspects.

Bastet is the daughter of Ra and Isis, and the consort of Ptah, with whom she mothered Maahes, a lion-headed war deity. Bastet was a protector of Lower Egypt, and as an aspect of Sekhmet, was associated with the 'Eye of Ra' equated with the disc of the sun and capable of shooting a violent ray, as an embodiment of Ra's wrath, itself equated with Sekhmet/Bastet. She was also a protector goddess of pregnancy, childbirth and protection from disease and evil spirits.

Cats in ancient Egypt were highly revered, certainly in part because of their ability to protect food from insects, mice and rats, and also to protect humans and animals from snakes. Cats were sometimes mummified along with humans in ancient Egypt (though other animal mummies are also present).

Geb

In contrast to most Eurasian mythologies, the Egyptians considered the sky feminine, as the goddess Nut, and the earth masculine, a 'father nature' personified as the body of the god Geb. This is a useful thing to remember for all magical systems, Tarot included, that draw on spiritual ideas of 'divine masculine' and 'divine feminine'. These are never truly fixed, and there is nearly always a way to find both masculine and feminine aspects in any principle or concept. This will hopefully furnish one with the power of doubt whenever spiritual teachers or systems try and overreach with fixed ideas of masculine or feminine, something that I unfortunately see frequently.

Geb, as 'father nature', does all the things that a mother nature is capable of. His laughter was said to cause earthquakes, he allowed the crops to grow (like Demeter and Persephone), and he also had a feared aspect as the god of snakes, an animal which is generally considered a symbol of evil in all Eurasian cultures.

Geb was the father of Osiris, Isis, Set, Nephthys, Nehebkau (a snake god), and in some sources Horus. (Elsewhere Horus is the son of Osiris, the version most applicable to Tarot, and sometimes Horus is also the reincarnation of Osiris). Like many Eurasian myths, Geb and Nut were initially said to be pressed together in embrace and were separated by the air god Shu, allowing room for life on Earth. The underworld is said to be in Geb's body.

In Greco-Roman- ruled Egypt, Geb became associated with Cronus, in their role as fathers of the gods.

Harpocrates/Har-Pa-Khered

Harpocrates was the Greco-Egyptian adaption of Horus the Child, 'Har-Pa-Khered', into a new god of silence and secrets. It is thought that the Greeks, seeing the hieroglyph for 'child', or statues referencing this hieroglyph, misunderstood the symbol to refer to the gesture of silence, a finger held to the mouth. The original Egyptian connotation may have instead been a child sucking their finger.

In the most common version of the story, Horus was the child of Osiris and Isis. Osiris was murdered by his brother Set, and dismembered. Isis, his sister/wife, found his body parts and put them back together. She then had sex with the corpse and produced Horus. Horus became the god of the morning sun, which rose each day victorious after the nightly battle against darkness. Horus avenged his father's death by defeating Set, and became the ruler of Egypt, of whom pharaohs of this era where incarnations.

As Harpocrates, he became associated with secret societies and mystery traditions, though more in Greece and Rome than in Egypt itself. Around the turn of the first century CE, terracotta statues of Harpocrates became popular throughout the Roman Empire.

Harpocrates was a favourite deity of Aleister Crowley, who associated him with Aiwass, a being, possibly of his own creation, whom he considered the minister of Harpocrates and whom he channelled in order to write *The Book of the Law* (1909), often considered Crowley's central spiritual text by his followers. Crowley made many unique associations with Harpocrates, associating him with the divine state of primordial possibility before the beginning of creation: 'He contains everything in Himself, but is unmanifested.'[112]

In this sense, Crowley assigned Harpocrates the Hebrew letter Aleph, and connected him to the Fool card in the Tarot. For Crowley, the idea of Horus the Child represented his prophecy of a new aeon, a sexually liberated age that he said would break free of the restrictions of Crowley's Victorian era. After his death, Crowley became a libertine symbol during the counterculture movements of the 1960s. This Dionysian age of 'sex, drugs and rock'n'roll' was considered by some to have been heralded by Crowley's own rebellion and antinomian lifestyle during his life.

---

[112] Aleister Crowley, *Liber AL vel Legis: The Book of the Law* (1909), section I:7.

My favourite of Crowley's associations, however, is between Harpocrates and Harpo Marx, the silent comedian of the Marx Brothers. Though the similarity to Harpocrates and the Fool is perhaps a coincidence, the character of Harpo was a combination of a vaudeville clown, a mime, and a brilliant musician playing the harp (an instrument with classical Greek connotations), which is where he got his name. Harpo wears a coat which seems to contain an infinite number of props which he can produce at any moment out of 'nothing' (Ein Soph), and with which he communicates instead of words, like a god speaking the world into existence. During a 1933 solo tour of Soviet Russia, the actor Arthur 'Harpo' Marx also conveyed secret messages in and out of the country by taping envelopes to his leg.[113] In Crowley's Thoth Tarot, Harpo Marx, as Harpocrates, is depicted in the face of the Fool card, offering a humorous insight into how Crowley saw mythology represented in the world and media around him.

Heka

Both the name of a god and the Egyptian word for magic. According to Egyptian literature (Coffin Texts, spell 261), Heka existed 'before duality had yet come into being'. In this sense, he is akin to the forming principle (which Crowley associated with Harpocrates in the previous entry), a possible precursor to the concept of Keter in Kabbalah, and a possible source for the Greek concept of the Logos: the boundary that is formed around a concept, in order that one thing may be differentiated from another, as well as the concept of the inner principle, or purpose of a thing or concept.

Heka was said to have been created at the beginning of time with Atum, a god who spoke himself into existence, just as YHWH was said in Kabbalah to speak or write the world into existence via the Hebrew alphabet. This principle, call it Heka, Logos or something similar, is one of the most important in all of philosophy, and it was taught to the West through the Greek Heraclitus. As such, it is also core to any form of magic that involves speech, writing or symbols, such as the Tarot.

As a primordial force that is present in all creation, Heka is also similar to the concept of Kia in the magical theory of Austin Osman Spare,

---

[113] 'None Swifter Than These: 100 Years of the Diplomatic Courier Service' (2018), US Department of State, Bureau of Diplomatic Security https://www.state.gov/none-swifter-than-these-100-years-of-the-diplomatic-courier-service/dcs Last retrieved 4 April, 2024.

which was used by Chaos magicians such as Peter J. Carroll. In this theory, magic is the manipulation of the forming principle, Kia. While matter cannot easily be brought in and out of existence by magic, it is thought by Spare and Carroll that one can negotiate with Kia, just before the moment of manifestation, nudging it one way or another in order to grant one's will. Put more simply, before every event, the universe must make a decision on how that event will unfold. Chaos magic aims to push these decisions towards the will of the magician.

Hermanubis

Another Greco-Egyptian god, Hermanubis is the syncretisation of Anubis with Hermes, both of whom are psychopomps: deities who can lead the soul to the afterlife or else allow magicians to commune with spirits, the dead and other gods.

Hermanubis had a cult of worship in the Egyptian town of Sa-ka, called Cynopolis by the Greeks, meaning 'city of dogs'. Hermanubis also made occasional appearances in Roman and later Renaissance literature.

He is depicted as a jackal, or dog-headed god holding the Caduceus, the staff of Hermes featuring two intertwined snakes and wings. To the Greeks, Hermanubis represented the Egyptian priesthood, especially the mystical search for truth.

Heru-Ra-Ha (Thelemic mix of Horus of the Horizon, and Harpocrates)

Not a true Egyptian god in the historical sense, but rather another deity syncretised by Aleister Crowley, in his visions and channelling, which produced his *Book of the Law*. Here Heru-Ra-Ha is a mix of Hoor-paar-kraat, Horus the Child, as Harpocrates, and Ra-Hoor-Khuit, Horus of the Horizon. Crowley used this syncretic consideration as a way to discuss active and passive forces (respectively Horus of the Horizon and Harpocrates), present in his prophesied 'Age of Horus'.

Horus

One of the most important of the ancient Egyptian gods, his depictions and descriptions are diverse enough that he may be better understood as a family of distinct, related gods. This tendency to spilt up spirits into different aspects, though perhaps confusing to a modern thinker, is necessary in order to understand mythology, theology and any explanation of the spiritual, symbolic or conceptual space. Because they are not confined to bodies, spirits are freer to change form and to interlink in complex ways.

Horus is most often depicted as a falcon-headed god, and his name means 'falcon'. He is the first known national god of Egypt, especially of Upper Egypt. The pharaohs of this time were considered incarnations of Horus during their lifetime, and were associated with Osiris after death.

Horus is usually said to have been the son of Osiris and Isis, and as Horus the Younger he is associated with the morning sun, the avenging of the murder of Osiris by his brother Set, and the foundation of the Egyptian Empire. In other versions of the myth, however, he was the son of Hathor, a sky goddess, and of Ra, a sun god. In still other versions, he is the brother of Osiris and Isis rather than (or perhaps as well as) their son. This is possible through Osiris' rebirth. In yet another conception of the myth, Horus is both Osiris' son as well as the reborn Osiris himself.

When Horus was represented as a god of the sky, his right eye was said to be the Sun, and his left eye the Moon. In his form as Horus the Elder (Heru-ur), brother of Osiris, he is the son of Geb and Nut, Father Earth and Mother Sky. Here he is the upholder of cosmic order and truth, Ma'at, necessary for his role in maintaining the Empire.

As Horus the Child, he is considered an early template for the Christ Child, with Isis as Mary Mother of God, from Catholic Christianity. As a state and solar god, Horus was sometimes merged with Ra as Ra-Horakhty. For other versions of Horus, see the entries for Harpocrates (Horus the Child) and Heru-Ra-Ha (Thelemic deity).

Isis

A major goddess dating at least as far back as 2686 BCE, in her most well-attested myth Isis is the sister and wife of Osiris, bringing him back to life after his murder by his brother Set. Horus is born of the union of Isis with the corpse of Osiris, and in some versions of the myth Horus is himself a reborn aspect of Osiris. Horus then avenges Osiris by defeating Set and establishing the spiritual foundations of the Egyptian Empire. The early pharaohs were said to be incarnations of Horus during their lifetimes and reigns, therefore Isis was the divine mother of Pharaohs. She was invoked in prayer and magic by Egyptians for healing, love and fertility.

During the New Kingdom (approximately 1550–1070 BCE), Isis incorporated attributes of the sky goddess Hathor, who was prominent in early Egyptian religion. In the first millennium BCE, Isis and Osiris became the two most widely worshipped of the Egyptian gods and Isis absorbed many of the qualities of other goddesses, including in neighbouring kingdoms such as Nubia and Kush. At the height of her worship, she was the protector of the empire, the governess of the sky and nature, and the goddess of fate. During the Greek rule of Egypt, Isis became popular amongst the Egyptian Greeks and she gained a new consort, Serapis, whose cult was deliberately established by the Greek Pharaoh Ptolemy I Soter (367–282 BCE) in order to unify the Egyptians and the Greeks in his empire. Serapis was a syncretic Greco-Egyptian deity combining Osiris and Apis, a bull-god who was the son of the goddess Hathor.

The worship of Isis was widespread until the rise of Christianity in the fourth to sixth centuries CE. At least in her iconography, Isis' image was incorporated into the worship of Mother Mary, especially in statues and paintings: a goddess with the infant god on her knee, first Horus and then the child Christ.

Isis played an important role in Egyptian funerary rites regarding grief, and the conveying of spirits from death to the afterlife.

In modern feminist neo-paganism, Isis has become an important symbol of the empowered divine feminine principle. This was helped by Isis' association with numerous other goddesses throughout Egyptian, Greek, North African and Roman history, allowing Isis to eventually become generalised as an icon of femininity itself.

Khepra/Khepri

A scarab-headed god of the dawn. As scarab beetles lay their eggs in dung, they became a symbol of life emerging from non-life (and value from what is not valuable). As the sun appeared each morning, it was said to be born anew from the underworld, and thus the dawn was associated with Khepra the scarab god. As the scarab rolls the dung ball across the earth, Khepra was thought to roll the sun-disc across the sky.

No cult of Khepra is recorded, so he is assumed to be a sub-deity or aspect of the god Ra. Sometimes he is part of a trinity, with Khepra the morning sun, Ra the midday sun, and Atum the evening sun. In any case, Khepra was the symbol of renewed life and jewellery. Ornaments depicting scarabs were common amulets amongst the ancient Egyptians.

Khonsu

A falcon-headed god of the moon who is sometimes the same deity as Horus. As a separate deity, his father was Amun and his mother Mut, of the primordial waters of Nu. In one creation myth, Khonsu is the serpent who fertilises the cosmic 'world-egg'. His name means 'traveller', which may refer to the movement of the moon through the night sky. In this manner, he marked the progression of time, due to the importance of the moon for the creation of calendars. He was the god of monthly time cycles such as the fertility of women and livestock. As a light source, he was also invoked to offer protection at night. He was also prayed to as a healer.

Ma'at/Isfet

Like many Egyptian deities, Ma'at was both a concept and a person. She was divine order, truth, law, morality, charity and justice, and functioned all the way from the personal and societal level to the cosmic. She regulated the seasons, the stars, the behaviour of mortals as well as gods, and was the force that allowed chaos to form matter. Her opposite destructive and/or evil force was Isfet, which when personified, became Apep (Apophis). Together they formed a dichotomy Ma'at/Isfet, with one being necessary for the other. This cycle was present in life/death, flood/drought, peace/war, day/night, truth/deception and many other dichotomies.

By the Eighteenth Dynasty (c. 1550–1295 BCE), Ma'at was said to be the daughter of Ra, (now a creator god) who had become the dominant national god, and who conferred state authority. Ma'at was deeply connected to the role of the pharaoh, who was supposed to uphold and achieve this moral order for the nation.

Ma'at was sometimes said to be the wife of Thoth, the god of writing, language, philosophy, magic, and communication, who was also said to maintain the universe and to be an example of a being who properly maintains the concept of Ma'at. In this role she and Thoth were associated with scribes, who as the backbone of law, communications, logistics, accounting, political discourse, bureaucracy and taxes were sworn to uphold Ma'at and to eschew corruption and crime.

Ma'at had another important role, as a judge of the dead through the rite of weighing a dead soul's heart. Upon death, a soul of a dead person would be delivered to Ma'at by Anubis. Here she would weigh the person's heart on a set of scales against a feather. If the heart was light (moral) as the feather they would be allowed into the afterlife. If their heart was heavy (corrupted) they would be consumed by the monster Ammit (see Anubis).

When personified, Ma'at is depicted as a young woman wearing an ostrich feather (the same that was used to weigh the dead). In other images she also has wings attached to her arms. Ma'at was in in some myths the sister of Shu, the god who held apart (like Atlas of the Greeks) Mother Sky (Nut) and Father Earth (Geb).

Montu

A falcon-headed god of war, often linked to the scorching effects of Ra, or to Horus. All three were depicted as falcon-headed, and Ra and Horus were also sometimes syncretised as Ra-Horakhty.

Montu was the god of warriors and bravery on the battlefield and was considered the upholder of Ma'at (righteous justice and cosmic order). As Montu-Ra, he was the deity of Upper Egypt, with Atum Ra the deity of Lower Egypt, especially during the Middle Kingdom (c. 2055–1650 BCE) when he was the supreme state god before being eventually supplanted by Amun.

Montu was sometimes also depicted as a white bull with a black snout, or as a bull-headed man (during the late period of the seventh to fourth centuries BCE). The Greeks associated Montu with Ares.

Mut

Also known as Maut and Mout. In one of the creation myths, Mut is a primordial goddess born of the formless waters of Nu (or Nun), who in turn births all of creation through parthenogenesis. She was the mother of Khonsu, a moon god, and the wife of Amun-Ra. Together these three were worshipped as a trinity at the Egyptian capital city of Thebes, especially during the Middle Kingdom (c. 2055–1650 BCE) and New Kingdom (c. 1550–1070 BCE). Mut was also worshipped as a lioness goddess in Upper Egypt, similar to the Lower Egyptian goddess Sekhmet.

Nu/Nun

In yet another gender inversion, at times the primordial waters (previously discussed through the feminine Nut) were represented by a male god called Nu or Nun, a formless chaos of endless potentiality from which all creation was spawned. I personally find contemplating both the masculine (Nu) and feminine (Nut) aspects of spiritual concepts to be magically useful.

Nut

Nut is Mother Sky, and the consort of Geb, who is Father Earth. She is often depicted as a naked woman, arched over her husband, her body forming the sky. She is the daughter of Shu (god of the air and wind) and Tefnut (goddess of moisture, dew and rain), and her children are Osiris, Isis, Set and Nephthys. In some versions, especially Greco-Egyptian, she is also the mother of Horus.

Common to many Eurasian mythologies is the theme of the separation of the 'world parents'. In this case Geb and Nut are born pressed together, allowing no space for things to live. Shu, god of the air, separates them, allowing life. Shu's name means 'one who holds up' and he is often depicted between the two, with his feet on Geb, and his arms pushing up the sky. In this way he bears a relation to the Greek Atlas, and the Māori Tāne.

Though Nut was formerly the goddess of the night sky only, over time she became the sky more generally. By extension, Nut was the goddess of all the heavenly bodies. Her body was also considered a barrier protecting the order of the Earth and its systems from the chaotic space outside. The toes and fingers of her four limbs were said to touch the four cardinal directions. In this way she was a goddess of orientation. She was also considered a protector of the dead, with the inside of sarcophagus lids often being painted with her image.

Crowley has his own curious interpretation of the goddess Nut, whose name he spells Nuit, perhaps in order to make it the same as the

French word for 'night'. Crowley was apparently fluent in French and was fond of playing such word games, which helped convey his esoteric meanings but are frequently not etymological. Crowley seems to have further conflated Nut with the concept of Nu. Nu, regarded by the Egyptians as masculine, is the primordial formless waters from which all creation was formed, a concept similar to the Hindu Brahman, the Kabbalistic Ein Soph, or the Orphic night.

Nuit is an important concept in Crowley's religious system Thelema. She represents endless potentiality, in contrast to the masculine Hadit, which is all in a single point, a singularity or monad. Hadit has no true Egyptian equivalent. These deities are described in Crowley's *Book of the Law* and elsewhere in his writings.

Osiris

As the religion of ancient Egypt was highly centred around the themes of death and the afterlife, Osiris, the reborn god, was one of the most widely worshipped. He is usually depicted as a green-skinned man with mummy-wrapped legs, a crown and a crook and flail. These are symbols of the farming of animals and crops. He is the god of rebirth, regrowth, fertility, agriculture, vegetation and the afterlife. In myths, Osiris is usually the son of Geb (Father Earth) and Nut (Mother Sky). His sister and wife is Isis, and his other siblings are Set, Nephthys (Nebet-Het), and sometimes Horus the Elder.

The most famous myth of Osiris is of his resurrection:

Osiris had risen to become a king amongst the gods. Set, his brother, grew jealous. Set threw a party which Osiris attended. At the party he brought out a coffin made for a king and in the spirit of mischief, invited the party-goers to lie in the coffin. Several tried but found that they didn't fit. Osiris had his turn, and suddenly Set and his conspirators slapped the lid on top and nailed the coffin shut. The coffin was then weighed down with lead and thrown into the Nile. Osiris drowned, and the rising waters of the Nile, personified as the god Nu, dragged the coffin out to sea. Isis, in mourning, vowed to find his body and walked the Earth in search of it, asking if any saw Osiris as she went. Through a divination, Isis discovered that the coffin had washed out to sea after losing its weights and washed up on the shores of Byblos, Phoenicia (now Lebanon, over 400km away). Where the coffin had landed, a tamarisk tree had grown (a flowering tree which can grow in barren soil and from salt water).

When Isis found the coffin, she released it from the tree and brought it back to Egypt. It is here that in some versions of the myth she conceived a child by having sex with the corpse. In another version she had turned into a kite bird and conceived magically by flying over the body.

The body was returned to Egypt, and though it was hidden, it was discovered by Set, who dismembered it into fourteen pieces which he scattered around the land. Isis again went in search and collected all the parts excluding the penis which remained lost. She then embalmed the body and mummified it in the traditional Egyptian rite. This act of magic restored Osiris who went on to eternal life in the underworld. Isis then gave birth to Horus the younger, who become the archetype of the pharaohs. Set was now jealous of Horus' kingship, and Horus, forewarned by Isis, engaged his uncle in battle. During the fight, Horus lost an eye, which became the moon (his strong eye being the sun), and in revenge he castrated Set. A tribunal of the gods was raised to settle the matter and the eventual verdict was Horus' victory and Set's redemption in his appointment as the defender of Ra.

Osiris, in the underworld, took on the role of watching over the judgement of the souls by Ma'at, the weigher of hearts. When the soul's heart was lighter than the feather of Ma'at, a sign of morality, it would be guided by Osiris towards paradise on a solar barque (sailing ship).

In Greco-Egyptian times, the Greeks associated Osiris with Dionysus, the central deity of the Orphic religion.

Ptah

A confusing deity that took on many roles at different times. As a creator deity who spoke the world into being (from a mound of earth), he was similar to Atum. He was depicted as a mummified man, sometimes with green skin, similar to Osiris. At other times he was a dwarf like the god Bes. He shared many of the same attributes with Osiris and was sometimes syncretised with him as Ptah-Sokar-Osiris. As an underworld god he was revered by blacksmiths, miners (as the provider of metals), and craftspeople. In other myths he was linked to Ra or Aten.

Ptah is not well attested in early Egyptian literature, but over time became the sovereign deity of the city of Memphis. Despite the difficulty in pinning him down to one role, Ptah was an important god, and it is from his name that the word Egypt is derived. The word comes from a name for Memphis meaning 'the temple of the soul of Ptah' (ḥwt-k3-ptḥ). The Greeks took this term and abbreviated it to 'Aígyptos' and then applied it to the whole country. The true Egyptian name for the country was Kemet (or Kumat), meaning 'black land', from the dark soil that the flooded Nile provided.

Ptah's wife was sometimes said to be Sekhmet. The Greeks associated Ptah with Hephaestus, the smith-god.

Ra/Re

Perhaps the most recognisable of the many Egyptian solar deities, he was especially associated with the sun at midday. Ra was the king of the gods for a time and was the sovereign god of Egypt and the god of pharaohs for much of Egypt's history. Like Horus, with whom he was sometimes conflated (as Ra-Horakhty), he is a falcon-headed god. In the New Kingdom between 1570 and 1069 BCE he was fused with Amun as Amun-Ra. He was often considered the creator of all living things, with humans having been created from his tears and sweat.

One of Ra's primary roles was to sail the 'solar barque', a sailing ship containing the sun, across the daytime sky and through the underworld during the night, through a subterranean section of the Nile. In the underworld he transformed into a ram-headed god (like Amun). Every night Apep (Apophis) would attack the boat, they would battle, and Ra would emerge with the sun, victorious every morning. At other times, Ra was combined with Atum, Khepri, Aten, or Montu all of whom are solar gods.

Ra could also be a vengeful god, with his eye being a ray-like weapon, that was often personified itself as a goddess, Sekhmet. When angry, she would attack those who had disturbed Ra. When calm, she became the goddess Hathor or the cat-goddess Bastet.

Sekhmet

A Lower Egyptian lioness goddess (similar to the Upper Egyptian Mut), who was a manifestation of the 'Eye of Ra', a ray-like weapon of the sun, she was also often considered the angry form of either Hathor or Bastet. Sekhmet is a goddess of violence, battle and plagues who likes to drink blood.

(See also Bastet.)

Set

The vengeful brother of Osiris and Isis. (See also entries for Osiris, Isis, and Horus.) He is a god of the desert, storms, disorder, violence, and foreigners. His parents were Geb and Nut.

Set was depicted with the head of an unknown animal referred to by Egyptologists only as the 'Set animal'. Nobody has been able to decipher which animal his depictions represent.

Solar deities

As Egypt was one of the longest enduring empires in history, its mythology underwent a huge amount of variation over its 4000 years. The sun was the dominant feature of their mythology, and was deeply connected to their concept of state authority. The pharaohs were believed to be incarnations or descendants of the sun, and thus different dynasties chose different state religions with different solar deities, many of whom were syncretised from earlier god-forms.

In total, there were more than 2000 Egyptian deities and hundreds of them associated with or conceptualised as the sun. Many of these also served as creator gods. Amongst the more well know solar deities are:

- Amun, creator deity sometimes identified as a sun god.
- Aten, god of the sun, the visible disc of the sun.
- Atum, the creator and finisher of the world, who represents the sun as it sets.
- Bastet, cat goddess associated with the sun.
- Hathor, mother of Horus and Ra and goddess of the sun.
- Horus, god of the sky whose right eye was considered to be the sun and his left the moon.
- Khepra, god of the rising sun, creation and renewal of life.
- Ptah, god of craftsmanship, the arts, and fertility, sometimes said to represent the sun at night.
- Ra, god of the sun, often the creator of the world.
- Sekhmet, goddess of war and of the sun, sometimes also of plagues, and the creator of the desert.
- Sopdu, god of war and the scorching heat of the summer Sun.

Shai

The concept and god of fate. His name means 'that which is ordained'. Some of the time, he was considered a goddess, Shait, the feminine form of the same name. He was said to determine the length of each human's life and to determine their fortune. In some myths it is Shai who judges souls after death rather than Ma'at.

During Atenism, the sun-disc religion of the religious reformer Pharaoh Akhenaten, Shai was considered an attribute of Aten. Later, Ramses II claimed to be the lord of Shai (fate). Shai first appeared in the Eighteenth Dynasty. In contrast to the related concepts of Ma'at (divine order/justice) and Isfet (disorder/evil), Shai is a neutral force, capable of bringing either fortune or misfortune.

Shai was sometimes said to be the husband of Meskhenet, goddess of the birth brick (a ritual implement used to support the mother during childbirth and covered in protective spells). She was the creator of the Ka, a part of the soul or vital essence breathed into the child by her at birth, which determined the difference between a living and a dead person. At other times Shai was the husband of Renenutet, the goddess who would give a child their 'Ren' or true name. Shai was at other times the husband of Shepset, a hippopotamus goddess of childbirth.

As Shai is also the Egyptian word for 'pig', Shai is sometimes depicted as a pig with a serpent's head.

Sopdet/Sothis

Sopdet referred to the star Sirius, as well as being a goddess. The star would periodically disappear throughout the year, and its reappearance coincided with the beginning of the periodic Nile flood, which was necessary for the growing of crops. This marked the beginning of the Egyptian new year, and thus Sopdet was both a goddess of the flood and fertility, and the goddess of the new year and thus new beginnings.

She was the wife of Sah, the constellation Orion, and their child was Sopdu, the planet Venus. These are the three brightest stars of the Egyptian northern winter sky. The Greeks called her Sothis and combined her with Isis. At other times Sothis was combined with Anubis or Osiris in a male version of the deity.

Sphinx

A mythological creature important to both the Egyptians and the Greeks. In the Egyptian tradition, the sphinx is a (usually benevolent) guardian. The word 'sphinx' is Greek. It is no longer known what the carvers of the Great Sphinx of Giza called the creature or the monument, but it is understood by archaeologists to have been created during the Old Kingdom, roughly 2558–2532 BCE.

In the New Kingdom, which began between 1570 and 1544 BCE, the sphinx was considered a depiction of Hor-em-akhet, 'Horus of the Horizon'. Its face bears a strong resemblance to the statue depictions of the Pharaoh Khafre, of the Fourth Dynasty, which would date its construction to roughly 2500 BCE.

In Greek tradition, the sphinx, while also a guardian, is a dangerous creature with the head of a woman, the body of a lion, and the wings of a bird. She challenges those who come to her to answer a riddle, and then eats those who fail to answer correctly. The sphinx therefore became associated in esotericism as being a spiritual or metaphorical guardian of occult knowledge.

Thoth/ḏḥwty

An ibis or baboon-headed god of the moon, wisdom, knowledge, writing, calendars, record-keeping, science, magic, art and judgement, Thoth is the Greek version of his name, borrowed from the Coptic, Thōout. His Egyptian name is 'ḏḥwty' pronounced 'diḥautī' or 'tihauti'. The word Thoth may therefore not originally be a pronunciation, but rather an abbreviation, in which each letter forms a syllable: Thoth → TeeHoTeH, or something similar. In any case the original pronunciation is not well understood.

In mythology, Thoth was an important god, serving as the scribe to the pantheon. In Egyptian culture, scribes held a privileged position in an empire that relied on extensive record-keeping, accountancy, logistics and priestly texts.

Thoth was a god of balances, present during the judging of the soul by Anubis and Ma'at, and was said to remark whenever the outcome of the judgement was exactly even. In this sense he was stronly linked to Ma'at, the goddess of divine justice, and she was normally considered to be his wife. Thoth was also often said to be the balancer of forces in the universe, including the stars, the heavens and the earth. He therefore had a role in setting all disputes.

Thoth was the god of astrology, which was very important to the Egyptians, and the Egyptian astrological methods laid the groundwork for the Hellenistic astrology that is most popular in the West today. As a moon god, Thoth governed short cycles of time and is said to have created the calendar. Similarly to Atum, Thoth was sometimes said to have created himself from nothing. Thoth had a female counterpart who shared many of his attributes called Seshat.

To the Greeks, Thoth was the same deity as Hermes and they attributed to him the invention of geometry, mathematics, writing, astrology, astronomy, medicine, theology, and oratory.

Norse gods

In this section I have kept the Old Norse spellings of the names. There are two special letters in Old Norse that were once also used in English:

The letter ð (eth) is pronounced as a voiced 'th' as in the word 'this'.

The letter þ (thorn) is pronounced as an unvoiced 'th' as in the word 'thanks'.

There are also some different vowels:

Ö is pronounced 'aw'.

Ǫ is pronounced like the 'o' in the word 'lot'.

Æ, the letter ash, is pronounced like the vowel in the word 'day'.[114]

In Old Norse the 'r' sounds are rolled.

The letter J is pronounced like the English letter Y.

Baldr

The son of the god Óðinn and the goddess Frigg, and brother to Thor. His name means 'brave' and 'prince'. He was the most popular and beautiful of the male gods and was said to shine with a radiant light. His beauty extended to his wisdom, his voice and his words.

The love that the other gods had for him incited the jealousy of Loki, who was the second most charming of the gods. To protect him, his mother Frigg made every living thing and object vow not to hurt

---

[114] This letter differs from the pronunciation in modern Icelandic, where it is pronounced like 'eye', or in Old English where it is pronounced like the vowel in 'bat'.

Baldr. All complied except the plant mistletoe, which was somehow passed over, perhaps because it was deemed insignificant (like Loki felt in his jealousy). Loki took note of the mistletoe and fashioned an arrow from this wood.

Later, having (almost) succeeded in making Baldr invulnerable, the gods were having fun by hurling dangerous items at him, knowing that he couldn't be hurt. To them it was a hilarious comedy. Loki slipped up to Baldr's blind brother Höðr, who was feeling left out of the game. Giving him the special arrow and a bow Loki whispered to him which direction to shoot. To the shock of the other gods and of Höðr who took a moment to realise what had happened, the arrow pierced and killed Baldr. The gods, apart from Loki, were grief stricken.

Frigg went to the goddess of the dead, Hel (who is Loki's daughter), and asked that Baldr be restored to life. Hel agreed, but only if all things alive and dead were to weep for Baldr's death. Frigg went around the world asking for each person, and thing, to cry for Baldr. All complied except one giantess, Þökk, who was Loki in disguise. So Hel deemed that Baldr must remain in the land of the dead, and Frigg and the gods were held to their agreement. Loki was discovered, imprisoned and tortured, until Ragnarök, the fated final battle of the gods.

The symbolism of this story presents us with both the concept of a perfect man, Baldr, and an exploration of how evil people think. Loki hated Baldr for the very qualities that other people loved him for. This is the bitterness that turns beauty into something terrible and wants to destroy what is good. Loki's act started a chain of cosmic disorder and it was never again fully restored, causing a slow decline which eventually led to the end of their world.

Fenrir

Fenrir is a wolf-god who is the child of Loki and the Jötunn woman Angrboða ('the one who brings grief'), and who is forsworn to kill Óðinn during Ragnarök.

As Fenrir became an adult wolf, he started to become giant in size, and this scared the gods. When Óðinn and the other gods received an oracle which predicted the danger that Fenrir would bring, they sought to bind Fenrir to forestall the destiny. They did this by daring Fenrir to break through various chains and shackles, pretending it was a game. Fenrir, knowing his own enormous strength, complied and even though each chain was bigger than the last, he broke through the bonds every time. Finally, the gods brought out a thin rope made by the dwarves from six impossible, or difficult to obtain, ingredients:

- The sound of a cat's footfall
- The beard of a woman
- The roots of mountains
- The sinews of the bear
- The breath of the fish
- The spittle of the birds.

Fenrir, seeing the thin rope, initially refused to be bound by a mere ribbon as there is no prestige to be gained by breaking such a bond. He eventually complied only if a god would put his right hand in the wolf's mouth. The dutiful warrior god Týr complied and when Fenrir found himself unable to break the bonds he bit off Týr's hand. The symbolism is that of the high price of trying to overcome fate.

Forseti

The god of justice and reconciliation, he was the son of Baldr, and lived in Baldr's hall Glitnir ('the shining one'), which was made of gold and silver. Forseti is mentioned only twice in Old Norse literature, so we know very little about him, though he seems to be a god who was invoked by judges, lawgivers and governors in order to improve their counsel.

Freyja/Frigg

These two were probably originally the same goddess as their names are cognate and they have similar roles. Frigg is the wife of Óðinn ('the crazed/inspired one'), whereas Freya (meaning 'lady') is married to Óðr ('crazy/inspired'). Frigg/Freyja is the deity who gave us the name of the day Friday. She was said to be a powerful sorceress, with the power of foresight, and extremely beautiful. There are many stories in which various gods, dwarves and Jötunn tried to take her as a bride.

She rode on a chariot pulled by cats, and was a goddess of fertility, agriculture, and sex. She also taught Óðinn the art of 'seiðr', a form of seer magic forbidden to men, a taboo which Óðinn broke.

Freyr

The brother of Freyja, his name means 'lord', and may also belong to another root word meaning 'fecund'. Freyr was a male fertility god, and the god of harvests, peace, prosperity and fair weather. As one of the kindest of the gods, he was later associated with Jesus, and was depicted similarly, as a handsome, youthful man with long hair and a beard. He also ruled over Álfheimr, the realm of the elves. He owned Skíðblaðnir, a sailing ship, that always had a fair wind in its sails, and which was able to be folded up and put into a pocket. Freyr also rode Gullinbursti, a large boar, instead of a horse. For a time, Freyr possessed a magic sword which was able to fight by itself, but he gave this up to his vassal Skírnir in exchange for him wooing the Jötunn maiden Gerðr on Freyr's behalf. Though successful, this loss of the sword had consequences when Freyr was made to battle at Ragnarök without it.

Together with his sister Freyja, their father Njörðr, and a number of other gods, Freyr was one of the Vanir. This was a clan of gods who were once at war with the dominant Æsir, ruled by Óðinn. At the end of the war Freyr and Freyja went to live with the Æsir, as part of a peace pact.

Freyr was also called Yngvi.

Heimdall

A son of Óðinn, Heimdall was a guardian god who kept watch for invaders at the rainbow Bifröst, which was at the junction of the earth and the sky. He was said to be the whitest of the gods and to be 'emerald-toothed'. He possessed the signal-horn Gjallarhorn, the sounding of which was foretold to mark the beginning of Ragnarök. He was said to have nine mothers, nine being a central and oft-occurring symbolic number for the Norse. There is much discussion about what this means, but it would make sense that the number nine would tie Heimdall to many concepts including the nine worlds of the world tree and the nine daughters of Ægir and Rán, who personified waves of the ocean.

Hel

This was the goddess of death, and the realm of the dead, which was also called Hel. This is cognate to the word 'hell' in English, which originally meant 'cave' or 'concealed place'. Though we now associate this in English with a place of torment, the term was originally more neutral, and referred only to a mysterious and dark place, symbolising the silent state of death. The goddess Hel was a daughter of Loki and she ruled over Niflheim, the 'misty place' of which Hel was a region. She was a goddess of the duality of life and death, and this was apparent by her appearance, which is half 'flesh-coloured' and half 'blue' (the old Norse word 'blá' also meant 'black'), suggesting that she was, in appearance, half alive and half dead. She governed the portion of the dead who died of sickness or old age. These were the souls that did not make it to the hall of Óðinn, Valhǫll,[115] nor Fólkvangr, the field of Freyja, both of which were reserved only for those who died bravely in combat.

Loki

A complex trickster god who rode the line between good and evil, order and chaos. He is my favourite villain in all of literature, but despite many depictions of him in pop culture, his use as a character is generally not as well written as he is in the Eddas, which are the original Icelandic source material for nearly everything we know about Norse mythology.

Loki was the blood brother of Óðinn and therefore at least as old as him. Despite this, his age is not apparent to the other gods, and he frequently goes on adventures with Thor, Óðinn's son, who he often manipulates. He is one of the gods with the most stories told about him. Loki is a shapeshifter, often appearing as animals and old women, and he seems to possess the powers of those creatures he takes the form of.

---

[115] Though the spelling 'Valhalla' is common, it is not grammatical in Old Norse. The original word is Valhǫll, were hǫll simply means 'hall'.

One day, a wall builder came to the gods and made a bet that if he could not complete a fortress wall for the gods before three seasons were over, then he would forfeit his payment. The price was to be both the sun and moon, and also Freyr's hand in marriage. Though this was a terrible price, Loki—who thought he had a sure bet—talked the gods into accepting the bet, with his charm. Over time, it became clear that both the wall builder and his horse, Svaðilfari, were magical, and that he was going to win the bet if something was not done about it. After failing several times to slow the builder's progress, Loki turned himself into a mare in order to distract the magic stallion. The stallion left the job to copulate with the mare, and soon Loki, remaining in the form, gave birth to Óðinn's eight legged magic horse, Sleipnir. Loki was therefore a god of androgyny, something mistrusted by the patriarchal Norsemen.

Of the gods' magic items, many were procured as the result of Loki's chaotic tricks and pranks, and these benefits often came from the great risks that Loki took, often due to his pride and his bragging. As such, Loki represents the type of risky chaos from which great ideas and inventions come. Both Óðinn and Loki were chaotic gods, but Óðinn represented the type of chaos that brings new order, while Loki's chaos was much riskier. While in the short term it produced many benefits, it ultimately brought death and destruction to the gods. In this way I see a lot of Loki in chaotic cult leaders like Charles Manson. Brilliant and charming, these are nevertheless destructive men, who first bring enjoyment to their followers. Over time, their leadership decays into violence as they become resentful. These people can be spotted by observing their manner and their effects. It is hard for instance to tell how old they are, and they are often surrounded by younger people, especially women, whose gullibility and lack of confidence they manipulate to their own end. They are charming until crossed and then they are full of rage. It is nearly impossible to tell whether they are cheekily joking with or insulting those around them with their teasing, and they will frequently escalate things just to test people.

Loki is humour and good fun turned bad. He represents bitterness and resentment buried until it seethes. He preferred to be the centre of negative attention than to be ignored, and resented it when others were praised instead of him. As the second most beautiful and charming male god after Baldr, he orchestrated Baldr's death out of jealousy. (See Baldr.)

By upsetting the order of Asgard, Loki was ultimately the harbinger of Ragnarök, the final battle and death of the gods.

Óðinn (Odin)

The ruler of the gods and the creator of many things, including human beings, he gave one of his eyes in exchange for wisdom or inner sight. He was a powerful magician and shape shifter. He gained the knowledge of the Runes by sacrificing himself to himself for nine days and nights[116] on the brink of death, hung on Yggdrasil,[117] the world tree. He also obtained the secrets of Seiðr, or seer magic, from Freyja, breaking a taboo which forbade its use by men.

Óðinn travelled the worlds in disguise as "Hárbarð" (greybeard), the form in which he is the template for most wizards: old, long-bearded, wearing a traveller's robe, a traveller's staff (the disguised spear Gungnir), and a wide-brimmed hat. Gandalf the Grey and Father Christmas both owe their image to this form.

Óðinn had two ravens called Huginn and Muninn, 'thought' and 'memory', spies who brought him knowledge from afar. He was a general and a schemer, a god of raiders and tacticians. His throne was Hliðskjálf, the high seat from which he was able to observe all realms.

In every battle he chose who was to be spared, who was to be victorious, and who was to die. Those who fought bravely were carried off to his hall, Valhǫll (Valhalla), by the Valkyrja (Valkyries), where the men feasted, drank and fought until they were to be called to the final battle at Ragnarök. There Óðinn was destined to be swallowed whole and alive, fighting the giant wolf Fenrir.

The day Wednesday is named after Óðinn, from the Anglo-Saxon (Old English) version of his name, Woden or Weden. The Romans associated Óðinn with Mercury (Hermes). I like to think of him as Hermes grown up into an old man, whereas Hermes is depicted as a child god in many surviving Greek myths. Where Hermes was playful, like a child, Óðinn was darker and scheming. Even when having fun,

---

[116] Nine is the mystical number of the Norse, referring to the number of worlds which are home to the gods, giants, elves, human beings, monsters and the dead. This number reoccurs many times in their stories.

[117] Yggdrasill means 'Óðinn's horse', a euphemism for a gallows, as Óðinn hung himself.

Óðinn's humour is dark, such as his verbal sparring with Thor (Þórr), while in disguise as a ferryman in the darkly funny story Hárbarðsljóð (The Lay of Greybeard). Both Hermes and Óðinn enjoyed bending or breaking the rules, and bringing ideas and inventions back from chaotic and liminal spaces.

The Norns

These were the Norse fates. Like the Greek fates, they were depicted as three women, Urðr (one's fateful path),[118] Verðandi (the present), and Skuld (debt, or obligation). They were located at the well Urðarbrunnr, beneath the world ash tree Yggdrasil, and they watered its roots. They were said to be there from the beginning of a person's life until their death, spinning the threads of life, and routing the destinies of human beings and gods alike.

Fate, obligation, oaths and debts were very important to all old Germanic cultures, including the Norse and the Anglo-Saxons.

The Valkyrja (Valkyries)

These were the female spirits who guided those who were to die bravely in battle to Óðinn's Valhǫll, where they were to feast, fight and drink until they were to be called upon to fight at Ragnarök. The name Valkyrja means 'choosers of the slain'. The northern lights (aurora borealis) were said to be caused by the reflections of the Valkyrjas' armour.

Thor (Þórr)

Thor was the red-headed god of thunder, storms, strength and temper tantrums. Where Óðinn and Loki were underhanded and scheming, Thor was direct, violent and honourable. He was the strongest of the gods, and they depended on his strength and readiness to keep invaders at bay, especially the Jötunn. In stories he is frequently with Loki, his travelling companion on adventures, who pretends to be his sidekick, but frequently manipulates him and those that they come across.

---

[118] Urðr is cognate to the Old English word 'wyrd', the Germanic concept of fate and duty.

Thor possesses the magic hammer, Mjǫllnir, which always returned to his hand no matter how far it was flung, the iron-gripped gloves 'Járngreipr' which were required to wield the hammer, and which allowed him to crush boulders, and a belt of power called Megingjörð, which doubled his strength.

Thor was the son of Óðinn and Frigg. His wife was Sif, who possessed beautiful golden hair, fashioned by the dwarves. He gives his name to the day 'Thursday'.

At Ragnarök, Thor was destined to fight the serpent Jörmungandr. Though he was said to have defeated it, he was only able to take nine steps afterwards before he died from the serpent's venom.

Týr

The god of soldiers, who was most famous for bravely sacrificing his right hand to the cause of binding the great wolf Fenrir (see Fenrir). In some accounts he was a son of Óðinn, but in others he was the son of the Jötunn Hymir. Where Óðinn is a scheming and tactical god of war, a general, Týr is brave and direct to a fault. For this reason, I think of him as a god of foot-soldiers and those on the frontline of battle.

Not as much is known about Týr as some of the other Norse gods but the etymology of his name holds some fascinating clues. The word Týr derives from the reconstructed Proto-Germanic root 'Tīwaz', which is cognate with the Greek 'Zeus' (pronounced 'Tsee-oos' or 'Thee-oos'), and the Latin 'Deus', all meaning 'god'. The same root-word combined with 'pater' meaning 'father' gives us 'Jupiter' (Deus-Pater, meaning God-father). All of these go back to a Proto-Indo-European root 'dey-wós', meaning 'heavenly one'. This shows that Týr is an evolution of a very ancient god-form and while we are short of mythological evidence, it has led some to suggest that Týr was the original head of the Proto-Germanic gods, and that Óðinn was developed or imported later, usurping his position.

The story of Týr losing his hand seems to suggest that while Týr is the bravest of the gods, he would be a reckless leader. The old Norse lived in an unstable time of great migration, raiding and trade, and in this complex world only the most shrewd would win the biggest rewards. For this reason, the Vikings (a term meaning approximately 'raiders') chose the devious trickster god Óðinn as the king of the pantheon over the more honourable Týr.

The Romans associated Týr with Mars. His name gave us the word Tuesday.

Gods from other cultures

Anansi

A trickster god from the Akan people of West Africa, who usually took the shape of a spider. In the tales he has a remarkable ability to talk and trick his way into getting what he wants, often to the benefit of humankind.

In the Americas and especially Jamaica, he became a folk hero to the enslaved people of African origin because of his ability to trick more powerful animals and gods, all despite his own weakness or apparent disadvantages. Amongst other feats, Anansi bought all of humanity's stories from the sky god Nyame for the price of the four deadliest animals, who he tricked into various traps.

Babalon

This was Aleister Crowley's sexually empowered reimagining of the 'Whore of Babylon' from the Biblical Book of Revelation. He also referred to her as the 'Scarlet Woman', a Victorian English euphemism for a sex worker. For Crowley, she represented a kind of universal mother who manifested all matter in the universe, and also a universal lover figure.

Her name actually appears to have come from John Dee's magical journals (from around the beginning of the seventeenth century), which hugely influenced Crowley, and the word Babalon was said to be Enochian, a language claimed, in Dee's memoirs, to have been transmitted to Dee and the medium Edward Kelley by angels. The word Babalon was said by Dee to mean 'wicked', something which suited Crowley's cult of moral inversion just fine. There is, of course, a connection to the ancient state of Babylon, which to the Hebrews represented a rejection of the one true God. Crowley was trying to reform Christianity into something more empowering and liberating than the version from his upbringing in the Plymouth Brethren. This was and is a very regimented sect of Christian separatists who believe in an impending apocalypse.

Crowley loved the company of liberated women, but it would be hard to class him as a feminist by modern standards. Despite this, Babalon became a feminist, sex-positive symbol in Thelema[119] and in the counterculture movement of the Sixties and Seventies. The male counterpart to Babalon was To Mega Therion, the 'great beast' with which Crowley self-identified. This apparently came from a nickname his mother would call him when he misbehaved as a child.

Baphomet

A curious deity with a convoluted history. Originally appearing in a letter about the siege of Antioch by the French crusader Anselm of Ribemont in 1098 CE, and probably an evolution or mispronunciation of the name 'Mohammed', the word took on a heretical connotation. It was used again in trial documents for the inquisition of the Knights Templar starting in 1307 CE. In this context it was somewhat of a conspiratorial and demonic term resulting from Christian hysteria.

The Templars became fashionable in popular culture again in the nineteenth century, especially in speculative conspiracy theories. Here the concept of Baphomet took on an identity as an occult deity. Éliphas Lévi wrote about and depicted the deity in his 1884 work *Dogme et Rituel de la Haute Magie (Dogma and Rituals of High Magic)*, a book which, in translation, was one of the sparks for the occult revival in the English-speaking world.

Here Baphomet was depicted as a horned hermaphrodite, which is also very similar to the image on the Devil card in many Tarot decks. As with many pop culture symbols, Baphomet is a dangerous demon to some and a rebellious figure of moral liberation for others. In the Sixties, the Church of Satan, led by Anton LaVey, appropriated Lévi's image for their movement and the symbol can now be found, like many other appropriated symbols, tattooed upon many 'rebellious' people who identify as satanists. Whatever floats your boat.

---

[119] Crowley's occult religion that he founded.

Brahman

The most abstract conception of God or Godhead in Hinduism, it is a universal unseparated 'all' from which all existence comes. Something like this can be experienced with a 'heroic dose' of magic mushrooms or similar psychedelic drugs, and comes after the 'ego-death' experience, which is an experience of the shedding of the self, into a state of pure awareness.

Brahman is actually a nearly universal concept and is roughly the same as Ein Soph from Kabbalah, Nyx from Orphism, the Monad from Gnosticism, Te Po (or Te Kore) from Polynesian mythology, 'The Father' from the Catholic and Orthodox Trinity, and many others, and this similarity across cultures may represent a 40,000+ year old concept.[120]

Brahman is related to the god Brahma, the creator god of the Trimurti, the trinity of supreme divinity that includes Vishnu and Shiva.

Coyote

A trickster god and a powerful magician who takes the form of a coyote, and is sometimes a creator along with a spirit called the Earth-maker. He is in the mythology of diverse groups of First Nations people from throughout the Americas. He is said to have been responsible for the capture of fire, the sun, and for the cunningness of humans, who he created after creating the animals. Though neither a benevolent nor malevolent figure, in some myths he is said to be responsible for the evils of the world. As a cultural figure and a god, he shares some common characteristics with the god Raven.

Kali

A Vedic goddess of destruction, death, birth and transformation, she is associated with the release or destruction of the ego which is necessary for 'moksha', or release from samsara, the timeless wheel of life, death and reincarnation. She is also often associated with the self-restriction of ascetic forms of yoga, where one must give up earthly things in order to find a balance necessary for higher spiritual experience.

---

[120] For further information, read E. J. Michael Witzel, *The Origins of the World's Mythologies* (Oxford: Oxford University Press, 2013).

Amongst other roles, she serves as a guardian of destruction, with whom the universe has made a deal in order to keep worse things at bay. She is therefore necessary to the cosmic order, and a symbol of the temporary nature of the human experience. She is also associated with time and is revered by many as the 'great mother', as well as the bringer of death. In this role she is similar to Chronos in Greek mythology. Many have adopted her as a symbol of the complexity of the divine feminine, which is core to Indian philosophy and mythology but harder to find in the West.

Legba

A psychopomp god of the religion Voudou, who stands at the boundaries between the spirit world and the human realm, and is often associated with the crossroads, itself a symbol of the crossing-over point of life, death and the spirit world.

Originating with the Yoruba and Gbe peoples of west Africa, Legba is also a popular deity in Louisiana, Haiti and beyond. Syncretised with the trickster devil of European folklore, and the Devil as the tempter of sin in Christianity, he is the deity behind the 'deal with the Devil' in blues and rock 'n' roll legend, who offers one fame in return for dedicating one's soul to hedonism and sin. As such, Legba became an approachable god of fortune as well as a liaison who can introduce one to other spirits.

He is very recognisable in Voudou iconography as a handsome black man in a suit, sometimes driving up in a fine carriage, or later a car, or characterised as either being a skeleton in a top hat, coat and tails, or having a skull painted on his face. He is said to be fond of whisky, bourbon and cigars, and is usually depicted with these.

Mithra

An extremely ancient deity of both the Avestan (ancient Iranian) and Vedic cultures, and therefore older than both, going back to at least 3000 BCE. He is associated with the Sanskrit Vedas as well as Zoroastrianism, and was later revived in a classical Roman military cult, Mithraism, which is thought to have influenced Christianity.

He was a god of oaths, light, justice and the sun, and may have been the archetype of the perfect man, a mantle later taken up by Jesus.

His name means 'that which causes to bind' in Indo-Iranian, hence his association with oaths. In the Iranian tradition he guarded the gates of paradise, only allowing entrance to those who were worthy. As the Roman Mithras, he was depicted wearing a Phrygian cap and battling a bull. His followers took part in a mystery cult, undertook initiations, acknowledged each other by secret handshakes, and met in underground temples.

This mystery cult, with its grades of initiation and the secret meetings, has lead many, especially occultists, to put forth the idea that the cult of Mithras could be a precursor to modern secret societies such as Freemasonry, which later gave rise to magic societies such as the Golden Dawn.

Raven

A creator and trickster god, or group of related gods, shared widely by the indigenous people of Siberia and the Pacific northwest coast of USA and Canada. Stories about him are diverse but he is variously said to have been involved in the creation of the world, to have given humans their cunning, to have obtained fire for humans, and to have released the sun, moon and stars from captivity. His similarity across such a wide group of cultures and regions suggests either that he is a very old god, that there was communication between these groups, or that there was a coincidental formation of stories based on interaction with ravens, or as practitioners would have it, spirit contact with a related entity.

Shiva

A complex deity in Hinduism who is usually understood in the West to be a god of necessary destruction. He is part of the cycle of life and death, bringing about the end of things in order to make room for new things.

As is often the case, the original concept is far more nuanced. Shiva is part of the Trimurti, a Hindu trinity which also includes Brahma the creator, and Vishnu the preserver. Together they form a cycle of universal life and death. In Shaivism, one of the major Hindu traditions, Shiva takes on attributes of the whole trinity, being himself the creator, preserver and destroyer.

Tables of correspondences

The suits

	Element	Qualities	Gender	Sense	Roles	Temperament	Court card	Signs by element	World
Wands	Fire	Hot & Dry	Masculine/ Active	Sight	Artists, inventors, magicians, consultants, solo sportspeople	Choleric	Kings	Aries, Leo, Sagittarius	Atzilut (Emanation)
Cups	Water	Cold & Wet	Feminine/ Passive	Taste	Counsellors, healers, clergy, poets, singers, mothers, carers	Phlegmatic	Queens	Cancer, Scorpio, Pisces	Briah (Creation)
Swords	Air	Hot & Wet	Masculine/ Active	Smell	Academics, soldiers, lawyers, judges, nobility, scientists, teachers, advertisers, inventors, engineers	Sanguine	Knights	Gemini, Libra, Aquarius	Yetzirah (Formation)
Pentacles	Earth	Cold & Dry	Feminine/ Passive	Touch	Merchants, farmers, miners, craftspeople, fashion industry, factory workers, tradespeople	Melancholic	Pages	Taurus, Virgo, Capricorn	Assiah (Manifestation)

The Major Arcana

	Astrological concept	Letter	Sefirotic Path	Alchemical concept	Deities	Meaning
0 Fool	Primum Mobile	Alef א ox	11 Keter to Chokhmah	Prima Materia	Har-Pa-Khered, Horus the Child, Harpocrates, Pan, Dionysus, Bacchus, Loki, The Child Hermes	First cause. Something out of nothing. A know-nothing.
I Magician (Juggler)	Mercury ☿	Bet ב house	12 Keter to Binah	Mercury ☿ (alcohol)	Thoth, Mercury, Hermes, Heka, Óðinn (after his stay on Yggdrasil)	A master. A fully realised and balanced person.
II Priestess (Popess)	Moon ☽	Gimel ג camel	13 Keter to Tiferet	Consciousness	Isis (as the priestess), Nut (Nuit), Artemis, Diana, Luna, Selene, Hecate, Freyja	Knowledge from personal experience. Occult wisdom. Higher consciousness.
III Empress	Venus ♀	Dalet ד door	14 Chokhmah to Binah	Salt (ash)	Isis (as the mother), Mut, Demeter and Persephone, Ceres, Venus, Juno, Hera, Frigg	Mother nature, fertility, food and the sensual world. Motherhood.

(*Continued*)

(Continued)

	Astrological concept	Letter	Sefirotic Path	Alchemical concept	Deities	Meaning
IV Emperor	Aries ♈	Heh ה window (Tzaddi in Crowley's system)	15 Chokhmah to Tiferet (28 Netzach to Yesod in Crowley's system)	Sulphur (oil)	Amun (a ram-horned god), Horus (as a sky god), Jupiter, Minerva, Athena	Fatherhood. Ordered society, authority, morality, rules and governance.
V Hierophant (Pope)	Taurus ♉	Vav ו a nail or a hook	16 Chokhmah to Chesed		Osiris (as psychopomp), Charon, Kerubim, Legba, Freyr, Ma'at	Institutions, initiations, education, religion, dogma, and cultural belief systems.
VI Lovers	Gemini ♊	Zayin ז sword (Duality)	17 Binah to Tiferet	The chemical wedding, or synthesis	Eros and Psyche, Orpheus and Eurydice, Castor and Pollux, Adam and Eve. Also known as The Lover	Faith in love or in partnership. Synthesis.
VII Chariot	Cancer ♋	Chet ח boundary/ fence	18 Binah to Gevurah		Apollo (as the sun charioteer), Óðinn (as leader of the great hunt), Merkabah (God's angelic chariot), Horus (as the avenger of his father Osiris), Thor (as Charioteer)	Taking control of one's world. Ambition.

VIII Strength (XI in some decks)	Leo ♌	Tet ט serpent	19 Chesed to Gevurah	Hercules, Thor, Vesta, Hestia, Bastet, Sekhmet	Taming oneself toward order. Mental health. Patience. Mentally and emotionally overcoming setbacks. The charming of a wild force.
IX Hermit	Virgo ♍	Yod י hand	20 Chesed to Tiferet	Atum (the god who creates himself), Óðinn (as 'Hárbarð'—Greybeard the Wanderer), Persephone (as she who bridges life and death), Anubis (as psychopomp)	Committing to a spiritual path outside of one's upbringing. Introspection.
X Wheel of Fortune	Jupiter ♃	Kaf כ palm of the hand, a spoon, and the state of being bent in submission	21 Chesed to Netzach	Sphinx/Hermanubis/Typhon (or Sphinx/Set/Typhon), the Hayyot, Fortuna, Tyche, the Fates, the Norns, Shai	A good or bad fortune. Seeing life events as temporary cycles.

(Continued)

(Continued)

	Astrological concept	Letter	Sefirotic Path	Alchemical concept	Deities	Meaning
XI Justice (VIII in some decks)	Libra ♎	Lamed ל ox goad (or yoke)	22 Gevurah to Tiferet		Themis (divine justice), Justitia, Dike (goddess of moral order), Athena (as the judge), Raguel (Kabbalistic angel of justice), Forseti, Ma'at (as goddess of universal balance), Mithra (law and order)	Judgement from outside. Being tested by society or an institution. Developing morality.
XII Hanged Man	Neptune ♆	Mem מ water	23 Gevurah to Hod		Óðinn (as a sacrifice to himself), Jesus on the cross (God incarnate sacrificed to God the creator), Neptune and Poseidon (as the god of the unconscious), Prometheus. Negatively aspected: Loki.	Rebelling against societal norms for a cause or for personal identity. A self-inflicted burden in a hope of achieving growth.
XIII Death	Scorpio ♏	Nun נ fish	24 Tiferet to Netzach		Mars (as a bringer of death), the Grim Reaper, Osiris (as the slain god resurrected, and as a psychopomp), Christ (slain and resurrected), Kali (as the destroyer who allows rebirth), Hel, Hades (when he interacts with the human realm)	The difficult shedding of that which has served its purpose. Grief.

XIV Temperence	Sagittarius ♐	Samekh ס support/pillar/prop, or medicine	25 Tiferet to Yesod	Homeostasis	Michael, Aphroditus, Hermaphroditus, Holy Guardian Angel, (Crowley says: Diana the huntress, Virgin Artemis)	A rebalancing. Taking time to improve one's health and habits. Taking charge of one's emotions. Coming out of a depression.
XV Devil	Capricorn ♑	Ayin ע eye	26 Tiferet to Hod		Satyr, The Devil, Satan, Baphomet, Loki (as a fall into corruption from resentment), Set, Pan (hedonism, and submission to a wild nature), Dionysus/Bacchus (as gods of intoxication)	Addictions to things that one knows are unhealthy. Associating oneself with people or institutions that one disagrees with morally.
XVI Tower	Mars ♂	Peh פ mouth	27 Netzach to Hod		Mars/Ares (defeat in war), Montu, Shiva (the destroyer)	A collapse of faith, institutions or authority due to corruption. Disasters that unveil corruption.

(Continued)

(Continued)

	Astrological concept	Letter	Sefirotic Path	Alchemical concept	Deities	Meaning
XVII Star	Aquarius ♒	Tzaddi צ fish hook (Crowley assigns it to Heh)	28 Netzach to Yesod (Crowley assigns it to 15 Chokhmah to Tiferet)		Ishtar, Venus (as the morning star), Lucifer (as the morning star who sheds light on what was hidden), Nuit (as 'mother heaven'), Babalon, Sirius/Sopdet/Sothis (the star that precedes the flooding of the Nile), Juventas/Hebe (goddess of youth), Ganymede/Ganymeda	Piety. Taking on a higher purpose or aligning oneself with an idealistic goal.
XVIII Moon	Pisces ♓	Qof ק back of the head	29 Netzach to Malkut		Kephra, Selene, Luna, Diana/Artemis (as night huntress), Hecate, Khonsu, Legba	Normally hidden things become noticeable to those who look. A journey through the liminal space between consciousness and unconscious.

XIX Sun	Sol ☉	Resh ר head	30 Hod to Yesod	Apollo, Helios, Baldr, Adam and Eve (in the garden), Heru-Ra-Ha (Thelemic mix of Horus of the Horizon, and Harpocrates), Ra, Aten, Horus and many other Egyptian sun gods	An innocent joy. A pleasant 'lightbulb moment' where things become clear and simple. Being in the moment with love energy. Rose-coloured spectacles.
XX Judgement (Aeon)	Pluto ♇ (non-traditional)	Shin ש tooth	31 Hod to Malkut	Anubis (as weigher of souls), Jesus resurrected, Osiris resurrected, Gabriel, Fenrir, Hephaestus/Vulcan (surviving his fall)	Old crimes or pain come back to haunt. A new path is discovered by unburying the past. 'Skeletons in the closet.'
XXI World	Saturn ♄	Tav ת a cross, or mark	32 Yesod to Malkut	Saturn, Chronos, Gaea, Brahman, Ptah, Geb, Ophion and Eurynome	A perspective of the big picture is gained. An acceptance of one's place in the scheme of things. Finally understanding how the parts fit into a big system. Global situations.

The court cards
(The timings follow the zodiacal correspondences)

	Element	Letter	Astrology	Timing (based on the sun)	World	
Kings						
Wands	Fire	Yod ʼ			Atzilut	Masculine authorities or older men.
Cups	Fiery properties of Fire	Yod ʼ	21st degree of Scorpio to 20th degree of Sagittarius	12th November to 11th December	Atzilut of Atzilut	A cult leader or successful public or motivational speaker. A fiery male performer.
Swords	Fiery properties of Water	Yod ʼ	21st degree of Aquarius to 20th degree of Pisces	10th February to 10th March	Atzilut of Briah	An emotional man or masculine person who is loyal and protects his family.
Pentacles	Fiery properties of Air	Yod ʼ	21st degree of Taurus to 20th degree of Gemini	11th May to 10th June	Atzilut of Yetzirah	A judge, impartial and distant. Rational to a fault. A good advisor for difficult decisions.
	Fiery properties of Earth	Yod ʼ	21st degree of Leo to 20th degree of Virgo	13th August to 12th September	Atzilut of Assiah	A guardian, or keeper of a tradition. A master craftsperson or worker in a highly skilled profession.
Queens	Water	Heh ה			Briah	Feminine authorities or older women.

APPENDICES 269

Wands	Watery properties of Fire	Heh ה	21st degree of Pisces to 20th degree of Aries	11th March to 9th April	Briah of Atzilut	A feminine artist, actor or musician or an imaginative mother. A woman who succeeds in a masculine position due to her femininity.
Cups	Watery properties of Water	Heh ה	21st degree of Gemini to 20th degree of Cancer	11th June to 11th July	Briah of Briah	A mystical woman or feminine person with great intuition. A counsellor. A psychic.
Swords	Watery properties of Air	Heh ה	21st degree of Virgo to 20th degree of Libra	13th September to 12th October	Briah of Yetzirah	A feminine scholar, politician, activist, military commander, or public authority. An expert.
Pentacles	Watery properties of Earth	Heh ה	21st degree of Sagittarius to 20th degree of Capricorn	12th December to 10th January	Briah of Assiah	A conservative woman of means who is a protector of nice things.
Knights	Air	Vav ו			Yetzirah	Skilled practitioners. Peers.
Wands	Airy properties of Fire	Vav ו	21st degree of Cancer to 20th degree of Leo	12th July to 12th August	Yetzirah of Atzilut	A 'prima donna'. A singular talent who is difficult and dramatic.
Cups	Airy properties of Water	Vav ו	21st degree of Libra to 20th degree of Scorpio	13th October to 11th November	Yetzirah of Briah	An escapist, romantic poet type. Very talented but unstable, prone to addictions. An artist, musician, writer or actor. Very charming to a group of people.

(*Continued*)

(Continued)

	Element	Letter	Astrology	Timing (based on the sun)	World	
Swords	Airy properties of Air	Vav ו	21st degree of Capricorn to 20th degree of Aquarius	11th January to 9th February	Yetzirah of Yetzirah	A brash, over-confident daredevil.
Pentacles	Airy properties of Earth	Vav ו	21st degree of Leo to 20th degree of Virgo	13th August to 12th September	Yetzirah of Assiah	A skilful, hardworking and down-to-earth masculine person who works with their hands.
Pages	Earth	Heh ה			Assiah	Apprentices, youth, beginners
Wands	Earthly properties of Fire	Heh ה	The space occupied by Cancer, Leo and Virgo	21st June to 22nd September	Assiah of Atzilut	A beginner, or one who is seeking prestige and the attention of those who have more power.
Cups	Earthly properties of Water	Heh ה	The space occupied by Libra, Scorpio and Sagittarius	23rd September to 21st December	Assiah of Briah	A kind, innocent idealist. A true believer and a romantic.
Swords	Earthly properties of Air	Heh ה	The space occupied by Capricorn, Aquarius and Pisces	22nd December to 20th March	Assiah of Yetzirah	A beginner who feels they are an expert as soon as they have taken a 101 class. An edgelord. A nerd.
Pentacles	Earthly properties of Earth	Heh ה	The space occupied by Aries, Taurus and Gemini	21st March to 20th June	Assiah of Malkut	A hard-working apprentice.

The Minor Arcana
[The angels follow the Golden Dawn attributions]

	Sefirah	Astrological Timing (Crowley)	Decan Timing (Shem HaMephorash)	Angel	World/Sefirah	
Aces	Keter				Keter	Beginnings and inspiration.
Wands	Fire in Keter			Archangel Michael	Keter of Atzilut	Inspiration from novelty. A new creative undertaking.
Cups	Water in Keter			Archangel Gabriel	Keter of Briah	A new emotion or potential relationship.
Swords	Air in Keter			Archangel Raphael	Keter of Yetzirah	A new endeavour. A new debate or new field of study.
Pentacles	Earth in Keter			Archangel Uriel	Keter of Assiah	A career or financial opportunity.
Twos	Chokhmah				Chokhmah	A decision

(Continued)

(Continued)

	Sefirah	Astrological Timing (Crowley)	Decan Timing (Shem HaMephorash)	Angel	World/Sefirah	
Wands	Fire in Chokhmah	21st March to 30th March	Mars in Aries	Vehuel והואל Day 21st March	Chokhmah of Atzilut	A new exploration.
				Daniel דניאל Night 26th March		
Cups	Water in Chokhmah	21st June to 1st July	Venus in Cancer	Eiael עיאל Day 21st June	Chokhmah of Briah	Mutual benefit. A new relationship.
				Habuiah הביה Night 26th June		
Swords	Air in Chokhmah	23rd September to 3rd October	Moon in Libra	Iezalel יזלאל Day 23rd September	Chokhmah of Yetzirah	A rational decision.
				Mebahel מבהאל Night 28th September		

APPENDICES 273

Pentacles	Earth in Chokhmah	22nd December to 31st December	Jupiter in Capricorn	Lecabel לכבאל Day 22nd December Vasariah ושריה Night December 27th	Chokhmah of Assiah	Juggling resources, balancing the books.
Threes	Binah				Binah	
Wands	Fire in Binah	31st March to 9th April	Sun in Aries	Hahasiah ההשיה Day 11th April Imamiah עממיה Night 6th April	Binah of Atzilut	Advancement and commitment Ambition. Making a decision.
Cups	Water in Binah	2nd July to 12th July	Mercury in Cancer	Roehel לאהל Day 1st July Iabamiah יבמיה Night 6th July	Binah of Briah	An emotional connection with others.

(*Continued*)

(Continued)

	Sefirah	Astrological Timing (Crowley)	Decan Timing (Shem HaMephorash)	Angel	World/Sefirah	
Swords	Air in Binah	4th October to 13th October	Saturn in Libra	Hariel הריאל Day 3rd October	Binah of Yetzirah	A heartache. Ideas negatively affecting the emotions.
				Hakamiah הקמיה Night 8th October		
Pentacles	Earth in Binah	1st January to 10th January	Mars in Capricorn	Iehuiah יהויה Day 1st January	Binah of Assiah	An apprenticeship. Showing one's works for the first time.
				Lehahiah להחיה Night 6th January		
Fours	Chesed				Chesed	Stability, or a hurdle
Wands	Fire in Chesed	10th April to 19th April	Venus in Aries	Nanael נגאל Day 10th April	Chesed of Atzilut	Early results.
				Nithael נתהיאל Night 15th April		

Cups	Water in Chesed	13th July to 22nd July	Moon in Cancer	Haiaiel האיאל Day 11th July Mumiah מומיה Night 16th July	Chesed of Briah	Dissatisfaction with what one has.
Swords	Air in Chesed	14th October to 23rd October	Jupiter in Libra	Loviah לואיה Day 13th October Caliel כליאל Night 18th October	Chesed of Yezirah	Time out. A rest for one's mental health.
Pentacles	Earth in Chesed	11th January to 20th January	Sun in Capricorn	Chavakiah חבקיה Day 11th January Manadel מנדאל Night 16th January	Chesed of Assiah	A miser. Saving for a rainy day.
Fives	Gevurah				Gevurah	Unpredictability

(Continued)

(Continued)

	Sefirah	Astrological Timing (Crowley)	Decan Timing (Shem HaMephorash)	Angel	World/Sefirah	
Wands	Fire in Gevurah	23rd July to 1st August	Saturn in Leo	Vehuiah והו Day 23rd July	Gevurah of Atzilut	A struggle for an initiation. Friendly competition.
				Ieliel ילי Night 28th July		
Cups	Water in Gevurah	24th October to 1st November	Mars in Scorpio	Levuiah לוו Day 23rd October	Gevurah of Briah	Crying over spilt milk. A failure to focus on what one has.
				Pahaliah פהל Night 28th October		
Swords	Air in Gevurah	21st January to 29th January	Venus in Aquarius	Aniel אני Day 20th January	Gevurah of Yezirah	Spoils of war. A debate won, sometimes by trickery.
				Haamiah חעמ Night 25th January		

Pentacles	Earth in Gevurah	20th April to 29th April	Mercury in Taurus	Mebahiah מבהיה Day 20th April	Gevurah of Assiah	Pride against accepting charity.
				Poiel פויאל Night 25th April		
Sixes	Tiferet				Tiferet	A win or a loss
Wands	Fire in Tiferet	2nd August to 12th August	Jupiter in Leo	Sitael סיטאל Day 2nd August	Tiferet of Atzilut	A parade under leadership. A group success.
				Elemiah עלמיה Night 7th August		
Cups	Water in Tiferet	2nd November to 11th November	Sun in Scorpio	Nelchael נלכאל Day 2nd November	Tiferet of Briah	Nostalgia.
				Ieiaiel ייאל Night 7th November		

(Continued)

(Continued)

	Sefirah	Astrological Timing (Crowley)	Decan Timing (Shem HaMephorash)	Angel	World/Sefirah	
Swords	Air in Tiferet	30th January to 8th February	Mercury in Aquarius	Rehael רההאל Day 30th January	Tiferet of Yezirah	An old trauma. Taking one's problems with one.
				Ieiazel יאיזל Night 4th February		
Pentacles	Earth in Tiferet	30th April to 10th May	Moon in Taurus	Nemamiah נממיה Day 30th April	Tiferet of Assiah	Charity to others.
				Ieialel ייללל Night 5th May		
Sevens	Netzach				Netzach	Drama and tension
Wands	Fire in Netzach	13th August to 22nd August	Mars in Leo	Mahasiah מהשיה Day 12th August Lelahel ללהאל Night 17th August	Netzach of Atzilut	'Kick against the pricks'. Taking on a battle on principle, where one is certain to take a loss.

Cups	Water in Netzach	12th November to 21st November	Venus in Scorpio	Melahel מלהאל Day 12th November	Netzach of Briah	Debauchery/hedonism. Temptation.
				Haiviah ההויה Night 17th November		
Swords	Air in Netzach	9th February to 18th February	Moon in Aquarius	Hahahel ההההאל Day 9th February	Netzach of Yezirah	The theft of ideas. A sneak.
				Michael מיכאל Night 14th February		
Pentacles	Earth in Netzach	11th May to 20th May	Saturn in Taurus	Harahel הרחאל Day 10th May	Netzach of Assiah	Impatience.
				Mizrael מצראל Night 15th May		
Eights	Hod				Hod	Action and change

(*Continued*)

(Continued)

	Sefirah	Astrological Timing (Crowley)	Decan Timing (Shem HaMephorash)	Angel	World/Sefirah	
Wands	Fire in Hod	23rd November to 2nd December	Mercury in Sagittarius	Nithhaiah נתהיה Day 22nd November	Hod of Atzilut	A speedy delivery or sudden change.
				Ha'aiah האאיה Night 27th November		
Cups	Water in Hod	19th February to 29th February	Saturn in Pisces	Veualiah וויליה Day 19th February	Hod of Briah	Quitting.
				Ielahiah ייליה Night February 24		
Swords	Air in Hod	21st May to 31st May	Jupiter in Gemini	Umabel ומבאל Day 21st May	Hod of Yezirah	Self-doubt.
				Iahhael יההאל Night 26th May		

Pentacles	Earth in Hod	23rd August to 2nd September	Sun in Virgo	Achaiah אכאיה Day 23rd August	Hod of Assiah	Diligence.
				Cahethel כהתאל Night 28th August		
Nines						
	Yesod				Yesod	Resolution and conclusion
Wands	Fire in Yesod	3rd December to 12th December	Moon in Sagittarius	Ierathel יהרתאל Day 2nd December	Yesod of Atzilut	A last stand, usually successful.
				Saeehiah שאהיה Night 7th December		
Cups	Water in Yesod	1st March to 10th of March	Jupiter in Pisces	Sealiah סאליה Day 1st March	Yesod of Briah	Hospitality.
				Ariel עריאל Night March 6th		

(Continued)

APPENDICES   281

(Continued)

	Sefirah	Astrological Timing (Crowley)	Decan Timing (Shem HaMephorash)	Angel	World/Sefirah	
Swords	Air in Yesod	1st June to 10th June	Mars in Gemini	Anavel אנואל Day 31st May	Yesod of Yezirah	Anxiety, depression, nightmares.
				Mehiel מחיאל Night 5th June		
Pentacles	Earth in Yesod	3rd September to 12th September	Venus in Virgo	Haziel החזיאל Day 2nd September	Yesod of Assiah	Comfort.
				Aladiah אלדיה Night 7th September		
Tens	Malkut				Malkut	
Wands	Fire in Malkut	3rd December to 12th December	Saturn in Sagittarius	Reiaiel רייאל Day 12th December	Malkut of Atzilut	Final stage before a new cycle A burden, taking on too much.
				Omael אומאל Night 17th December		

Cups	Water in Malkut	1st March to 10th of March	Mars in Pisces	Asaliah עשליה Day 11th March	Malkut of Briah	A family celebration.
				Mihael מיהאל Night 16th March		
Swords	Air in Malkut	11th June to 20th June	Sun in Gemini	Damabiah דמביה Day 10th June	Malkut of Yezirah	Defeat, despair.
				Manakel מנקאל Night 15th June		
Pentacles	Earth in Malkut	13th September to 22nd September	Mercury in Virgo	Laviah לאיה Day 12th September	Malkut of Assiah	Affluence.
				Hahaiah ההיה Night 17th September		

REFERENCES

Bibliography

Agrippa, Henry Cornelius, *Three Books of Occult Philosophy* (1533), ed. Donald Tyson (Rochester, VT: Inner Traditions, 1993).

Carroll, Peter J., *Liber Null & Psychonaut: An Introduction to Chaos Magic* (New York: Weiser, 1987).

Cicero, Chic, and Sandra Tabatha Cicero, *Self-Initiation into the Golden Dawn Tradition* (Woodbury, MN: Llewellyn Publications, 2002).

Crowley, Aleister, *The Book of Thoth: A Short Essay on the Tarot of the Egyptians* [1944] (New York: Weiser, 1969).

Crowley, Aleister, *Liber AL vel Legis: The Book of the Law* (1909).

Dawkins, Richard, *The Selfish Gene* (Oxford: Oxford University Press, 1976).

Encausse, Gérard, aka Papus, *Le Tarot Des Bohémiens: La Clef Absolue de la Science Occulte* [1889] (Paris: Dangles, 1990).

Freeman, Ari, *Pragmatic Magical Thinking: Real Magic Explained* (London: Aeon Books, 2023).

Freeman, Ari, *Tarot for Sceptics: The Practical Usage of Divination for Psychic Results* (London: Aeon Books, 2025).

Kaplan, Aryeh, *Meditation and Kabbalah* (Newburyport, MA: Weiser, 1982).

Kerényi, Carl, *Dionysos: Archetypal Image of Indestructible Life*, tr. Ralph Manheim (Princeton: Princeton University Press, [1976] 1996).

Kubik, Gerhard, 'The African matrix in jazz harmonic practices', *Black Music Research Journal* 25(1) (2005).

Lévi, Éliphas, *Transcendental Magic, its Doctrine and Ritual* [*Dogme Et Ritual de la Haute Magie*, 1856], tr. A.E. Waite (London: Rider & Company, 1896).

Pico della Mirandola, Giovanni, *Syncretism in the West: Pico's 900 Theses* (1496), tr. S. A. Farmer (Tempe, AZ: Arizona State University, 1998).

Regardie, Israel, *The Golden Dawn: The Original Account of the Teachings, Rites, and Ceremonies of the Hermetic Order* [1940], 7th edition, ed. John Michael Greer (Woodbury, MN: Llewellyn Publications, 2016).

Reuchlin, Johann, *On the Art of the Kabbalah, De Arte Cabalistica* (1517), tr. Martin Goodman and Sarah Goodman (Lincoln, NE: University of Nebraska Press, 1993).

Wang, Robert, 'Introduction', in Johann Reuchlin, *On the Art of the Kabbalah, De Arte Cabalistica* (1517), tr. Martin Goodman and Sarah Goodman (Lincoln, NE: University of Nebraska Press, 1993).

Wang, Robert, *How the Modern Occult Movement Grew Out of Renaissance Attempts to Convert the Jews* (Marcus Aurelius Press, 2003).

Wilson, Colin, *The Occult* (London: Watkins, 1979).

Witzel, E. J. Michael, *The Origins of the World's Mythologies* (Oxford: Oxford University Press, 2013).

Web pages

Anon., https://hermeticorderoftheroundtable.angelfire.com/files/pentagram-rituals.html.

Anon., https://hermeticorderoftheroundtable.angelfire.com/hexagram-rituals.html.

Eno, Brian, and Peter Schmidt. (2022). *Oblique Strategies*. http://stoney.sb.org/eno/oblique.html. Last retrieved 4 April 2024.

Glaser, Rabbi Yom Tov. (2016). *The Meaning of the Ten Sefirot*. https://www.youtube.com/watch?v=Y1AH84vCoSo. Last retrieved 3 December 2023.

Leitch, Aaron. (1998). *Shem ha-Mephoresh, The Divine Name of Extension*. https://cdn.preterhuman.net/texts/religion.occult.new_age/occult_library/Leitch_A-Shem_Ha-Mephoresh.pdf. Last retrieved 5 December 2023.

US Department of State, Bureau of Diplomatic Security (2018). 'None Swifter Than These: 100 Years of the Diplomatic Courier Service', https://www.state.gov/none-swifter-than-these-100-years-of-the-diplomatic-courier-service/dcs. Last retrieved 4 April 2024.

INDEX

A∴A∴ 50
Aaron (biblical) 77, 212
abracadabra 85
Abramelin, Book of 77
Abramelin ritual 78, 82, 156
abstinence xvii, 216
Abulafia, Abraham ben Samuel 38
Adam (the first man) 35, 40, 54, 81, 84, 262, 267
addiction xvii, 29, 161, 265, 269
aeon (time period) 193–194, 232, 267
Aeon (god) 193, 199
Africa 37, 39, 43, 236, 255, 258
Agrippa, Henricus Cornelius 49–51, 53–54, 82, 86, 98, 215
Akkadians 194
Akkadian language, 208
alchemy 51, 86
 solvé et coagula 64
Alemanno, Johannan, 44
Altshuler, Aharon Meir 79
American dream 155
American First Nations people 257

Anatolia 214–215
androgyne 14, 191
angels
 Chayot 75, 263
 Cherubim 75–76
 Gabriel 77
 Holy Guardian Angel 77–78, 265
 Mal'akh 74
 Michael 76, 78, 92, 114, 265, 271, 279
 Ophanim 75
 Raguel 79, 264
 Raphael 77–79, 93, 271
 Raziel 84, 86
 Uriel 78–79, 93, 271
Anglo-Saxons 253
antisemitism 46
Apollonian (philosophy) 10, 13, 196
Aramaic 6, 5, 84
Argonautica 215
Armenian 51
Artificial Intelligence
 ChatGPT 183–186
artists xv, 81, 114, 175, 260

ash tree 218
  Yggdrasil 253
Asia 43, 218
astral plane 190
astrology
  Aquarius xviii, xx, xxii, xxiii, xxvi–xxvii, 8, 17–18, 25–27, 33, 95, 102, 130, 145, 260, 266, 268, 270, 276, 278–279
  Aries xvi, xx, xxiv, xxv, 9–10, 12, 17–18, 20–21, 27, 30, 32, 93, 96, 99, 130, 135–136, 171, 262, 269, 272–274
  ascendant 20
  Cancer xvi, xxi, xxiv, xxv, 11–13, 17–18, 22–23, 32, 97, 100, 130, 138–139, 262, 269, 272–273, 275
  Capricorn xvii, xxi, xxii, xxiv–xxv, 8–9, 17–18, 25, 33, 95, 101, 130, 144, 260, 265, 270, 273–275
  cardinal signs 19
  Chiron 15
  Crystallinum 6
  decans xii, 30–31, 34, 131, 135
  detriment xxv, xxvii, 17–18, 20–27, 32–33
  domicile (ruling planet) xxiv, xxv–xxviii, 17–18, 20–27, 32
  ecliptic 19, 27, 30
  exaltation xxv–xxvi, 17–18, 20–27, 32–33
  fall xxiv, xxviii, 17–18, 20–27, 32–33
  firmament 6, 75
  fixed signs 19, 21, 75
  Gemini xvi, xx–xxi, xxiii–xxiv, xxvii–xxviii, 9–13, 17–19, 21–23, 28, 32, 69, 97, 99, 130, 137–138, 198, 260, 262, 268–270, 280, 282–283
  Jupiter xvii, xx–xxi, xxiv–xxviii, 6–10, 17–18, 21–23, 25, 27, 29, 32–33, 62, 69, 93–95, 97, 99–102, 130, 137, 139, 141, 144, 158, 224, 263, 273, 275, 277, 280–281
  Leo xvi, xx–xxii, xxiv–xxvii, 8–11, 13, 17–19, 22–23, 28, 32, 69, 75, 93–94, 98, 100, 130, 139–140, 260, 263, 268–270, 276–278
  Libra xxvii, xxi, xxiii–xxiv
  Mars xvii, xx–xxi, xxiv, xxv–xxviii, 6–7, 9–12, 17–18, 20–22, 24–25, 28–30, 32–33, 62, 69, 93–97, 99–102, 130, 135, 137, 140, 142, 144, 146–147, 264–265, 272, 274, 276, 278, 282–283
  Mercury xvi, xx–xxi, xxv–xxviii, 6–7, 12, 14, 17–18, 21, 23, 25, 27, 32–33, 94–97, 99–102, 130, 136, 141, 261, 273, 277–278, 280, 283
  Moon xvi, xviii, xxi, xxiv–xxvii, 6–7, 9, 11–13, 17–18, 21–22, 24–25, 27–28, 32–33, 64, 68, 70, 94–97, 99–102, 130, 136, 139, 141, 143, 145, 261, 272, 275, 278–279, 281
  Moon sign 20, 221
  mutable signs 19, 21, 23, 25–26, 98
  Neptune xvii, xx, 8–10, 14, 16, 18, 22–23, 26–27, 29, 130, 264
  Pisces xviii, xx, xxvii–xxviii, 8–10, 17–18, 26–27, 33, 96, 102, 130, 146–147, 260, 266, 268–270, 280–281, 283
  Pluto xviii, xx–xxi, 9–10, 12, 15–16, 18, 21, 24, 26, 29, 130, 267
  Polarity 18, 20–26
  Sagittarius xvii, xx–xxi, xxiii–xxiv, xxvii–xxviii, 8–10, 12–13, 17–19, 24–25, 26, 29, 33, 69, 95, 98, 101, 130, 143, 260, 265, 268–270, 280–282
  Saturn xviii, xx–xxii, xxv, xxviii, 6–9, 15–18, 20, 22, 24–26, 29–30, 32–33, 61, 71, 94–97, 99–102, 130, 137, 139, 141, 143, 146, 267, 274, 276, 279–280, 282

INDEX 289

Scorpio xvii, xx–xxi, xxiii, xxiv, xxvi–xxvii, 9–12, 16–19, 24–25, 29, 33, 69, 75, 95, 101, 130, 142, 260, 268–270, 276–277, 279
Sun xviii, xx–xxii, xxv–xxviii, 6–7, 10–13, 17–19, 22, 24, 26–28, 32–33, 63, 69, 72, 74, 94–97, 99–102, 130, 136, 138, 140, 142, 144, 267, 273, 275, 277, 281, 283
Sun sign 20
Taurus xvi, xx, xxiii–xxiv, xxvi–xxvii, 8, 10, 12–13, 17–20, 21–22, 28, 32, 69, 75, 96, 99, 130, 136–137, 260, 268, 270, 277–279
Uranus xx, xxii, 8, 14–16, 18, 21–22, 24, 26, 29, 130
Venus xvi, xx–xxi, xxiv–xxviii, 7, 10–11, 17–18, 20–21, 23–25, 27, 32–33, 94–97, 99–102, 130, 136, 140, 143, 158, 261, 266, 272, 276, 279, 282
Virgo xvii, xx–xxii, xxiv, xxvii–xxviii, 11–13, 17–19, 23–24, 28, 32, 69, 94, 100, 130, 134, 140–141, 201, 260, 263, 268–270, 281–283
Athens 195, 197, 207, 218, 220
Atlantis 219

Babylon 208, 255
Babylonian 3, 6, 40, 76, 93, 194
Bacon, Roger 82
Bahir (Sefer) 37–39, 82, 84, 87
Barrett, Francis 54
Bible
    Exodus 2, 38, 81, 87–88
    Ezekiel 75
    Genesis 105, 121, 230
    King James Bible 88, 105–121
    Psalms 105–121
Bible literalism 35
bliss 63, 66
Boaz and Jachin 59

Book of Enoch 76, 78–79
Book of Esdras 79
Brahman 71, 194, 257
Buddhism 87, 145, 194, 216
Burney, Venetia 15

caduceus 211–212, 234
Canaanites 48, 194, 224
capitalism 153
Carnival (festival) 200
Carroll, Peter J. 174–175, 234
Castor and Pollux 198–199, 262
Catholicism 36, 45, 78
chakras 35, 41
    Sahasrara 71
Chaldean 6, 30, 208
    Chaldean Oracles 208
Challis, James 14
Champollion, Jean-François 52, 54
Chaos (primordial state) 179, 199, 211, 222, 225, 227, 237, 239, 251
Chaos magic xii, 78, 174, 234
charisma xxi
charm xvi, 2, 9–10, 23, 63–64, 73, 136, 160, 180, 210, 215, 246, 251, 263, 269
Christianity (see also Bible, Bible literalism, and Catholicism) 4, 34, 36–37, 45, 50, 54–55, 77, 87, 187, 195, 221, 226, 236, 255–256, 258
Christian fundamentalism 35
Christian Kabbalah 38, 40–42, 44, 46–48, 51, 53, 81, 86
Christian magic 76, 87, 187
Church of Satan 41, 256
Colman Smith, Pamela 34
Comte de Mellet 42, 86
consciousness (states of) xii, 10, 13, 44, 60–61, 66, 68, 127, 201, 207, 216
consciousness (universal, see also Brahman) 61
Copernicus, Nicolaus 3
Cordovero, Moses ben Jacob 39
corruption 238, 265

cosmology 4, 6
  geocentrism 4
Couch Adams, John 14
counselling 156
Court de Gébelin, Antoine 42, 86
Cronus 195, 199–200, 206, 211, 213, 218, 223
Crowley, Aleister 24, 30–31, 34, 41, 49, 65–66, 78, 87, 194, 232–233, 240, 256
  Thoth deck 2, 127–128, 156, 194, 262, 265–266
cult leader xx, 27, 251
cultural appropriation 81
cyclopes 199, 218–219

d'Arrest, Heinrich Louis 14
daredevil 179
Dawkins, Richard 104
Deconstructionism 152
  Derrida, Jacques 151
Dee, John 41, 129, 255
Derrida, Jacques 151
Dionysian (philosophy) 10, 13, 196, 232
Dionysian mysteries 202–203, 216
DNA 212
Dowson, Godfrey 127
dreams 13, 16, 27, 29, 108–109, 111, 115, 120, 137–138, 197, 220
dreams (ambition) 186–187, 190
drugs 16
  amanita muscaria 202
  opium 203
  psilocybin 202
  sex, drugs and rock'n'roll 201
Dungeons and Dragons 127, 162, 171

Eddas 250
ego 2, 25, 27, 61–63, 180
egotism 24
ego-death 61, 257
Egypt (modern) 39
Egypt (ancient) 3, 48, 53–54, 65, 88, 211–212
Egypt (Greco-Roman) 200

Egyptian astrology 30
Egyptian hieroglyphics 51
Egyptian mythology 87, 127, 201–203, 208–209, 216, 222, 224–246, 267
engineers xv, 260
England 37, 182
Enlightenment (era) 3, 152, 191
  pre-Enlightnment 34
enlightenment (spiritual state) 44, 61, 63
Eno, Brian 175
etheric energy 190
Ethiopian 51
Etruscans 214–215
Europe 2, 36, 54
European Union 155
Eve (the first woman) 262

faculty X 175
farming 195, 240, 260
fashion (clothes) xv, 138, 260
fate xvii, xxviii, 168, 222, 247–248
fate (gods of) 236, 244, 253, 263
Father (trinity) 230, 257
fatherhood xix, 8, 28–29, 199, 214, 220, 223–224, 226, 254, 262
fatherless 209, 223
Father Christmas 252
father Earth 200, 202, 231, 235, 238–240
father sky 208, 223
Felkin, Harriet 128
feminism 50, 221, 236, 256
Ficino, Marsilio 4, 37, 46
First Nations (American) 257, 43
fixed signs (astrology) 19, 21–22, 24, 26, 75, 98
fixed stars 6, 71, 75
flow state 61, 175
folie à deux 11
fractal 66
France 35
French (language) 11, 240
Freemasonry 54, 59, 143, 172, 259
fundamentalism 35

Gemara (Jewish text) 83
gematria 70–71, 84–85
geocentrism 3–4
German 47, 84, 175
German (language) 69, 77
Germany 36–37, 49
Germanic 228, 253–254
Glaser, Yom Tov 40
Gnosticism 35, 43, 193, 216, 230, 257
gnostic mass 82
Godhead 43–44, 71, 84, 225, 257
gods (see also Heroes)
    Aeon 193–194, 199, 267
    Aion 194, 199
    Aiwass 232
    Amun 224–226, 229–230
    Anansi 255
    Anubis 227, 234, 244–245, 267
    Aphrodite 11, 194–195, 199
    Aphroditus 195
    Apollo 10, 195–197, 203, 208, 212–213, 218–219, 221, 262, 267
    Apophis 129, 222, 227–228, 237, 242
    Ares 9, 196, 198, 210–211, 238, 265
    Artemis 196–197, 214, 218, 221, 261, 265–266
    Asclepius 196, 212
    Astarte 194
    Astraea 201
    Aten 225, 228–230, 241–244, 267
    Athena 196–198, 210, 220, 262, 264
    Atlas 220
    Atum 230, 233, 237–238, 241, 243, 246
    Babalon 255–256, 266
    Bacchus 201, 261, 265
    Baldr 246–248, 251, 267
    Baphomet 195, 256, 265
    Bastet 230–231, 242–243, 263
    Castor and Pollux 198–199, 262
    Ceres 200–201, 204, 261
    Charon 206–207, 262
    Christ 45, 47, 77, 212, 228, 249, 258, 264, 267

Christ child 235–236
Chronos 194, 199, 258, 267
Coyote 257
Cronus 8, 195, 199–200, 206, 211, 213–214, 218, 223, 231
Cupid 76, 203–205
Cybele 201
Demeter 199–202, 204, 220
Devil 195, 221, 256, 258, 265
Diana 196–197, 208, 261, 265–266
Dike 201, 222, 264
Dionysus, 201–203, 210, 214, 216–217, 220, 228, 241, 261, 265
Eris 211
Eros 69, 203, 210, 262
Fates 222, 253, 263
Faun 220–221
Fenrir 247–248, 252, 254, 267
Forseti 248, 264
Fortuna 205, 263
Freyja 248–250, 252, 261
Freyr 249, 251, 262
Frigg 246–248, 254, 261
Furies 218
Gaia 199
Ganymede 205, 207, 266
Geb 200, 208, 231, 235, 238–240, 243, 267
God (Judeo-Christian) 6, 35, 38, 40, 42–44, 46–47, 55–56, 71, 74–76, 79–81, 83–84, 91, 106–121, 153, 181–182, 235, 255, 264
Grim Reaper 199, 264
Hades 200–201, 206–207, 217, 219, 223, 264
Harpocrates 232–234, 261, 267
Hathor 235–236, 242–243
Hebe 207, 211, 266
Hecate 197, 207–208, 214–215, 221, 261
Heimdall 249
Heka 208, 233, 261
Hel 247, 250, 264
Helios 196–197, 204, 208–210, 213, 221, 267

292 INDEX

Hephaestus 209–211, 242, 267
Hera 196, 199, 202, 204, 209–211, 223–224, 261
Hermanubis 234, 263
Hermaphroditus 195, 265
Hermes 12, 195–196, 210–213, 218, 219, 234, 246, 252–253, 261
Hermes Trismegistus 54
Hestia (Vesta) 213–214, 263
Höðr 247
Horus 129, 194, 231–232, 234–243, 245, 261–262, 267
Hyperion 209, 221
Isis 129, 194, 201, 228, 231–232, 235–236, 239–241, 243–244, 261
Janus 214
Jesus 45, 47, 77, 212, 228, 249, 258, 264, 267
Jörmungandr 228, 254
Jötunn 247–249, 253–254
Juno 196, 199, 202, 204, 209–211, 223–224, 261
Jupiter (see also Jupiter under Astrology) xvii, 8–9, 158, 196, 205, 223–225, 254, 262
Justitia (see also Dike and Themis) 201, 264
Juventas (see also Hebe) 207, 266
Kali 257, 264
Khepra (Khepri) 236–237, 243
Khonsu 226, 237–238, 266
Legba 258, 262, 266
Leto 196–197
Loki 246–247, 250–253, 261, 264–265
Luna (see also Moon under astrology) 13, 221, 261, 266
Ma'at 201, 225, 227, 235, 237–238, 241, 244–245, 262, 264
Maenads 203, 217
Maia 211, 213
Mars (see also Mars under astrology) 7, 9, 11, 196, 255, 264, 265
Mercury (see also Mercury under astrology) 7, 12, 211, 213, 252, 261

Metis 198
Minerva 197, 262
Mithra 209, 264
Mithras 258–259
Moirai (fates) 222
Montu 238, 242, 265
Mother Earth xvi, 194
Mut 226, 237–239, 242, 261
Neptune (see also Neptune under astrology) 16, 219, 264
Ningishzida 212
Njörðr 249
Norns (fates) 222, 253, 263
Nut 200, 208, 231, 235, 238–240, 243, 261
Nymphs 197, 199, 209, 216–218, 221, 223
Nyx 43, 206, 211, 257
Óðinn 211, 246–254, 261–264
Óðr 248
Olympians 8, 199, 206, 211, 213–214, 217, 223
Orpheus 51, 203, 206, 215–217, 262
Osiris 129, 194, 202–203, 216, 225, 227–228, 230–232, 235–236, 239–241, 243, 262, 264, 267
Pan 216, 218–219, 221, 261, 265
Persephone 200–202, 205–207, 217, 219, 231, 261, 263
Phanes 199
Pluto (see also Pluto) under astrology) 15, 206–207
Poseidon 199, 206–207, 210, 219–220, 223, 264
Prometheus 15, 200, 211, 264
Psyche 203–205, 262
Ptah 226, 230–231, 241–242, 243, 267
Ra 224–226, 231, 235, 237–238, 241–243
Ragnarök 247, 249–254
Raven 257, 259
Rhea 199, 223
Satan 41, 78
Saturn (see also Saturn under astrology) 8, 199–200
Satyrs 203, 217, 221, 265
Sekhmet 230, 242, 263

INDEX   293

Selene 209, 214, 221
Set 235, 239–241, 243
Shai 244, 263
Shiva 257, 259, 265
Shu 230, 239
Sirius 222, 244, 266
Sol 196, 208–209, 267
Sopdet 244
Sopdu 243–244
Thanatos 206
Theia 209, 221
Themis 201, 222, 264
Thor (Þórr) 246, 250, 253–254, 262–263
Thoth 237–238, 245–246, 261
Titans 8, 15, 198–200, 202, 206, 209, 217–219, 221, 223
Tyche 205, 263
Typhon 51, 211, 222–223, 228, 263
Týr 254
Uranus (see also Uranus under astrology) 15, 195, 199, 217–218, 223
Valkyries 252–253
Venus (see also Venus under astrology) 9–11, 158, 194–195, 203–205, 261, 266
Vesta (Hestia) 213–214, 263
Vulcan 209, 267
Weird Sisters (see also Fates) 222
Zephyrus 204
Zeus (see also Jupiter) 8–9, 196, 198–202, 205–207, 209–211, 213, 218–220, 222–226, 254
Goetia 82, 105
Golden Dawn 2, 30, 34, 38, 41–42, 44, 49, 52, 54–55, 58, 71, 77–79, 82, 84, 86–87, 91, 93, 98, 122, 127–129, 158–159, 228, 259
Gottfried Galle, Johann 14
Greco-Roman 4, 193, 199–200, 231
Greece 36
Greece (ancient) 65, 194, 202, 210, 226, 232
Greek language 7, 37, 48, 51, 74, 129, 193–194, 202, 206, 208, 218, 223, 226–227, 234, 242, 244, 245, 254

Greek Magical Papyri 78
guitar 62, 196

healing xvi, xxvi, 79, 114, 120, 187, 196, 236
Hebrew (language) 34–44, 46–51, 55–56, 58, 60, 76, 81–83, 87–92, 98, 105, 127
Hebrew Bible (Torah) 2, 36, 81, 83
Hebrew alphabet 1, 68–71, 84, 86, 232–233
hedonism xvii, 62, 258, 265, 279
heliocentrism 3
hermaphrodite 191, 195, 199, 256
    hermaphroditus 265
hermeticism 41, 45
Hermetic Order of the Golden Dawn 2, 30, 34, 38, 41–42, 44, 49, 52, 54–55, 58, 71, 77–79, 82, 84, 86–87, 91, 93, 98, 122, 127–129, 158–159, 228, 259
heroes
    Achilles 206, 210
    Bellerophon 198
    Heracles (Hercules) 198, 207, 210, 263
    Jason 198, 215
    Odysseus 198, 209, 217, 219
    Perseus 198
    Theseus 220
Herschel, William 14
Hesiod 195, 207, 211, 218
Hieroglyphs 51, 53–54, 78, 232
Hinduism 35, 43, 66, 71, 87, 194, 240, 257, 259
Holocaust 37
Holy Roman Empire 50
Holy Spirit 45, 55
    Shekhinah, 55
Homer (ancient Greek writer) 215
    Odyssey 127, 219
Hyksos 224

Icelandic 246, 250
I Ching 127, 176
India 6, 217, 258
intoxication 13, 265

INDEX

intuition xvi, 13, 29, 59–60, 83, 132, 154, 171, 174–175, 269
Isaac the Blind 37–39, 82
Ishtar 194, 266
Islam 4, 37, 77, 87, 225
Islamic Empire 38
Islamic magic 76
Israel (modern nation) 37
Israel (ancient) 76–78, 88, 113, 155
Italy 4, 36, 44, 47, 78, 214
Italian (language) 38
Italian people 44

jazz music 2, 126–127
Jesus 47, 77, 212, 228, 249, 258, 264, 267
Jews (see also Judaism) 35–53, 76, 79, 81, 84, 189, 194, 225
Jodorowsky, Alejandro 165–167
John the Baptist 77
Judaism (see also Kabbalah, and Jews) 36–37, 45, 47, 56, 76, 78, 83, 225
   Haredim 39
   Hasidim 39–40, 84
   Orthodox Judaism (see Haredim and Hasidim above) 35, 39, 84
   Pharisees 35
   Rabbinic 35–36, 83
   Sephardic Judaism 36, 39
Jung, Carl 103
   anima xvi, 13, 205
   animus 11
   individuation xvii, 10
   shadow xvii, 16, 24, 130, 210
   synchronicity 157

Kabbalah 34–124, 127, 172
   Ein Sof 194, 230, 233, 257
   Shem HaMephorash
   Tree of Life (see also Sefirot below) xii, 1–2, 38, 44, 49, 52, 56–60, 66, 68, 93, 131
   Sefirot xii, 38, 40, 44, 52, 55–58, 60, 65–66, 68, 71, 261–266
     1 Keter xii, xvi, xxiv, 56–57, 60, 63–65, 67, 71–72, 233, 261, 271
     2 Chokhmah xvi, 57, 60–61, 65, 67, 71–72, 153, 261, 266, 271–273
     3 Binah xvi, xxv, 57, 60–61, 65, 67, 71–72, 261–262, 273–274
     4 Chesed xvi–xvii, xxv, 57, 60, 62–63, 65, 67, 72–73, 91, 262–263, 274–275
     5 Gevurah xvi–xvii, xxv–xxvi, 60, 62, 65–67, 72–73, 91, 262–264, 275–277
     6 Tiferet xvi–xvii, xxvi, 57, 60, 62–63, 65–67, 72–73, 79, 154, 261–266, 277–278
     7 Netzach xvii–xviii, xxvii, 57, 60, 63–67, 73, 172, 262–266, 278–279
     8 Hod xvii–xviii, xxvii, 57, 60, 63–67, 73–74, 79, 264–265, 279–281
     9 Yesod xvii–xviii, xxvii–xxviii, 57, 60, 64–67, 73–74, 147, 172, 262, 265, 266–267, 281–282
     10 Malkut xviii, xxviii, 57, 60, 64–65, 67, 73–74, 266–267, 270, 282–283
Kaplan, Aryeh 74, 104
Kelley, Edward 129, 255
Key of Solomon 86
kings
   Ahmose 224
   Akhenaten 225, 229–230, 244
   Alexander the Great 7, 226
   Amenhotep III 228
   Amenhotep IV 229
   Augustus 195, 201, 211
   Emperor Frederick III 47
   George III 14
   Julius Caesar 195
   Pharaohs 224–225, 232, 235–237, 241–245
   Ramses II 226, 244
   Tutankhamun 225, 229–230
Kircher, Athanasius 51–53, 55, 82, 86, 93, 98, 124

Koran 77
Kush (kingdom) 225, 236

Latin (language) 36–38, 49, 82, 198, 205, 211, 223, 254
LaVey, Anton 41, 256
Le Monnier, Pierre Charles 14
Le Verrier, Urbain 14
Leitch, Aaron 85, 88, 92
Lesser Ritual of the Pentagram 78
   Rituals of the Hexagram 82, 122, 158
Lévi, Éliphas 42, 53–54, 78, 86, 98, 195, 256
liminality xviii, 13, 16, 26, 146, 207, 253, 266
Loans, Jacob 47
logos (philosophy) xiii, 59, 208, 233
Luria, Isaac ben Solomon 38–39, 55, 58
Luxon, Christopher 186

Madaurensis, Lucius Apuleius 203
magicians xii, xv, 2, 4, 34, 41, 44–46, 51, 80–83, 85–87, 89, 105, 122, 127, 129, 156–158, 160, 162–164, 174–175, 181, 190–191, 211–213, 234, 252, 257, 260
   chaos magicians 78, 234
manifestation xv, xx, 43, 57, 64, 74, 86, 157, 175, 234
Manson, Charles 27, 251
martyr 225
   self-martyr xvii, 26
Marx, Harpo 233
Marxism 149, 152–153
materialism 4, 56, 189–190
Mathers, MacGregor 77, 82, 87, 93, 128–148
Mattern, Marcus 122
Mayans 217
medieval 4, 37, 78
   middle ages 194
menstrual cycle 13
Merkabah 35, 75–76, 262
military xxi, 50, 115, 182, 196, 210, 226, 258, 269
mining xx, 24, 206

Mirandola, Pico della 34, 44–46, 81, 83, 86
Mishnah 35–36, 39, 83
Mithraism 258
Mohammed (Islam) 77, 256
Monad (see also Brahman) 43, 194, 225, 230, 240, 257
Moses (biblical) 40, 53, 76, 88
   Sixth and Seventh Books of Moses 105, 212
Moses de León 39
Moses ben Jacob Cordovero 39
Mother Mary (see also, Virgin Mary) 77, 182, 235–236
motherhood xvi, 167–170
music 11, 62, 73, 109, 125–126, 140, 176–177, 187, 195–196, 212–213, 215–218
   music theory xii, 125
musicians xv, 175–177, 215–217, 233, 269
   jazz musician 2
   music producer 175
Mycenaeans 202

NATO 155
necromancy 207
Nehunya ben HaKanah 39, 82
neo-Nazis 37
Neoliberalism 153
Neoplatonism 35, 45
new age 2, 157, 160, 189, 221
New Zealand 183–186, 192
Newton, Isaac 190
Norse 222–223, 246–255
Nous 194
Nubia 225–226
numerology 14, 18, 65, 68, 70, 84
   Neo-Pythagorean numerology xii–xiv

Oblique Strategies 175–177
Oedipus Aegyptiacus 51, 86, 93, 124
Olympians 8, 199, 206, 211, 213–214, 217, 223
Olympic Games 197

Olympus 209–210, 214
Ordo Templi Orientis 49
Orion (constelation) 222
Orphism 43, 45, 51, 199, 203, 215–216, 230, 240–241, 257
    Orphic hymns 215

Pacific 43, 259
Palestine 155
Papus (Gérard Encausse) 84
Parcae (fates) 222
Parker, Charlie 126–127
Pentagrammaton 47, 50
Persia 2, 48, 65
Pharisees 35
Philochorus of Athens 195
philosophers
    Aristarchus of Samos 3
    Aristotle 3–6, 215
    Corbin, Henry 190
    Heraclitus 233
    Hicetas 3
    Nietzsche, Friedrich 10, 13, 196
    Philolaus 3
    Plato (see also Platonism and Neoplatonism) 4, 55, 190, 193, 219
    Pythagoras xii–xiii, 34, 48, 65, 216
philosophy 29, 64, 86, 106, 109, 118, 195, 199, 233, 237
    Idealism 190
    Hermetism 86
    Neoplatonism 35, 45
    Perennial philosophy 45
    Platonism 37, 45, 48, 55, 86, 190, 193, 219
Phoenicians 48, 194, 202
Phrygians 201
pyrrhic victory 155
playing cards 165, 172–174
Pleiades 211
poetry/poets xv, xxi, 16, 27, 84, 109–110, 195, 260, 269
political parties
    ACT party (New Zealand) 186
    National Party (New Zealand) 186

politics xxi, 9, 20, 36–37, 111, 114, 151–154, 156, 165, 184–186, 238, 269
    Marxism 149, 152–153
politician xxi, 9, 262, 269
popes (historical) 45–46
    Alexander VI 46
    Innocent VIII 46
    Nicholas V 36
    Sixtus IV 36
Popess 169, 261
    Pope Joan 169
Postmodernism 149, 151–152
    Deconstructionism 151–152
Pragmatic Magical Thinking 35, 41, 80, 104
Pranayama 159
prima donna xxi, 269
primum mobile xvi, 6, 60, 71–72, 261
psychic xii, 175, 269
psychology 86, 103, 159
    flow state 61, 175
    narcissism xxi
psychonaut 27, 61
    Liber Null & Psychonaut 174
psychopomp xvi, 208, 211–212, 234, 258, 262–264
pyrrhic victory 155
Pyrrhus of Epirus 155

queens (historical)
    Elizabeth I 181–183

Rabbinic Judaism 35, 37, 39, 48, 83
radio surfing 186–187
reductionism 153
    post-reductionism 191
Regardie, Israel 59, 93, 128
reincarnation 203, 216, 231, 257
religion xvi, 36–37, 41, 53, 87, 110, 112, 118, 182, 189, 191
Renaissance 4, 36, 46, 49, 75, 82, 86–87, 192, 205, 234
Reuchlin, Johann 37, 47–50, 81–83, 86, 90–91, 98, 105

Rider Waite Smith (deck) 2, 127, 149, 167, 170, 172, 174, 226, 228
Rigveda 218, 258
Rishis (Sat, Chit and Ananda) 66
Rituals of the Hexagram 82, 122, 158–160
rock stars
   Bowie, David 187, 201
   Hendrix, Jimi 201
   Little Richard 201
   Morrison, Jim 201
   Plant, Robert 201
   Presley, Elvis 201
romance xv–xvi, xx, 11, 28, 63, 132, 161, 170, 171, 174, 178, 202, 205, 269
Romantic movement 219, 221
Rome 53, 194, 196, 211, 232
Romeo and Juliet 11
Romulus 196
Rosetta Stone 52, 54
Rudd, Thomas 82, 105
Russia
   Russia-Ukraine war 37
   Soviet Russia 233

Sammonicus, Quintus Serenus 85
satanic 189
   satanists 256
scarab 236–237
Schmidt, Peter 175
science
   chemistry 86, 117, 121
   electromagnetism xxii
   gravity xxii, 8
   physics 43, 45, 86, 117, 121
   quantum physics 42, 56
seasons 30, 201, 206, 237, 251
   autumn xvii, xxii, xxiii, 24–25
   spring xxiii, 20–21, 30, 194
   summer xxii–xxiii, 22–23, 220, 243
   winter xxiii, 25–27, 200, 206, 244
Sefer Bahir 37–39, 82, 84, 87
Sefer HaRazim 84
Sefer Raziel 84, 86
Sefer Yetzirah 37–39, 71, 84

Sefirot xii, 38, 40, 44, 52, 55–58, 60, 65–66, 68, 71, 261–266
   1 Keter xii, xvi, xxiv, 56–57, 60, 63–65, 67, 71–72, 233, 261, 271
   2 Chokhmah xvi, 57, 60–61, 65, 67, 71–72, 153, 261, 266, 271–273
   3 Binah xvi, xxv, 57, 60–61, 65, 67, 71–72, 261–262, 273–274
   4 Chesed xvi–xvii, xxv, 57, 60, 62–63, 65, 67, 72–73, 91, 262–263, 274–275
   5 Gevurah xvi–xvii, xxv–xxvi, 60, 62, 65–67, 72–73, 91, 262–264, 275–277
   6 Tiferet xvi–xvii, xxvi, 57, 60, 62–63, 65–67, 72–73, 79, 154, 261–266, 277–278
   7 Netzach xvii–xviii, xxvii, 57, 60, 63–67, 73, 172, 262–266, 278–279
   8 Hod xvii–xviii, xxvii, 57, 60, 63–67, 73–74, 79, 264–265, 279–281
   9 Yesod xvii–xviii, xxvii–xxviii, 57, 60, 64–67, 73–74, 147, 172, 262, 265, 266–267, 281–282
   10 Malkut xviii, xxviii, 57, 60, 64–65, 67, 73–74, 266–267, 270, 282–283
self-destruction xvii
sex 24, 29, 63–64, 106, 194, 205, 224, 232, 241, 249
   abstinence 110, 216
   gender 12, 50, 131
   gender inversion 200, 202, 208, 231, 238–240
   sexuality 9, 11, 203, 220–221, 255
   sex, drugs & rock'n'roll 201
   sexual liberation 232, 255–256
   sex worker 255
Sforno, Jacob 47
Shaivism 259
Shakespeare 222
Shekhinah 55

significator 128–131, 133, 135, 147–148, 182
Simeon ben Yochai 39
Sirius 222, 244, 266
Smart People Traps 80
Snell, Lionel 78
Solomon (biblical) 38, 105
    Key(s) of Solomon 86
    Temple of Solomon 59
Spain 36–38, 182
    Al-Andalus 36, 38
    Sephardic Jews 36, 39, 47
    Spanish Armada 181
Spare, Austin Osman 175, 233
sphinx 76, 187, 245, 263
Spiritualism 145
sportsperson xxi
storms xx, xxii, 110, 219, 243, 253
Sufism 35
synchronicities 157–158, 164

talismans 121–122, 189
Talmud 36, 47, 83
Tantra 41
Taoism 10
Tarot de Marseilles xvi–xvii, 1, 42, 125, 166–167
television 127, 165
temperament
    choleric temperament xv, 260
    melancholic temperament xv, xxi, 260
    phlegmatic temperament xv, 260
    sanguine temperament xv, 260
temptation xxvii, 11, 200, 205, 258, 279
testosterone cycle 13

Tetractys xiii
Tetragrammaton 47
thirty-two paths (Kabbalah) 44, 71–74
    (1–10, see Sefirot)
Thoth deck xvi–xvii, 2, 31, 127–128, 149, 172, 194, 226, 228, 233
Thracians 210, 215
Three Books of Occult Philosophy 49–50, 53, 86, 215
Tombaugh, Clyde 15
Torah 2, 36, 81, 83
Turkey 36, 201
tyranny 200

Ukraine 37
United Nations 155

Vedas 218, 258
Vedic astrology 19
Vigenère, Blaise de 82, 105
Virgin Mary (see also Mother Mary) 182
Voudou 258

Waite, Arthur Edward (see also Rider Waite Smith deck) 34, 54
Wang, Robert 36–37, 46–47
Wicca 145, 208, 221
Wilson, Colin 175
witch xii, 50, 87, 207
Witzel, E. J. Michael 48, 257

Yates, Francis 46
Yoga 145, 257
    breath Yoga 159

Zohar 39–40

www.ingramcontent.com/pod-product-compliance
Ingram Content Group UK Ltd.
Pitfield, Milton Keynes, MK11 3LW, UK
UKHW021925181125
465179UK00001B/2